A MIGHTY TEMPEST

A MIGHTY TEMPEST

MICHELLE & RACHELLE HAMILTON

Wolgemuth & Hyatt, Publishers, Inc.
Brentwood, Tennessee

Published February 1992. First Edition.
Printed in the United States of America.
97 96 95 94 93 92   8 7 6 5 4 3 2 1

Wolgemuth & Hyatt, Publishers, Inc.
1749 Mallory Lane, Suite 110
Brentwood, Tennessee 37027

Library of Congress Cataloging-in-Publication Data

Hamilton, Michelle.
A Mighty Tempest / Michelle and Rachelle Hamilton.
p.   cm.
ISBN 1-56121-111-7
1. Hamilton, Michelle—Journeys. 2. Survival (after airplane accidents, shipwrecks, etc.) 3. Hamilton, Michelle. 4. Hamilton, Rachelle. I. Hamilton, Rachelle. II. Title.
G530.H218   1992
910.4—dc20   91-39235
CIP

Dedicated to the One
Whom even the winds and the sea obey

CONTENTS

ACKNOWLEDGMENTS

A SPECIAL THANK-YOU TO THE FOLLOWING PEOPLE (in alphabetical order) for the sacrifice of self in order that all may be blessed.

Angeline and Natalie Hamilton: For making this family a cocoon of strength and a sanctuary from which we can all draw support, enduring and unconditional love, and constant encouragement.

Captain Baudillo Pactao and the entire crew of *The Alyss Star:* For rescuing me from the depths of the ocean and the jaws of death and also for the tenderness and compassion you showed me. All of you went above and beyond the call of duty. May God reward you abundantly with treasures in heaven.

Brian Kane: For all the hours you tirelessly and uncomplainingly helped us type the manuscript. You were truly a lifesaver.

David Lonergan: For your wonderful spirit of generosity for the twelve hundred dollars you furnished Rachelle for the hire of the aerial plane search and your words of encouragement that instilled in Rachelle the will to keep on fighting.

Esther D. Lambert: To one of God's special people. This acknowledgement of thanks is just a token gesture of appreciation for selflessly giving up your apartment in order that we would have a place in which to write this book. Without you this book would not have come to fruition. Your immeasurable insight and undying support of us and this work have been truly inspiring.

Jackie Mitchum and Steve Conway: For going out on a limb to take care of us during our sojourn in America. Your assistance was greatly appreciated.

Pastor Neil Wylkes and all the faithful warriors of Maroubra Baptist Church, Sydney: Our warmest thanks for all your prayers and support that enabled us to fight the good fight and keep the faith when the enemy was in hot pursuit and determined to thwart this project.

Sandy Williams: For opening your house and extraordinarily generous heart to us. You're one in a million!

Wolgemuth & Hyatt, Publishers: Our heartfelt thanks go to our publishers and friends, Robert Wolgemuth and Mike Hyatt, whose unique creative insight and marketing flair have made our dream a reality. You caught the vision for this book and looked upon what others thought to be a risk as a challenge, and for this you have our deepest admiration.

Finally, our warmest and sincere thanks go to all those people who generously helped us, you know who you are!

The LORD sent out
a great wind on the sea,
and there was a mighty tempest. . . .

For You cast me into the deep,
Into the heart of the seas,
And the floods surrounded me;
All Your billows and Your waves passed over me.
Then I said, "I have been cast out of Your sight;
Yet I will look again toward Your holy temple."
The waters surrounded me, even to my soul;
The deep closed around me;
Weeds were wrapped around my head.
I went down to the moorings of the mountains;
The earth with its bars closed behind me forever;
Yet You have brought up my life from the pit,
O LORD, my God.

When my soul fainted within me,
I remembered the LORD;
And my prayer went up to You,
Into Your holy temple.

(The Prophet Jonah)

A TONIC FOR THE SOUL

RACHELLE . . . 12 P.M., SATURDAY, MARCH 4, 1989, SYDNEY, AUSTRALIA. The plane taxied down the runway, engines whining to full power. I felt the same way, emotionally charging with excitement! To my amazement, the holiday that I had organized at a moment's notice had finally come together.

Here I was, strapped securely in my seat, but once again I still could not dispel the slight apprehension I felt about flying. Unbidden, three airline mishaps of the past few months came to my mind. I'd previously paid little attention to the air hostesses as they stood in the aisles demonstrating the aircraft's safety procedures, but in light of the recent events, I now strained to hear the location of exits and the usual emergency routine. My eyes followed the direction of her pointed finger, noting the exit nearest my seat. Watching the air hostess for what seemed like the hundredth time demonstrate the use of the life jacket, I wondered if it came to the crunch, would I really remember the procedure well enough to carry it out effectively?

Don't dwell on that, I told myself harshly. *If your number's up, there is nothing you can do about it. Relax, sit back, and enjoy the flight.*

The jet shifted as we began our ascent. My window seat offered a breathtaking view of the magnificent panorama of my hometown. There below me were the jewels of Sydney, encompassed by the majestic splendor of the harbor. The Harbor Bridge stretched its arms of steel toward the city, while enthroned on the harbor lay the impressive Opera House. The brilliance of its creative design was a sight to behold; the vast mass of gleaming white shimmered in the bright morning sunshine.

My heart swelled with pride at this, the adopted city I now called home. Surely, no other city on earth could equal its natural beauty.

A Tropical Paradise

The pilot's voice nudged me back from my thoughts: "We have reached our cruising altitude of twenty-five thousand feet. The weather conditions are fine, and our scheduled arrival in Singapore is at 7:35 this evening. We hope you enjoy your flight."

My daughter Michelle had sent an assortment of Boracay Island brochures to give me a taste of my holiday destination. In a whirlwind of frantic activity arranging the last-minute details, I'd skimmed hurriedly through the brochures, glancing only at the glorious colored photographs. Now with six hours at my disposal, I took them from my bag, relishing the idea of leisurely reading them. I opened one of the brochures on my lap and began to read:

Boracay Island—The Philippines

Serenity best describes this most endearing of tropical islands. Boracay is a tonic for the soul, owing its serenity to its physical isolation as much as anything else. About nine hundred and fifty kilometers [589 miles] south of Manila, the island is only 4 miles long and a little over one mile wide. It can only be reached by bunca (a boat similar to a catamaran) from the town Caticlan, located on the southernmost tip of the island of Panay.

Boracay is a poet's haven. You'll find cabanas beautifully set into dramatic hill slopes. Or choose a cabana on the beach, so you can simply stroll through the palm trees on the powder-fine white sand down to a sliver of vibrant, almost unreal, turquoise green sea.

Nature seems to have used Boracay as a model for all other tropical paradises. Mornings greet the soft, whispering waves of the sea and peer at the radiance of the green, swaying coconut palms. Evenings quietly set in with brushstrokes of exotic hues and the most stunning silhouettes of evening. Watch the sunset while you dine on sumptuous food at one of the stunning array of restaurants Boracay has to offer.

Enjoy the sun, sea and soul—for this will be a holiday you'll never forget.

I poured over these brochures, enraptured. It all seemed too good to be true! I could almost feel the sand as I imagined lying on it with the heat warming my body. A lengthy period of unseasonal rain in Sydney certainly enhanced the anticipation of the island pleasures in store for me.

Reunion with Michelle

My excitement was also heightened because I would soon see Michelle again. One year ago my daughter had seen an advertisement in the Sydney *Morning Herald* for a private tutor to teach conversational English in Tokyo. Within two weeks of applying she was accepted. In a flurry of activity Michelle left her job, obtained a visa, terminated the lease on her apartment, packed her bags, and flew away on a promising new adventure.

With her hopes, dreams, and ambitions tucked firmly in her heart, she was ready for the flight into the unknown. The timing was perfect: A two-year relationship with her American boyfriend had ended suddenly, leaving her bewildered and hurt. A change of environment seemed to be the perfect panacea for her first broken heart. Some would call her decision impetuous, but if the distance would benefit Michelle, then I encouraged the venture.

Conflicting emotions had assailed me! While a part of me urged her to take hold of her life and explore the world, another part was reluctant to see her go. Michelle's absence would leave a distinct void in our lives. For her twenty-one years we had hardly ever been separated. But I knew Michelle must follow her own destiny, and as a mother I was secretly relieved she had ended her mismatched romance. I also envied her carefree life with no encumbrances, responsibilities, or commitments. Michelle was a free spirit. I would have loved to pack up and jet to the other side of the world as she had. Unlike her, however, I hadn't the freedom to follow my desires. My heart was full of *maybe's* and *one day's*. And now, a year later, my own tropical paradise was awaiting me at the end of this flight.

"Excuse me, madam, would you prefer grilled fish or beef stroganoff ?" the hostess asked.

I snapped back to the present. "Oh, the fish, please."

The aroma of the meal wafted toward me, and I suddenly realized I was ravenous. I had barely noticed the woman sitting next to me, but now she glanced over and smiled.

"This looks good, doesn't it? I was getting really hungry," she commented.

"Yes, me too," I responded. "I was miles away and didn't realize until now just how hungry I was."

"I missed breakfast this morning which is something I never do, but with an early morning flight I didn't think it would be necessary. Oh well, now we won't starve," she told me good naturedly.

"I'd really made it! One glorious month's holiday was about to begin, and I was breathless with expectation."

Our conversation ceased as we indulged ourselves. After we had enjoyed the appetizing meal, the hostess removed our trays. My seatmate returned to her magazine, and I settled into a relaxed, contented mood.

Envisioning our reunion, I imagined Michelle and I would talk into the small hours of morning. We had an entire year's news to catch up on. I wondered how much she had changed. The year she had lived in Japan would undoubtedly have broadened her horizons. A small, unwanted thought crept in. Would we still retain our close relationship? She was now a grown woman, not my little girl. Extremely adventurous by nature, Michelle's curiosity for life was boundless. Even as a child I was unable to contain her. Now I hoped she still needed me and hadn't become so worldly that her mother was disposable and obsolete!

Only ten minutes more until we were to arrive in Singapore. I took out my cosmetics bag and touched up my lipstick. I didn't want to look even one year older!

I'd really made it! One glorious month's holiday was about to begin, and I was breathless with expectation. My stomach was doing somersaults when the captain's voice crackled over the intercom, "We trust that you have enjoyed your flight. If you care to adjust your watches, Singapore time is now 7:40 P.M. The temperature is seventy-seven degrees and the humidity is eighty-five percent. Thank you for flying Qantas. We hope you enjoy your stay in Singapore and that you will travel with us again soon."

I stood with my luggage cart, watching the endless procession of baggage moving around on the conveyor belt. Embarrassed, I claimed the canvas army bag as mine. There certainly was a disparity between the glamorous image I portrayed and the rugged, adventure-bound bag which accompanied me. As I dragged the conspicuous bag off the luggage conveyor, its unsuspected weight caused me to drop it, nearly sending me sprawling to the floor. Fortunately for me, a man behind me caught my arm as I went down and managed to save me from making a spectacle of myself. He manuveured the bag back onto the trolley. I smiled gratefully and then walked forward toward a mass of brown faces staring through the huge glass window.

I caught sight of her at once. Michelle's long blonde hair stood out among the crowd. My heart pounded against my chest as Michelle's arms waved furiously in the air. Happiness washed over me, and I couldn't wait to hold her again. Tears of joy threatened to flow down my cheeks. *Oh no,* I thought, *there goes my make-up.* I wanted to rush over and hold her immediately, but I had to be cleared by customs first. I must have an honest face, for he waved me through without question.

I pushed the awkwardly heavy cart through the double doors. Michelle called excitedly from behind the metal barrier. I couldn't contain myself any longer! Abandoning the trolley, I rushed to meet her, our arms encircling each other. Tears of pure joy released themselves unchecked as we held each other for what seemed like an eternity. Standing back at an arm's length, we appraised each other, laughing through our tears. A fresh wave of emotion swept over us as we hugged and kissed all over again. I took a long look at her: It seemed incredible that this strikingly beautiful young woman before me was my daughter.

Her long golden hair flowed down her back, curling at the ends. She appeared to be taller than I'd remembered, a little over five feet, six inches tall. Her skin glowed with a healthy tan, acquired, no doubt, on some exotic island. Michelle beamed me a self-conscious smile, for she knew that I was appraising her. The color of her fiery green eyes reflected her passionate zest for life. But more than this, they radiated an intelligence and sense of humor. Her natural, spontaneous generosity was born out of her genuine, humanitarian heart. The air around her seemed to crackle with raw vitality; she possessed the spirit of an Arabian thoroughbred, galloping fearlessly through life with carefree abandon. Michelle displayed the willfulness of a self-determined individual, impetuously snatching all that life had to offer without a moment's reflection. And she was my daughter.

My heart swelled with a mother's pride. It didn't seem possible that this was the same little girl who once had red-ribboned ponytails and missing front teeth. The duckling had been transformed into a beautiful swan. With arms linked, we made our way out of Singapore's Changi Airport, about to embark on the holiday of a lifetime—one I hoped would be so memorable that I'd delight in telling my grandchildren about it many years from now.

Two

TROPICAL AMBIENCE

MICHELLE . . . 7:30 A.M., THURSDAY, MARCH 9, BORACAY ISLAND. The morning sun danced playfully on the ripples of the shimmering ocean. I waded languidly through the crystal clear sea, occasionally kicking water into the air with carefree abandon. Dreamily soaking in the landscape, I came to the only conclusion possible: Boracay Island was idyllic!

The ivory sand felt as soft as baby powder between my toes, as a multitude of squeaky grains massaged the soles of my feet. The stunning colors of the ocean were breathtaking. Like an artist's brushstrokes on a canvas, the shades changed from a brilliant turquoise green, blending into an aqua, and finally merging into a deep midnight blue. Palm trees stood silhouetted against the backdrop of the morning sky. I stood there in awe of such natural beauty.

The ocean had an almost mystical aura, and I found it an endless pleasure to observe its ever-changing moods. At times it was a tranquil, velvety carpet of water, but at others a different face appeared, that of a powerful, unpredictable force. The ocean was a tonic for my soul, a place I headed for quiet contemplation and solace. It represented the enjoyment of hot summer days, tanning under the tropical sun. Memories of treasured childhood days surfaced, of bare-bottomed children playing blissfully under the sun; of colorful beachballs, sandpails, and shovels; of melting ice cream cones and long cool drinks.

The Tropical Atmosphere

Ahhh, another perfect day in paradise, I thought. *And splendid conditions for sailing around the island.*

I'd been waiting the last couple of days to attempt this adventurous challenge, but strong winds had prevented me from doing so. The weather conditions today, however, proved more suitable, with a slight sea breeze bringing relief from the already sultry heat.

Strolling back to our beachfront bungalow, I hoped Mum would be as enthusiastic as I was about the adventurous day I'd planned for us. I glanced at my watch before entering the bungalow. Ten past eight, an acceptable hour to wake Mum. No self-respecting person should still be sleeping on such a wonderful day, even if she were on holiday.

I quietly opened the door. The mosquito net was still draped, overhanging the bed. It reminded me of an exotic movie I'd seen as a child, set in Africa.

"Good morning. It's time you were up and about. It is a beautiful day," I said, breezing into the bungalow. "A superb day for sailing around the island. Do you feel up to it?"

"Why not?" Mum responded, shaking herself from sleep. "Let me take a shower and get dressed. Why don't you order us a cup of coffee and find out the situation on hiring a boat."

"Okay, sounds great to me." I agreed, heading out the door.

On entering the restaurant, I approached a Filipino waiter. "Excuse me, I believe you have some boats for hire?" I asked.

"Not me, ma'am, my boss," he said with a smile. "You'll have to speak to him, okay? I'll get him to come and talk to you at your bungalow."

"No problem," I assured him.

With that settled, I ordered our coffee and returned to the bungalow to begin dressing appropriately for the day. Rummaging through my backpack, I selected my blue and white striped bikini, blue shorts with a tropical design, and my favorite Ken Done cotton T-shirt. I also slipped on my black track shoes for a possible jungle trek on the other side of the island.

The Filipino waiter soon appeared with a silver tray bearing our morning coffee. He looked more suited to be serving on an elegant oceanliner, rather than at our Boracay beach cabana. Although finding it absurdly comical, we appreciated the gesture. He courteously placed the tray on the cane wicker table on the balcony, smiled shyly, then left.

It was an unaccustomed pleasure to be sitting on the balcony of a beachfront bungalow, leisurely sipping our freshly brewed coffee, contemplating the enjoyable pursuits we would indulge ourselves in today.

Oh well, I suppose I could get used to making these laborious decisions, I smiled smugly to myself.

I felt a warm satisfaction, watching the tension fall away from Mum like an unwanted winter overcoat. In the three days that we had been here, she was being wooed by the summer sun, the tropical atmosphere

"In my mind I'd always believed that Mum was invincible, destined for eternal youthfulness and health."

seducing her into a relaxed holiday mood. What an enormous relief! Mum represented a solid rock, an anchor for our close family of three girls. Usually she was a powerhouse of vital energy, endowed with an indestructible resilience, someone to marvel at in a mundane world.

"Impossible! It can't be done," was only a taunting challenge to her wells of resourcefulness. Invaluable words taught to us children came back to mind: "When you think you have done everything you can possibly do, know for certain you haven't exhausted all the avenues to the fullest. There is always another answer to the 'impossible' that you've yet to explore. Apply yourself and you will find a way through."

A Tonic for Mum

Her understanding of human nature penetrated the deepest aspects of people's hearts and minds. Her dynamic personality and continual enthusiasm, often in the face of insurmountable problems, intrigued me. Mum flatly refused to be beaten.

Wisps of sadness touched my heart, and I felt a tremor of childhood fear. In my mind I'd always believed that Mum was invincible, destined for eternal youthfulness and health. I'd always reassured myself of this without question. These past few days had scared me to see her so weary. She was now temporarily crushed under a barrage of unfavorable conditions, her fighting spirit reduced under an onslaught of pressures. Under normal circumstances, she would have laughed in the face of obstacles, accepting the opportunity to display her versatility and inventiveness. However, reoccurring minor illnesses during the last year—brought on by the stress of raising a family alone and the pace of city life—had taken their toll and, frankly, it worried me more than I was willing to believe or accept.

Mum, I realized with mild shock, was not as indestructible or infallible as I had naively believed as a child. For the first time I recognized this fact, as one adult to another, not as child to parent. A veil was removed from my perception; in a flash of reality her true vulnerability as a human being was revealed.

I glanced over at Mum sipping her coffee. With a hopeful heart I could see the tranquility of Boracay doing its work. In only a few short days since we arrived, Mum was being transformed back into the sparkling person I always knew her to be.

Her appearance was somewhat deceptive, and we dumbfounded many when they discovered we were mother and daughter. In fact, on several occasions some people absolutely refused to believe it. An abundance of thick blonde hair hung softly around her shoulders. She possessed chameleon-like eyes, which changed color mirroring her mood. In a state of high spirits her eyes reflected a shade of pale green, altering to the soft grey of a winter sky in her more reflective, gentle moods. Captivating good looks and naturally flowing confidence endeared her to almost everybody she met. A glowing, unblemished complexion, encompassing high cheekbones, helped her retain a youthful appearance.

Mum strove to rise above the level of mediocrity. Her life could be described as anything but boring. You could find her equally at home, at a business meeting, backpacking through the Orient, crewing on a yacht race, or mixing with overseas delegates. We overlooked the fact that her most ingenious meal was eggs on toast; cooking was just not her forte! Flexibility was the keyword—going with the flow of life, enjoying everything it had to offer, even though it was not always a bed of roses.

The letters and tapes I'd received from her during the year I was away in Japan were mostly disheartening. Judging by them, it was obvious she was overworked and stretched to the limit. Maintaining a pressured position with a major newspaper, as well as managing a home singlehandedly, had taken its toll. Since Mum's divorce, she had solely supported my two teenage sisters, financially and otherwise.

To be honest, I was becoming increasingly concerned about her health and well-being. She was finding it more difficult to cope with increasing daily pressures. This threatened the entire family's security, which Mum had always provided in loving abundance. During the past

"Mum, I realized with mild shock, was not as indestructible or infallible as I had naively believed as a child."

year, she had been plagued with bouts of ill health, no doubt aggravated by the strain of overwhelming responsibilities she carried.

Every letter I received proved the situation was worsening. At one stage, I was even seriously considering cutting my assignment short and returning home to Sydney, but in a sudden twist of destiny our problem was solved. Miraculously, a door was opened and an answer revealed.

An Opportunity of a Lifetime

I was preparing to fly to the Philippines when at the last minute, due to unforeseen circumstances, my travelling companion had to cancel our arrangements. She offered me her prepaid ticket, which could not be changed or refunded. I immediately thought of Mum! The turn of events seemed more than just a coincidence. I intuitively felt destiny was intervening. This would alleviate Mum from the pressures of her treadmill existence. One month in the Philippines, relaxing on a tropical island, would be the perfect tonic for her to regain her health and rejuvenate her spirit. Shaking with nervous excitement, I called her from Bangkok. Miraculously but not suprisingly, Mum was able to make it, and we met in Singapore ten days later!

We had a special relationship and shared many interests. I was born when Mum was only nineteen, so the generation gap barely applied. We always were friends in the true sense of the word. Now, after this month's holiday, I felt sure she would find a renewed vitality and zest for life once more. And we would both enjoy our time together.

Incredibly, here we were *fetê accompli,* sitting on the balcony of our beachfront bungalow on gorgeous Boracay Island, leisurely sipping our morning cup of coffee, in the most heavenly surroundings. And we had an entire month of this. Ahhhhh. . . .

With a burst of enthusiasm I began telling Mum what the day's plans were.

"It's going to be great. Perhaps we can sail around to the other side. The entire island is only about four miles long, so it shouldn't be too strenuous for you. When we get around there, we can sunbake, do a little snorkeling, and have a picnic. David mentioned that there are even some caves we can explore. It will be fun. What do you think? Are you game?" I questioned.

"Absolutely," she said, although I sensed a little reluctance in her voice.

I knew Mum wasn't that keen on the ocean, unless of course, she was on a luxurious boat. But her slight reticence did not deter me; I was determined to sail around the island anyway and have a wonderful day.

"Excuse me ma'am," said a man, interrupting our conversation. "You want to hire a bunca?"

"Oh, yes, do you have one for rent?"

"We have two. Do you want to see them?"

"Definitely. C'mon, Mum," I insisted, guiding her by the arm in a flurry of excitement.

Willy Gelito, the owner of Willy's Beachfront Cottages, escorted us down to the water's edge.

"Here we are," he said, pointing to a thirteen-foot pink sailboat. "How many people will be on the boat?"

"Oh, just the two of us," I said lamely. I immediately sensed his apprehension at letting two females take out his sailboat.

"Can you sail a boat?" He directed the question at me.

"Well, Mum can. She belongs to a yacht club at home."

He raised his eyebrow quizzically. His dubious tone of voice sounded an alarm in me.

Well, I conceded mentally, *the boat does look a little large for us to handle.*

Determined not to abandon the idea completely, I asked him: "Excuse me, you said you had another boat. Perhaps that would be smaller and more suitable?"

He pointed to a little crassly painted canoe with outriggers, lying abandoned on the sand. It couldn't have been longer than seven feet. I almost started to laugh but decided against it.

"But it has no sail!" I exclaimed.

He motioned toward two oars. "It is a bunca. You paddle it," he instructed. "Where do you intend going?"

"Oh, just around." I dared not tell him we were planning to take it around to the other side of the island. He might refuse to hire it, and I was desperate not to have my plans thwarted. Once I set my mind to something, my stubborn streak of determination would not be swayed by opinion or logic—not always a positive trait, but it did have its advantages!

"The boat is one hundred and fifty pesos for the day. Do you want it?" he shrugged.

"Shall we go for it, Mum? It is a little primitive, but what the heck, it will probably be fun."

She nodded.

"Okay, we'll take it. I'll just go and get some money and my bag and be back in a minute," I told him.

We walked back to the bungalow. I hurriedly began stuffing the necessary items into my cotton string bag: two walkmans, a selection of tapes, two sarongs, a camera, reading material, snorkel, flippers, and mask.

Rattling off the items as I came out the door, I asked Mum, "Can you think of anything else?"

"No, I think we've pretty well covered it, except maybe it would be a good idea to get a bottle of water and a few mangoes to take with us."

"Good thinking. I'll pick them up from the restaurant when I pay for the bunca. If you're ready, then let's go."

I loved pitting my skills against the elements; it exhilarated me. Paddling around the island would enable me to fulfill an exciting challenge. Sliding my moneybelt around my waist, I securely locked the door behind us and ran enthusiastically toward our little red rented rowboat.

In my exuberant mood, little did I know that this would be the last time I'd ever set foot on Boracay Island again.

THREE

A TORRENT OF WILD EMOTIONS

RACHELLE . . . 9 A.M., THURSDAY, MARCH 9, BORACAY ISLAND. The crystal clear water of the sea intrigued me. A school of electric blue and yellow fish darted directly beneath the canoe. I welcomed the distraction from the rising nausea I was feeling, due to the incessant bobbing of the canoe. Unable to resist, I dipped my hand into the soft, warm, and inviting water. I watched as the water parted at my cupped hand, leaving a ripple behind me. Farther below us, I observed swaying branches of seaweed flowing with the currents. Multi-colored coral adorned the rocks below, camouflage for a multitude of sea life which lived off the reef.

Floating on the top of the ocean was one thing, but being able to witness firsthand the teeming unseen world beneath the surface was another. Completely captivated by the window into that world, I forgot that five minutes earlier I'd wanted to go back to shore. My stomach, however, was not having such a good time. Suppressing the queasy sensation, I tried to focus my attention on a huge dark patch looming ahead of us.

Far below, I could see the sun's rays penetrating the depths. Plant life lifted up foliage to absorb the light. Now we were almost directly over the large reef which was just about eight feet below the surface. The rock appeared dark and ominous; then a large reef fish emerged from between the weeds.

"Look, Michelle, over there. Can you see him coming from between the weeds?" I asked excitedly as I pointed in the direction of the fish.

"Hey, he's a beauty. I'd love to put on my snorkel gear and go take a closer look."

"Please, don't. It makes me so nervous. Stay in the boat. Besides, we can see more from this perspective anyway."

"But, Mum, it's not the same as being under the sea and actually entering into their world."

"Maybe so, but just the thought of you under there has already made my hair stand on end. Wait till you get back and then you can snorkel around the rocks closer to the shore. We're out quite deep now!"

We had been paddling for approximately an hour now, and it was becoming increasingly more difficult to move against the current. The muscles in my arms were strained. Now I understood why the bunca came equipped with a small plastic bailer; it was continually filling with water. With only about six inches of free board, the bunca offered an open invitation for the sea to lap into the canoe, which it did with increasing regularity.

The Need to Touch Dry Land

For some unexplainable reason my mood had changed from enjoyment to anxiety. My eyes anxiously sought the shore; we had paddled out too far for my comfort. My stomach began fluttering nervously. Suddenly I wanted to be back on dry ground.

"Michelle, could you please take me back now? I've had enough. The water has turned too choppy for my liking and I'm feeling a touch seedy. I'm really sorry. I don't mean to spoil your day."

"Oh, Mum, don't be such a wimp. You said you wanted to come. Now where's your sense of adventure?"

"Deserted me, I'm afraid. I've experienced all I want to for one day. You know how nervous I am on the ocean. I think it was great of me even to venture out at all in this toy boat, which in my opinion is more suited to a backyard swimming pool."

"Okay, then," Michelle agreed reluctantly, the disappointment clearly showing on her face.

Extremely relieved, I dipped the oars into the sea, paddling strongly until the depth of the water was almost shallow enough for me to stand up. The pounding of my heart had subsided. I was grateful to be back within my own depth.

I enjoyed the ocean—to look at, admire, pay homage to its awesome power, or take in its waters on a hot summer day—but that's about as far as it went with me. There were so many unseen dangers lurking beneath its surface. I'd had more than enough trouble dealing with everyday threats, let alone flaunting unnecessary danger. After seeing the Spielberg movie *Jaws,* I had been haunted by nightmares for days, not that I was any water baby before!

"I enjoyed the ocean—to look at, admire, pay homage to its awesome power, or take in its waters on a hot summer day—but that's about as far as it went with me."

Standing up in the seven-foot bunca, I precariously balanced myself as I prepared to jump out. Bending down, I placed my hands on each side of the canoe, leaning my full weight on them, trying not to tip it over as I lifted up my right leg and placed it down onto the sandy bottom of the shallow water. Transferring my weight to the stable leg, I then lifted my other leg out of the canoe.

"Wonderful," I said, as I planted both feet on solid ground.

"Here's the key to the bungalow, Mum. What will you do for the rest of the afternoon?"

"I'll probably relax in the hammock and read for awhile. Michelle, I think you should come in as well. The water's not as calm as it was earlier on."

"Mum, I'm twenty-two years old. I've managed an entire year in Japan on my own, so I'm sure I can handle a day's outing in this child's canoe."

I gave up trying to convince her, realizing she was determined to have her own way. I relented only with a warning: "Please, Michelle, don't go out too far, will you?"

"No, I won't. See you later. Have fun."

Wading into the shore, I turned around to watch her glide off happily, singing with her walkman as she paddled in time to the music. Oh, well, she's happy. The young always have so much stamina. They seem fearless! Maybe they believe in their own immortality.

I was suddenly confronted with a sense of loss for my own youth. I pondered for a moment. At what age did fear replace daring? At one time, not so long ago, I would have felt cheated to have missed out on any action. Now I was content watching my children greedily devouring great chunks of life for themselves. Dragging my big toes in the sand and leaving a trail behind me, I sauntered up the beach to our bungalow in a reflective mood.

The day had become hot and sultry. Walking the twenty yards to the restaurant, I relished the thought of an ice cold mango shake. Mangoes, ice cream, yogurt, milk, and ice blended together made a refreshing drink.

My thirst prompted me to order two, which would last through the afternoon. Carrying them back to the bungalow, I noticed with some amazement that I had almost demolished one on the way. Collecting the walkman and a selection of choice classical tapes, my half-read novel, and the remains of the mango shakes, I settled into the hammock, anticipating a deliciously seductive afternoon.

Opening my book, I endeavored to read, but my mind kept wandering off. After several attempts to get into the novel, I gave up and succumbed to the afternoon delights. To Chopin's Minute Waltz in D-flat Major, I swayed gently to and fro, gazing up at the fluffy cumulus clouds as they drifted across the magnificent blue South Sea sky.

My thoughts were fleeting and scattered; I wasn't able to concentrate on any one subject for more than a moment. *What the heck, I don't have a care in the world,* I reflected. My lost youth, the regrettable past, the unknown future, the children's welfare—at this moment they were all far from me.

Staring out to sea, my attention was captured by a solitary windsurfer. The shocking pink and lime green sails assaulted the horizon. I was held transfixed as the board skimmed across the surface, at one stage almost becoming airborne. The rider seemed very competent as he maneuvered it through the choppy waters.

Instantly, I was aware that the sea had become quite a bit rougher, the glassy surface of the morning now gone. The wind had stirred up small churning waves. Michelle—in that little boat—came to the forefront of my mind, and an uneasiness crept through me.

Grabbing my sarong from the balcony railing, I tied it securely around me as I walked briskly towards the shoreline. From where I stood, the palm trees blocked my view of the other end of the beach. Shielding my eyes from the sun, I scanned the foreshore.

I breathed a sigh of relief as I sighted her about five hundred feet down the island, paddling fairly close to the shore. Thank goodness, she'd actually taken my advice for a change. I resumed my luxurious position in the hammock, and, to the emotionally charged melodies from the pen of Chopin, I drifted into a pleasurable afternoon siesta.

"Please, Be Home!"

Awakening some time later, I felt cramped and stiff. Beads of perspiration trickled down my back and forehead. Where my head had fallen forward onto my chest was now sticky. Yuk! A dip in the cooling ocean was the remedy. Snatching a towel, I ran down to the sea, dropping it onto the sand as I went. Without hesitation, I plunged into the surf, dunking right under for maximum relief. Ahh! That felt good. Refreshed, I stood up, squeezing the excess water from my hair.

As I did this, I noticed there were only a few people left on the beach. Long, early evening shadows streaked the sand. Whirling around, I looked at the sun. It was low in the sky. For goodness sake, it would soon be dusk. How long had I been asleep?

Clearing the salt water from my eyes, I once again peered down the southern end of the beach. By this time, I was sure I would see Michelle paddling her way home, but there was no sign of her. With a quickened step, I returned to the bungalow, dried off, and slipped on a cotton dress.

Locking the door behind me, I made my way down to the beach, hoping to meet up with her coming home. I took long, purposeful strides, my step quickening as I kept my eyes glued to the water's edge. I glanced at the molten sun as it descended in the glowing sky. Ripples of fear played up and down my spine. Though subtle, they nevertheless were early warning signs of my growing apprehension.

I strained to see what looked to be her bunca appearing from behind a rock about three hundred feet out. Was there one person or two in that bunca? I broke into a run, now needing action to deter the rising trepidation which threatened to take hold of me. No, there were definitely two people in there. Maybe she had taken someone on board for company? As it drew closer, my hopes were dashed. The person in the boat wore a bright yellow T-shirt. Definitely not Michelle!

From this vantage point, I was now able to see to the end of the point clearly. I wasn't mistaken; the sea was deserted! *Be calm,* I told myself forcefully as I broke into a run. Retracing my steps up the beach,

I now transferred my hopes to the possibility that she may have already arrived home, having approached the bungalow from another direction. Breathless from the exertion, I kept up my pace until our bungalow was in view. My heart was thudding hard against my chest, although thoughts of my own discomfort were not a consideration. With every step I prayed, *Please, be home, Michelle. . . . Please, be home!*

I stood staring at the vacant space where only this morning we had carried the bunca down to the water. Rooted to the spot, my mind searched desperately for another valid reason as to why she was not home. A reasonably logical answer came to my mind: She could have beached the boat at another place.

Not yet recovering my breath, I forced myself to keep on looking. Now my attention was focused on the chance that Michelle might have changed course during the afternoon and headed for the floating restaurant at the opposite end of the point from where I had been searching. *Yes, that's it,* I convinced myself with renewed hope. *She's gone to visit David and the crowd we had met several days before.*

Having yet another valid alternative as to why she had not returned, I subdued the melange of emotions that were stirring beneath the surface unvoiced. Halfway towards my destination, I met David on the beach.

"David, have you seen Michelle?" I asked, gasping out the words through a parched mouth.

"No, not today. Why?"

"Oh, my God, David, she took out a bunca for the day and hasn't come back yet." My fears rose to the surface, draining my face of color.

"Sit down for a minute and catch your breath. Now tell me exactly what has happened, Rachelle." He was calm as he took my arm and led me to a chair.

"We went out in a hired bunca this morning, planning to go around to the other side of the island," I explained. "After an hour or so, I'd had enough, so Michelle dropped me back on the beach and paddled off. She hasn't come back yet!"

"When did you see her last?" he asked.

"Around ten thirty—no, hang on, I saw her again at about eleven thirty," I said, with a tremor in my voice. "But it's almost dark, and I obviously expected her before now. There is no sight of her anywhere."

"Don't upset yourself, Rachelle. I think you're jumping the gun," David reassured me. "From what I know of Michelle, she seems a very

"I wasn't mistaken; the sea was deserted! Be calm, I told myself forcefully as I broke into a run."

capable young lady. I'll bet she's relaxing on another beach enjoying a cocktail while you are frantically worrying yourself for nothing."

"No, David, I know Michelle better than you. She wouldn't stay out like that. Even if she had been caught by the current and couldn't get back to this side of the island, she would have walked overland. It is not that far, you know. We were over there yesterday horseback riding, so she knew the way. Besides, I've been right down to the southernmost point. I would have seen her boat dragged up on the beach."

"Look, if it would make you feel better, I'll ask John if we could take his boat out to look for her. But I'm sure you're underestimating her. I bet she'll turn up large as life and wonder what all the fuss is about."

His reassuring confidence in Michelle's capabilities alleviated the rising panic in me. I desperately needed to be convinced that he was right. I did not wish to acknowledge the subliminal instinct which nudged the corners of my consciousness. Call it mother's intuition, but I inwardly sensed I would not find Michelle on the island. I didn't want to accept this primal information, let alone allow it to take root.

David, John, and I soon headed the forty-foot schooner out to sea. The churning machinery of the motor drowned out the whistling sounds of the strong sea breeze. We rounded the corner where the island tipped into the Pacific Ocean, where I'd last seen Michelle heading. I called out into the growing blackness of the night sea, "Michelle . . . Michelle." I called with my ears straining and my face contorted with concentration. We waited but silence reigned; my pleading calls went unanswered.

"Rachelle, we'll have to turn back now," John gently told me. "It's too dark to see anything. I doubt she'll be out here anyway. I bet she'll be waiting for you back at the bungalow."

I smiled weakly, trying to summon up enough courage to believe the possibility of his suggestion. Turning the boat around, we headed back to its mooring. There was still a chance Michelle had slipped through my search and would be waiting for me, and I clung desperately to that thought.

With supreme effort I suppressed the strangling lump in my throat which constricted my every breath. I shook uncontrollably! We steered into the berth. Even before the boat had moored properly, I leapt off into the knee-deep water. I possessed one single thought: to get to the bungalow and end this excruciating uncertainty.

She had to be there! My faith was running out of possibilities; this was the last plausible one. If she wasn't home, then there could only be one conclusion—she was out in that ocean.

No, I wouldn't accept that. She had to be home! Running along the dark deserted beach alone, I picked my way between the scattered rocks and trees, thankful that the moon gave enough light for me to move quickly.

Looking up into the vast open sky, I pleaded with a desperation I'd never known. *Dear God, please let her be home, please. This is too much for me to bear,* I prayed.

Up until now, drawing on the reserves of my inner strength, I had managed to contain the torrent of wild emotions behind a thin veneer of hope. I drew close to the moment which would reveal my joy or pain. In an excruciating, timeless instant, I stood paralyzed in agony. An impenetrable wall of reality confronted me.

She had not come home! The last threads of hope cementing me together caved in. I sunk to my knees in the sand, letting out a tormented howl from the very depths of my being.

FOUR

COLLISION WITH DESTINY

MICHELLE . . . 10:30 A.M., THURSDAY, MARCH 9, BORACAY ISLAND. The oars cut through the iridescent surface of the water with powerful precision. First one side, then the other. The bunca sliced effortlessly through the slightly buffeting waves. Just as I congratulated myself on mastering the technique of rowing, I tilted the oar the wrong way, managing to drench myself with an unwelcome spray of salty water. Well, that certainly doused my self-confidence!

Clad only in my bikini and shorts, I felt the sun beating down on my bare back. My skin felt invigorated by the heat of the sun's rays. Today was going to be a scorcher! My object of focus was the craggy, southernmost tip of the island. I had to maneuver the bunca around the tip if I wanted to get around to the other side.

Putting on my headphones, I pushed the play button on my walkman and turned the volume up to maximum. There was a momentary silence, then the raw, hardhitting voice of my favorite rock musician, Jimmy Barnes, came pounding through the walkman. The rhythm was contagious, and I began rowing in time to the intoxicating beat of "Freight Train Heart."

Initially, I had been annoyed with Mum for giving up so early, but now that she had, I was secretly pleased. I was free to do what I wanted and unleash my unmelodious voice as loud as I liked and no one would hear me, except some flying fish or a stray seagull. I was enjoying my solitude immensely, feeling as light and free as a summer breeze.

I marvelled at my exquisite surroundings; the clear blue sky was only interrupted by wisps of white cloud breaking up the monotony. I glanced over at the island, where waves of sweltering heat turned the entire island into a shimmering mirage. Swimmers and sun lovers adorned the ivory white strip of beach, giving it a flamboyant splash of color. A burning sensation began to well up in the muscles of my arms. What an exhilarating feeling it was to push your body to the limits. At this rate I wouldn't have to work out today!

Once again, I focused my attention on the tip of the island to see how I was progressing. Although I'd been rowing strenuously for quite some time, it registered with some surprise that I didn't appear to be getting any closer. In fact, I had the distinct feeling I was moving even further away from the shore. Maybe my perspective was a little deceiving as I was now parallel with the tip, although still quite a way out. I didn't seem to be able to maneuver the boat around it, and I couldn't understand why.

I reached into my bag to select another tape to play, slotted it into the walkman, and continued to row. This was undoubtedly proving to be more difficult than I had anticipated. Oh well, I wanted a challenge, and now I certainly had one. What the heck, the sun was shining, I was listening to my favorite music and holidaying on one of the world's most beautiful islands. So what if it wasn't all smooth sailing!

With renewed vigor I began paddling harder, determined to make it around the point. To my left, I noticed the approach of a brightly-colored fishing boat which passed quite close to me. Several of the fishermen waved cheerfully to me. I detected questioning looks on their faces and wondered if I appeared strange to them in some way. I couldn't understand why they were staring at me with such quizzical expressions. I glanced down to check if my bikini top had fallen off. No, everything was still in place. Possibly a blonde girl rowing on her own so far out was an unfamiliar sight.

Oh well, I was becoming accustomed to the locals looking bewildered at everything we tourists did. They really do think we're crazy, especially sunbaking. The idea of lying in the hot sun to get brown utterly confused them.

In Deep Water

Sometime later, I was struck by a disturbing realization. I had become so absorbed in my music and the laborious task of rowing that, unaware, I had drifted out a lot further than I intended. Underlying ripples of fear rose to the surface. I shook them off. Although I was now in deep water, literally, I still hated to give up so easily.

However, it was blatantly obvious even to me now that there was no physical way I was going to paddle this piddly little boat around the point. *Why continue this impossible mission?* I thought. *No, I'm going to call it a day.* I glanced at my watch; it was 1 P.M. Great, if I make good time I'd get back to the floating cocktail bar in time for a liquid lunch.

Turning the boat around with a new purpose in mind, I headed back in the direction I'd come from. Suddenly I was excited about the prospect of

---

"It was blatantly obvious even to me now that there was no physical way I was going to paddle this piddly little boat around the point."

---

meeting David while I was there. I'd met him over breakfast the first morning we had arrived on Boracay. Striking up a conversation together, we discovered we had an amazing rapport and much in common.

David had invited Mum and me on his friend's luxury cruiser for a day's outing. We planned to cruise around the island, but instead we got no more than fifty yards out to sea, only to tie up to the floating cocktail bar. Not surprisingly, we ended up spending a glorious day, drinking fabulous fruit and other exotic cocktails, and basking in the heat of the tropical sun.

Located approximately fifty yards from shore, the floating cocktail bar was the most ingenious idea I had ever seen. Made entirely of bamboo, it was about ten feet squared in an octagonal shape, kept adrift by polystyrene floats anchoring it firmly in place. Its unique aspect was its ability to be moved to different locations along the shoreline. The bamboo slats on the floor had been polished until smooth, and in its center stood the cocktail bar with stools surrounding it.

At the other end, casual chairs, cushions, and lounge chairs lay scattered around. Skimpily clad people from a variety of countries lazed casually under the tropical sun. A huge white tarpaulin sheltered the bar, offering a great escape when one got too hot. Alternatively, one could just roll off the side into the crystal clear water to cool off. This was the ultimate in self-indulgence, a simply fabulous way to spend a lazy afternoon in paradise.

I had felt very much like a film star sailing up in our cruiser. One of the local boys offered his hand as Mum and I stepped aboard, so to speak. I gave Mum a knowing look which she reciprocated. We certainly captured the attention of everyone; we had arrived in style, and everyone else had to swim the fifty yards from shore.

The scorching heat, however, made every surface red-hot to touch. The soles of my feet sizzled, which forced me to drop my film star facade and dash across the bamboo floor, flopping into a sheltered deck chair. John, the owner of the cruiser, ordered cocktails for everyone. Moving his chair closer to me, David asked if I could rub some sunscreen on his shoulders. I willingly obliged!

David was a charming companion. His sandy blonde hair was appealingly long, which I thought was very cute. His amber-colored eyes emanated a warm intelligence. He was twenty-six years old and close to six-feet tall. With his well-muscled body and golden brown tan, he was the epitome of a Californian. Gazing over at him sipping a Mai Tai, I had the distinct feeling that this was going to be a fantastic holiday.

American men had a certain charm that I found alluring. The ones I had met tended to be tall, good looking, and witty. But it was the timbre of their accent that attracted me, so masculine, yet easygoing and lighthearted. They had a casual attitude about life that I found particularly appealing. David fitted this category perfectly.

Nearing the moment I would see him again, I replayed over in my mind the things he had said to me. He was undoubtedly one of the most mentally stimulating men I had met in a long time. I discovered we were incredibly in tune, like kindred spirits. Although we had only known each other a few days, a rarely-found affinity existed between us. The electricity between us was tangible. With renewed vitality, I began paddling faster in anticipation of seeing him again.

I felt a stretch of unused muscles in my shoulders beginning to ache. By this stage, the novelty of my adventure had well and truly worn off. I was looking forward to a long, cold drink. The bottle of water I'd brought with me was now as tepid as warm bath water and would do little to quench my thirst. A cold drink would be worth waiting for. My parched mouth began watering at the tantalizing thought.

The early afternoon sun was like a blazing orb in the bright blue sky, hammering down on me relentlessly. Reaching into my bag I retrieved my sunscreen and poured a lavish amount into my hand, rubbing it into my shoulders which were becoming angry red. I could feel my nose sizzling as well; I knew I should put some zinc on it, but the last thing I wanted was David seeing me with a fluorescent green nose.

I decided a smearing of SPF 4 would have to suffice. After spending the last few months in Southeast Asia at several of its island resorts, I was fully aware of the damaging effects of the tropical sun. However, I was fortunate that my tanned skin was accustomed to the sun and not prone to burning. With the increased awareness of skin cancer in recent years, I had become more protective of my skin than ever before.

Now that that was taken care of, I returned to the job of maneuvering the bunca in the direction I wanted it to go. Easier said than done, though.

Tremors of concern again nudged at the corners of my mind. I ignored them, not wishing to acknowledge the truth—that I had drifted out recklessly far. *But no worries,* I reassured myself. *I'll alter course and cut across the bay diagonally.*

One thing I definitely knew: I was making headway as I was now parallel to the jagged rock formation I had sunbaked next to yesterday. Great, that meant I was virtually opposite our bungalow. *I wonder if Mum is still out there sunbaking.* Straining my eyes I scanned the beach, but she was nowhere to be seen! *Oh well, I'll catch up with her later.*

I wondered if I should paddle the boat in and return it now; then I could walk the rest of the way on the white beach. No, that would mean I'd have to swim the fifty yards out to the floating bar. Forget that, I'd arrive looking like a drowned rat. Now, was that any way to impress David? Absolutely not! *It's not that much further,* I reasoned. *I might as well row the rest of the way up there and besides, then I can tie the bunca up to the floating bar.*

Now that I'd made a decision, the slight uneasiness I'd momentarily felt ceased. Changing tapes again, I began singing along to U2's smash hit "I Still Haven't Found What I'm Looking For." A gnawing sensation in the pit of my stomach reminded me how hungry I was. I'd accidently skipped breakfast in my enthusiasm to get an early start. Soon mental pictures of my favorite foods filled my mind.

Think Logically!

I emerged slowly from my daydreams of food with the stark realization: I was undoubtedly even farther away from shore, although I was making a concerted effort to paddle directly toward it. My euphoric, lighthearted feeling instantly shattered. My heart began to beat faster! What on earth was happening? Why am I not getting closer to the floating bar? Although I was now opposite the bar, I must still be at least fifty yards out.

What can I do? Should I wave or call out? I wondered. I wanted someone to know I was having some difficulty in paddling the bunca back to shore. Judging by the distance, however, I was painfully aware that I was well out of earshot, and the shoreline was receding at an alarming rate. People were now just colorful dabs on the beach.

Flashing warning signs beeped on and off in my mind, signaling danger. I knew I was in trouble! Ripping out my earphones, I threw the walkman into my bag. I had to get serious!

Now Michelle, get a grip on yourself. Don't panic! You've got to think logically, I told myself. I had to change my strategy in order to know that I was making progress. I decided to set a closer goal for myself, so I searched for a reference point. Up ahead was a dark patch of coral which stood out in the otherwise transparent water. I made this my target.

While I paddled furiously towards it, my attention was focused solely on this point. As I glanced into the waters surrounding me, the wind whipped up a series of hostile little waves which I had to row against. This did not, however, obstruct my clear view of the sea floor. It was a frighteningly long way down!

The remaining shreds of confidence in my ability to get this situation under control were diminishing. With every unnerving discovery, I was faced with the alarming truth of my predicament. The bunca glided over the dark patch of coral I had focused on. Now as I looked around me, bewildered, the sea was a maze of reefs. I couldn't be sure whether this was the reef I had been aiming for or not.

I set another goal which was a reef about thirty feet ahead. I was afraid my underlying suspicions might be true, that in fact I was drifting farther out to sea. Gripping the oar tightly with both hands, I began paddling furiously. The oar sliced through the water with every determined stroke. My concentration was intense!

I found the once enchanting sea that now surrounded me very frightening. The surface of the water was choppy, although beneath it I could still sense the tranquility of this magical underwater world. In any other circumstances this would have been a breathtaking spectacle; however, this serene world now represented a dangerous threat to me. In spite of myself, I was mesmerized by the myriad sea life I saw swaying gently with the current. A school of shimmering neon fish darted nervously in and out of a cluster of sea anemones. An electric blue starfish clung precariously to the jagged reef. With a sudden intake of breath, I noticed an enormous rainbow-speckled fish appear on the scene. With lightning speed, jaws open, it moved in for the kill, disappearing almost immediately between the seaweed with a gullet full of neon fish.

I observed this encounter with awe. Swiveling my head to the left side of the bunca to see where he had gone, I was suddenly hypnotized by a giant grey stingray, his huge wings oscillating, propelling him through the water. Overcome by a sickening fear, I was so relieved to be in the safety of the bunca, protected from these fearsome creatures. I hoped to God that a wave wouldn't tip my fragile boat over, tossing me into the sea teeming with menacing danger. The mere thought of it petrified me!

I could feel anxiety becoming entrenched in me, but in order to keep control of the situation, I had to continually squelch these feelings with a blanket of artificial calm I had manufactured but certainly didn't feel. I longed to put down the oars and rest my aching arms. The tedious task of paddling was beginning to irritate me. I was tired, hungry, and ready to be home!

I was even prepared to suffer the embarrassment of signaling for assistance and being towed to shore. I could just picture it: wouldn't I be hassled by the guys? Intrepid Michelle would have to admit that the adventure turned out to be a failure. Well, I was saved from that indignity as there was not a boat in sight. But now I was faced with an even more daunting prospect: how was I going to get back to shore?

The next fifteen minutes were spent in the repetitive action of focusing on a reef and making a beeline towards it. This was the only way I could ascertain whether or not I was making any progress toward the shore. But how much longer could I go on pretending that everything was okay? I threw down my oars in frustration. Was this the reef I was targeting or not? I couldn't be sure. Looking about me in bewilderment, I noticed all the surrounding reefs were almost identical. How could I distinguish one from the other?

Suddenly, like a ton of bricks, the seriousness of my situation hit me. How on earth was I going to get out of this mess? What were my options? I could scream, but would anyone hear me? I doubted it. If I stood up in the bunca and waved my T-shirt, was there any possibility of anyone seeing me? I doubted it! My chances of being picked up by another boat were slim, considering the last boat I had seen was about four hours ago. After eliminating all possible sources of help, it was obvious that I had gotten myself into this and it was up to me to get myself out of it. But how?

Engrossed in my thoughts, I suddenly became aware that I was moving at an alarming speed straight out to sea! I was horrified by the distance I had traveled in a matter of only minutes. All the ground I had succeeded in covering by my persistent paddling had been in vain. Panic-stricken, I desperately wrestled with the grave reality of the dilemma. Bombarded with feelings too overwhelming to handle, my mind went completely blank. I couldn't think straight! My entire system froze with indecision.

I sat there traumatized for some moments before I willed myself to snap out of it. *Get a grip on yourself, Michelle. Every second lost in thought is ground I'll have to make up. As Mum would say, "thinking stops action."* With that injection of positive thought, I picked up my oars and paddled furiously, spurred on by my rising fear.

The adrenalin pumped through my veins, intensified by the imminent danger I faced. My entire attention centered on getting back to dry land; all other thoughts were obliterated! I could no longer afford to divert my concentration every few minutes by evaluating my progress by the reefs below me. I knew beyond a doubt that this current was a powerful force, and I would need every ounce of strength and ingenuity if I were going to escape from its hold.

Powerfully striking the water with the oars, I propelled myself forward. One-two to the right. One-two to the left. One-two to the right. Every cell and fiber in my body was engaged in the task. I felt devoid of all thoughts and feelings, operating on automatic with a sole purpose in mind: survival!

With every stroke, I was now in direct opposition to the strong current. After about fifteen minutes of this all-consuming effort, I was physically exhausted. I had to rest, even if it was just for a minute. A searing heat burned deep into the muscles of my arms as waves of excruciating pain tore at my limbs. Never before had I experienced pain as intense. I drew a long, deep breath in an attempt to slow down the wild pounding of my heart.

And I watched in horror as the bunca again began moving swiftly back out to sea. I had to resume paddling; there was no other choice! I was brutally tired, but I picked up the oars with resignation. *How much longer can I go on?* I wondered. Exhaustion was no longer a consideration. I demanded my body continue the battle; to give up the fight would mean to accept the inevitable. There was no escape; I had to endure. This was a do-or-die situation.

"Engrossed in my thoughts, I suddenly became aware that I was moving at an alarming speed straight out to sea! I was horrified by the distance I had traveled in a matter of only minutes."

As I clenched my fists tightly around the oars in a vise-like grip, the whites of my knuckles stood out. The friction of the splintered wooden oars against the soft palms of my hands had shredded them raw. I was in agony! I longed to give up the futility of it all. How absurd to attempt to struggle against the sea! But instincts stronger than my pain wouldn't allow me to quit.

I summoned all my inner strength to suppress the torrent of emotions threatening to consume me. To keep control of my emotions was imperative. I felt as if I were on a tightrope of acute tension, too scared to cry or feel any self-pity. To concede a single tear of submission would burst the floodgates, dissolving me into a vulnerable wreck. There could be no surrender, no retreat! This was not a game anymore; this was survival, and I was fighting for my life. The odds were against me and were increasing with every minute.

The setting sun in the early evening sky had turned from primrose to flaming orange, indicating precious daylight hours were dwindling. The time was 4:17 P.M., only one and a half hours before darkness. Could I get back to Boracay by then? It suddenly seemed a very long way away. After paddling nonstop for five and a half hours, I was agonizingly tired. My mind was willing, but my body was unable to endure the demands I was making on it.

I watched the shoreline receding; the only thing visible now was a slither of white sand. The horrific truth of my predicament struck me in a fresh wave of shock. I berated myself for such incredible stupidity. How had I let this situation get so out of hand, let it escalate to such life-threatening proportions? I felt so angry at myself, knowing I should have paddled the boat straight into shore at the first signs of difficulty, but in my carefree mood I was unwilling to spoil "this perfect day" on the ocean by heading in early.

Instead, I had recklessly continued believing I could rectify what had seemed at first only a minor problem. I knew all along I was going off course, but I believed, without a doubt, that with a little concentrated effort I would easily make it back in. I had even suspected then that the reason I'd started drifting out was due to a patch of turbulent water that I passed through. If only I could have seen then how wrong I was, that in fact the strong currents, not an isolated patch of rough water, drove me out to sea.

My difficulties had begun when I tried to get around the southernmost point. Without the protection of the island's land mass, I had ignorantly paddled into the direct path of the ocean currents, which then carried me along in their wake. From that point on, the situation had steadily worsened until now, and my life was in severe jeopardy.

Gripped in a deadlock of my own fear, I racked my brain for a solution. Wrestling with indecision, I had only two choices, both of which could be fatal. I could not afford to make another rash decision. I was now over four hundred yards from shore.

I could probably swim there by nightfall if I did it in slow, easy strokes, alternating between backstroke and breaststroke. When I got tired, I could float on my back until I regained my strength. Or better still, I could swim under the surface of the water, using the snorkel to breathe and my flippers to propel me. I assumed I could thus escape the strong currents that had taken me prisoner. I tried to evaluate how I thought my physical strength and resilience would hold out. It was an extremely long way, and my energy reserves were running on empty; but I was physically fit from working out daily. There was a fighting chance I would make it.

Looking down into the water, I clearly saw a mass of reefs swarming with sea life which were completely oblivious and unperturbed by my crisis. The irresistible allure of the ocean was now laced with petrifying images that released a sick, nameless sensation within me. A horrifying vision loomed up from the recesses of my mind. Huge, oscillating wings of steel grey swam past my masked face. Enveloped by the stingray's awesome wings, I saw myself being dragged down into a watery grave.

My heart palpitated wildly! Could I bare the ordeal of being submerged and exposed to these fearsome creatures in my struggle to reach the shore? I was haunted by the thought that if I didn't make it back before nightfall, I would be trapped in this dark and foreboding under-

"I knew all along I was going off course, but I believed, without a doubt, that with a little concentrated effort I would easily make it back in."

world at the mercy of these predators. My skin crawled at the very thought of it. Paralyzed with overwhelming dread, I knew I could not go through with this!

I was left with only one option—to stay in the bunca and wait to be rescued. This was certainly a grim alternative! I rationalized that I couldn't possibly leave the boat just floating out here. At the rate it was traveling, especially without my weight in it, within a short space of time it would be lost forever in the infinite expanse of the open sea. *Imagine,* I told myself. *The owner will have heart failure if I arrive back without his boat.* He would demand to know where it was. What could I tell him? *Oh, it is drifting somewhere out in the ocean.* I'm sure he would be extremely unhappy about my abandoning his boat.

Anyway, I reasoned, I had my moneybelt on me containing our passports, airline tickets, and travelers' checks. It wouldn't be overly sensible to let them be ruined, especially since the nearest passport office was nine hundred and fifty miles away in Manila. Not to mention, my camera, walkman, and other valuables in my bag would also be lost. When I weighed the pros and cons of the situation, it became apparent that to swim would not be the most logical decision.

Okay, Michelle, calm down. Keep your head clear. Now, do I have any other alternatives? No, I had exhausted them all. The only choice open to me was to stay put in the safety of the bunca and let the currents carry me to land. I placated myself with the assurance that it was impossible not to get caught by the safety net of the adjacent island of Panay, which I appeared to be heading directly toward. I presumed the bunca would be washed up on Panay's long stretch of coastline. It would mean, of course, a long trek and hiring a boat to take me back to Boracay. Then there was the problem of arranging for the bunca to be picked up from Panay. What an enormous hassle it would create. I promised myself that this was the last time I would ever go canoeing alone.

Actually, I was numbed by the new set of circumstances I was facing. I watched on helplessly as the bunca was carried farther and farther out. Oh God, this was even worse than rowing. The consuming effort of trying to get back to Boracay had at least kept my mind occupied. The stillness and inaction of sitting here idly had opened a trapdoor in my mind, releasing hideously morbid thoughts, even more shocking than my physical struggle had ever been. My impulse was to pick up the oars again and start rowing frantically to rid myself of the diabolical feelings that had taken over my senses. There was no escaping from myself; I had nowhere to run and nowhere to hide.

Collision with Destiny

The next fifteen minutes passed in a blur of fiendish thoughts. I sat there in utter disbelief. Suddenly, I realized that the bunca had shifted course! Instead of heading directly towards the island of Panay as I had presumed it would do, something disastrous had happened. I was now traveling parallel with the island about two hundred yards out.

My belief that I had been capable of paddling back to Boracay was an inaccurate assumption. But worse still, the safety net of Panay Island, where I was sure the current would carry me, and my last bastion of hope was incredibly dissolving before my eyes. This was all too much! All along, though I knew that I was in serious trouble, I was aware of the island of Panay and believed that, if worse came to worst, it was my safeguard. Now I was being transported not to Panay but parallel to it—hundreds of yards away.

But all was not lost! A plan was forming itself in my mind. Obviously, the course the bunca had now taken would not reach Boracay or Panay, but I had one last fighting chance. In my estimation, the bunca would pass reasonably close to the tip of Caticlan, the farthermost point of Panay. The terrible fear I had previously held about swimming among the gruesome creatures of the sea had been dwarfed in the face of an even more horrific realization: that of spending a night alone in the clutches of the cold ocean, engulfed in blackness.

With that thought, a decision was made. It was now 4:40 P.M.! At the stroke of five o'clock, I would take my chances and make a swim to Caticlan. Whatever the distance to shore, that was my appointed time. I calculated I would need a minimum of one hour to swim there. If I started any later than that, I would have to swim in darkness. That thought I found totally abhorrent.

I was now locked into a waiting game. Time was a paradox! In one way it seemed to stretch out into a nerve-racking eternity, the minutes ticking by in a frightening procession. At the other end of the spectrum, I was hurtled forward, closer and closer to my hour of dread. Time was the enemy I was unable to escape. Picking up my snorkeling equipment, I began putting it on piece by piece, preparing myself for the inevitable swim to shore.

I looked down at myself through the tight-fitting silicone mask. My vision was blurred by an array of saltwater drops which had formed over the glass. My body appeared contorted from the way I had squeezed myself sideways into the bunca, with my flippered feet hanging over the rim. Sucking in large gasps of air through the snorkel, I tried to control my breathing.

I could feel myself hyperventilating and could taste the bile rising in my throat as a spasm of nausea swept through me. Tearing the snorkel from my mouth, I lurched forward. My head dangling over the edge of the bunca, I dry retched until my stomach contracted with pain. I fell back to the bottom of the bunca, completely drained of all energy. How I was going to make that swim was beyond me, but I knew instinctively that it might be my only chance.

I scanned the ocean for John's cruiser for what seemed like the hundredth time. There was nothing! Where was everybody? I couldn't believe no one was out looking for me. Surely Mum must realize by now that I was missing. I clung desperately to the belief that any minute I would turn around and see Mum powering toward me in the boat.

I wanted to weep with frustration. She was my mother. Didn't she know that I was in trouble? These last few hours I had constantly sent her telepathic messages that my life was in severe danger. I wanted desperately to let her know that I hadn't stopped off for a drink around the other side of the island, which I was afraid she might be thinking. I pleaded for her to hear my cries for help, to come and rescue me now before it was too late.

Now I had five minutes left. I prayed, *Please come and rescue me before the clock strikes five.* She had only a few minutes left before my appointment with destiny. I found it inconceivable that my innocent venture had bought me to the brink of this life-threatening moment.

I was in dire need of a cigarette. I hoped my deliberately slow inhalation would serve as a pacifier, calming my nerves and giving me the courage to face the most frightening moment of my life, which was only two minutes away. My hands shook uncontrollably as I reached for the packet. Thank goodness they were dry! I placed the cigarette between my quivering lips and attempted to light it. I couldn't believe it. The lighter was soaking wet and refused to ignite. The irony of having dry cigarettes and a wet lighter was a catalyst that shattered my remaining fragile defenses. I let out a howl of frustration and black despair. Tears of anger and desperation burst forth with the fury of an erupting volcano.

Time had hurtled me forward to my appointed time. It was 4:48 P.M. I debated going now or waiting another two minutes. Obviously, nobody was coming to rescue me. *If I'm going to make it out of here alive,* I thought, *then it is up to me.*

With sickening dread, I raised myself into a sitting position, my legs hanging over the side of the bunca. My eyes were riveted on the island I was preparing to swim to. I didn't dare look into the water I was about to enter, with all the unseen dangers it contained. I knew with certainty that if I deliberated any longer, I would lose the edge and my courage would fail! Taking a deep breath, I summoned up all my strength. Grabbing hold of the side of the bunca, I leaned forward and prepared to jump.

Suddenly, the silence that reigned over the ocean was shattered as a loud, commanding voice from behind me said: "Don't leave the boat!"

FIVE

IN TOO DEEP

MICHELLE . . . 5:00 P.M., THURSDAY, MARCH 9, CUYO EAST PASSAGE. "What?" I said aloud. I had clearly heard the unmistakable words. A flood of relief washed over me. Someone had finally come to rescue me before I was forced to make the petrifying swim to shore. I released my grip on the bunca and swung around wildly, my heart beating fiercely in a state of apprehension.

There was no one in sight!

I was instantly engulfed by a wave of disappointment of such magnitude that I slumped back into the cradle of the bunca, fighting to gain control of the disintegration taking place within. As I lay there in shock, I tried to fathom who or what had said those words to me. Why shouldn't I leave the boat? If it wasn't Mum or a fisherman about to rescue me, then who was it?

It certainly wasn't a figment of my own mind, disturbed as I was. Somebody had spoken to me, and I'd heard the instructions loud and clear! Terror had returned with a vengeance, and indecision had been thrust upon me once again. I had resigned myself to make the perilous swim to shore, but now my feelings were ambivalent.

The last remnants of light were being chased away by the encroaching night. How would anyone find me in the dark? Would they even bother to go out looking?

To my horror I realized abruptly that even if Mum suspected I was in trouble and was out searching for me, she wouldn't be looking for me here, but around the other side of the island where she presumed I spent the day. And if I stayed in the bunca, I would be inevitably dragged along with the currents farther and farther out into the open sea. I felt sick with dread at the thought of spending the night out here, floating around in the darkness.

This traumatizing thought made me re-examine my decision to swim, which seemed my only hope. To swim or to stay with the bunca became the gravest ultimatum I'd ever been forced to confront, my very survival dependent on my making the right choice. The waves already were a lot bigger and more ferocious, and the wind was rising in velocity, whipping up the ocean into a tumultuous squall.

The thought of spending the night alone in the ocean compelled me to make a decision. I would stick to my original plan, no matter how hazardous, and attempt to swim to the shores of Caticlan, risking whatever the consequences might be. I was being carried farther from land every minute I procrastinated. This inaction could very well cost me my life. I had to act immediately.

My eyes sought the land. I looked longingly at the slither of firm earth I so desperately wanted to plant my feet upon. Positioning myself to jump, without warning, the same words were repeated with even more authority and conviction than previously.

"Don't leave the boat!" the voice said. The last time I was unsure, but now I knew without a shadow of a doubt that this instruction was not the product of my own chaotic mind. It distinctly originated from somewhere outside myself. The voice seemed to literally boom down from the heavens above.

Stunned by the power of the voice and the supremacy it conveyed, I squinted my eyes and gazed speculatively at the sky. Aloud I asked, "Is that you, God?"

My question hung poignantly in the air. I waited expectantly for a response, straining my ears for the reassurance I longed to hear. Nothing but the sound of the roaring swells of water crashing around me reminded me of my predicament.

This command I received was in total conflict with what I believed to be a logical course of action, namely to swim to shore. Nevertheless, the power of the voice had rendered me impotent and confused. I felt powerless to do anything except resign myself not to disobey and swim to shore, but to stay put in the bunca.

If that voice belonged to God, then I assumed He knew of the danger I was in. In His wisdom, maybe He could foresee the future and know the perils of swimming. Anyway, by now I was so scared and confused that I didn't have the strength or the nerve to do anything else but sit there immobilized, watching myself drift further out to nowhere.

Sunset

The sun had become a flaming ball of orange against the evening sky. It tinted the midnight blue water to gold. Dusk was falling fast! There was absolutely nothing more I could do, except wait and hope rescue would come. Stifling a sob, I felt a wave of helplessness wash over me. I longed to put my head in my lap and cry hysterically, to permit myself to weep until there was nothing left inside. But I couldn't allow myself to become so vulnerable. Besides, crying right now wouldn't give me the release I sought. To break down would shatter what little inner strength I had left, and it was imperative to save that reserve for what would undoubtedly be the most horrendously frightening night of my life.

"This command I received was in total conflict with what I believed to be a logical course of action, namely to swim to shore. Nevertheless, the power of the voice had rendered me impotent and confused."

I swallowed hard at the lump in my throat that felt like a dislodged golf ball. Lying back down in the bunca I removed the snorkel and mask but kept the flippers on and waited for the inevitable to happen—the impenetrable darkness to come upon me.

The very thought of being blinded by the inky blackness of night, alone in the ocean, seemed incomprehensible. Lying in the bottom of the bunca I began streaming with the sweat of utter panic as I visually digested the scene that awaited me. This brought to the surface of my mind the awful knowledge that fish feed at night. My stomach began to churn in motion to the sea surrounding me. I felt so horribly naked and exposed in this hostile environment, stripped of all my bravado and courage.

The movie *Jaws* came unbidden to mind. I mentally surveyed the minute, seven-foot bunca; it was so flimsy it was liable to fall apart at any moment, or, more likely, capsize. The chance of being swept overboard was an all-too-real possibility. If there were hungry sharks lurking beneath the surface, I wouldn't last a minute. Life had dealt me a bitter blow, but I had to rise above the fear and concentrate on survival. I would need all my wits about me if I wanted to make it. A moment's loss of concentration, one false move, could prove fatal. This was, however, easier said than done. I had for the moment managed to suppress the consuming fear, but before long I knew it would be back to haunt me.

It was now eight minutes past six! The sky had been transformed into a magnificent display of colors. On a royal blue backdrop, sunburst orange and slithers of magenta red and dusty pink lit up the sky. Under normal circumstances, I would have been rendered breathless by such beauty, but what it now represented simply sickened me. If only I could harness the sun and keep it with me.

I didn't see how I was going to make it through the night in the stormy, pitch-black ocean. I begged the sun not to desert me, but I knew it was an inevitable occurrence of nature. To restrain myself from having a complete emotional breakdown, I began to cling frantically to the belief that if I could just make it through the night, Mum would be here to rescue me tomorrow. By then she would have organized search-and-rescue parties to look for me at first light.

I began to whimper her name. "Mummy, I'm so scared. If only you were here with me, we could handle this together."

A logical thought wedged its way into my mind. *No, that would be worse. Who would know we were missing and come to search for us?* It was a bittersweet thought.

"Mum, help me," I called into the nothingness, as tears of self-pity stung my eyes. I held dear to the one belief that Mum would be here tomorrow, but it was all I could do to hold on to my dwindling hope. To my horror the waters around me had become progressively more turbulent, lifting the fragile bunca alarmingly skyward, then plunging it ferociously downward into another swell of white water. Because of the outriggers, the bunca moved sideways instead of meeting the waves head-on. This was disastrous! It was frighteningly obvious that it would only take a sufficiently large wave to simply knock the bunca over completely. Would I be capable of righting the bunca if it capsized? I hoped I'd never have to put that to the test.

The waves continually washed into the bunca. I glanced down at my belongings slopping around in about seven inches of water which had collected at the bottom. In a reflex action that had become second nature, I began bailing water again. Thank God the bunca had come equipped with the white plastic bailer. My shoulders felt as if they were being wrenched from their sockets, but I had to do what I could to stop the bunca from sinking.

My fear was blanketed by a mask of total numbness which pervaded my mind and body. I was numbed by the shocking reality that this was actually happening to me, numbed from the cold and saturated clothes that clung to my wet skin, numbed from the throbbing aches and pains that racked my body, numbed from the truthful fact that no one was coming to rescue me. I felt like an abandoned child, lonely, desperate, and petrified. My senses had been obliterated. I felt like a lifeless robot operating on auto pilot. I settled into a repetitive cycle: The waves flooded the bunca; I bailed water; I was capable of no more. It felt as if I were on the very edge of the world, about to be washed right over the side into nothingness. The sea appeared to be rolling toward a black void at the end of the earth and it was dragging me along with it. I was rendered impotent, with absolutely no control.

Now I could understand why at one time ancient explorers thought the world was flat, and they risked falling off the edge when they ventured out into the uncharted expanse of the ocean. I could see the perimeter of water surrounding me on the horizon, and it was almost impossible to believe it went on and on and did not just come to a halt, where I would fall off the edge into the stratosphere.

Nightfall

The sunset had now disappeared, leaving me to face the foreboding darkness alone, which seemed to infiltrate every part of my body until I couldn't separate myself from the night. The darkness and desolation had entered the core of me and refused to leave. I felt like a caged animal, forced into a corner with my back against the wall. I was trapped with no visible escape in sight, physically or emotionally.

Looking into the sky I noted the creamy whiteness of the moon; at least it hadn't deserted me and did shed a little light, so I wasn't in total darkness. However, I felt that it was also against me, united with the sun and sea in a sinister plot to terrify me to death, literally! The moon, I noticed, was nestled in a thick layer of storm clouds.

Gazing skyward, I gasped as the full implication hit me. The signs were evident; a storm was gathering and I would be caught in the midst of it. Was this some kind of horror movie? It didn't seem feasible that this was actually happening to me! My heart began thudding against my chest as complete panic set in. *Oh, please, don't let this be true . . . a false alarm . . . anything but what it appears to be.*

These tropical storms usually only last a few minutes, but in those few minutes the effects can be devastating. I'd experienced many in Thailand and knew they were laced with potential havoc. The bunca wasn't even long enough for me to lie down in and barely wide enough for me to squeeze sideways into; so I doubted its seaworthiness even to make it through the night, let alone through a storm. If I were honest with myself, I knew the bunca didn't stand a chance. Only a miracle would save me now. Oh, if only I had hired the bigger boat which had a sail, then I would have been able to direct it into land. But today had been a series of fatal mistakes, each new one surpassing the other in bizarre misfortune.

I wanted to scream with frustration and self-pity! How could I have been so incredibly stupid? Actually, maybe it wasn't stupidity so much as believing I was invincible, a superwoman or something. I'd been reckless, taunting the elements, facing any challenge with a devil-may-care attitude. Well, now I was paying the price. I had been made to face my own vulnerability and mortality. I'd tempted destiny with an attitude of supreme confidence in my own ability to overcome any obstacle.

I did, however, have a gut feeling that my predicament was no coincidence. I wondered briefly, *Is God trying to teach me something, get me to take a realistic look at myself and my life, or more likely bring me to a point of humility?* I had to admit that I certainly needed it. But wasn't this lesson a little extreme, in fact bordering on outrageous? I could have understood if He had allowed me to suffer a bit of discipline to bring me into line, maybe until five o'clock, then have someone come to rescue me, but this was taking it just a touch too far! What was equally frightening was that if I failed the test, would I get another chance?

I was ready to promise anything in return for my life. I wanted to be released from this nightmare, to be home, safe and secure. I felt I had more than learned my lesson already. *What is it you want from me, God? I'll do anything if You get me out of this mess—anything, I promise.*

I thought seriously about the other times in my life when I'd been in trouble, and the promises I'd made to God. Now when I thought back I realized that as soon as the crisis had passed and my prayers had been answered, God had been promptly forgotten, put on the back burner until the next time I was in trouble and needed Him. I'd reneged on my deals, too caught up in the swing of my own personal life. Now I felt remorseful, that I hadn't been sincere. I'd used God for my own selfish purposes and forgotten Him and the pledges I'd made! So why should He trust me again? Why should He help me now? I reasoned that I'd already proven I wasn't genuine in my previous promises, it was true, so why should He help me now?

"I thought seriously about the other times in my life when I'd been in trouble, and the promises I'd made to God."

This fact really frightened me. I felt so utterly alone, so terribly guilty for asking for God's help, but I had no choice. *There was nothing left to do. God was my last option, my only hope.*

I said aloud with an inner trembling, "God, if You are up there and are listening to me now, I want You to know that I'm scared with a fear I've never known. I'm sorry for what I've done in the past, but if it's in Your power to do miracles and change my situation, then I beg You to please help me. Do it now, God. Don't make me sweat it out through the night to prove a point. I get the message loud and clear and will change my attitude and my ways. I won't be neglectful of You anymore and will obey everything You say. Just please help me, God, I beg You!

"Don't let me die, not now, not here. I'm not ready yet! I suppose many people tell You that when they find out they have some terminal disease, that they aren't ready to die. But who's ever really ready to give up on life anyway, unless they are over ninety? I suppose it is fear of the unknown. What happens when we die? Where do we go? Is there really a heaven, or is that just a popular myth so people will not be afraid of death? I don't know what to believe, God. But I do know I'm not ready to die.

"Besides, I believe I've been a good person in my life; You know that. I've never intentionally hurt anyone; in fact, I've always gone out of my way to be caring and generous. I'd give my last cent to someone on the street, God, so why am I being punished? Aren't there enough wicked people in the world who deserve it far more than I? Murderers? Rapists? I know You have far more wisdom than I, but don't You honestly think that I'm being unduly punished? It seems to me to be a rather severe penalty for just reneging on my promises. Or maybe it's really the truth that only the good die young. When I watch the news, it surely seems that way. Nevertheless, You know that I'm in dire straits and I need Your help. Please do something. I'm begging You!"

I sat back, straining my ears, waiting for the forgiving words. I scanned the ocean for the boat that would appear and the helicopters that would fly down from the sky and pluck me from these treacherous waters. My desperate pleas were answered by a cold, stark silence that seemed to penetrate the air, chilling me to the very bone.

I was so utterly desolate, so terribly sorry for myself. *Nobody cares. Even God has forgotten me.* But then again who did I think I was—making deals with God, plea bargains for my life? I had nothing to offer God in return; besides I didn't even know what He wanted of me. I realized then, with a calmness I didn't know I had, that if I were to make it out alive, I would have to rely totally on my own ability. Expecting a miracle was wishful thinking and childish. I needed to use all of my resourcefulness, tenacity, and wits if I did not want to die.

I snapped to attention when I caught sight of a light on Caticlan, flashing off and on. My heart jumped in response, thrilled by the evidence of human life. Was that John's boat signaling its whereabouts to me? Since I hadn't been found, maybe they had rigged up this device for me to locate them in the dark. The light was approximately two hundred yards away to my left, so I would have to battle against the currents in order to reach the signal. The odds were a hundred to one that I would make it all the way, but if I could only get close enough to scream out for help, possibly they would hear me.

My sense of helplessness evaporated as I spun into action. Picking up the oars, I frantically paddled toward the flashing light. I barely felt the pain shooting up my arms as I rowed powerfully, in anticipation of being rescued. My vicious strokes pounded the choppy seas with a desperate urgency. This was my last chance!

The howling wind had whipped the ocean into a violent turmoil. I was oblivious to the gallons of salty water crashing upon me. If only I could get there in time, I would spend the night in a warm bed. The bunca was filling up with water to a dangerously high level; I could see I would have to stop again and bail. Throwing the oars to one side, I grabbed the plastic bailer and began bailing with frenzied motions until I managed to rid the bunca of enough water to make it safe.

It was a race against time, one I couldn't afford to lose. I was petrified that they would leave if they didn't find me soon. I wanted to scream out, "Don't leave. Please wait for me. I'm on my way," but I knew it was useless. The wind would rip the words from my mouth before I barely said them. No, I would have to wait till I was closer. I wished I had a couple of flares that I could set off, although I hadn't assumed they'd be necessary for a leisurely day's outing.

I had spent today assuming too much and yet not enough.

Studying more closely the flashing light I was heading for, I unexpectedly made a shocking discovery. Now I could plainly see that it was not John's boat signaling to me as I had believed, but in fact a lighthouse at Caticlan, the tip of Panay.

"Oh no!" I groaned, feeling the agony of my disappointment. My shoulders slumped forward as I let the oars fall to the bottom of the bunca. In my dire need, my eyes had played a trick on me. My last hope of being plucked from the ocean tonight dissolved before my eyes. I was doomed!

The disappointment I felt seeped through me like a cancer eating away at my very being. The idea of swimming to safety had been taunting me all day. First, I was going to swim to the floating restaurant, then to Boracay, then to the shores of Panay Island, and now finally Caticlan on the tip of Panay's Island where the lighthouse was.

Now I was heading into the infinite expanse of the open seas. The lighthouse was my last sighted contact with land and my last contact with humans. I had the sense of being captured by an alien adversary. I could go into battle or surrender myself to its superior powers. Physically and emotionally I was at the end of my rope. I knew I was worn down by the struggle, my energy running on empty.

Taking a deep breath, I gave up the fight and slowly removed the flippers. Twisting my body into a contorted position, I managed to squeeze down into the bottom of the bunca, my hips firmly wedged between the sides. Lying on my stomach, with bent knees, I hung my feet over the end of the bunca. To prevent my face from being submerged in the sea water at the bottom, I rested my forehead on my rolled up sarong. This position only barely enabled me to breathe, made more difficult by a plank of wood that dug sharply into my ribs.

My body was in agony; however, my mind was experiencing a far worse torture. Fear had become so embedded in me that I continually tasted a metallic bitterness in my mouth. My need to escape from this situation was so great that it called for the extreme. I couldn't bear to look at the sea around me any longer; it had become a raging beast. The waves had taken on a ghoulish appearance; each white-crested wave had claws and long tongues of foaming water lashing out to grab hold of me, to claim me. Burrowing myself as far as I could into the hull of the bunca, I tried to escape the reality.

Instant replays of me as a little girl flooded my mind. As a child I used to curl myself up into a ball, pulling the covers over my head, taking refuge from the grisly night monsters who danced about on my bedroom walls. It had worked for me then; I believed what I didn't see couldn't hurt me. If the images became too scary, then I'd employ a childhood tactic to escape from the terrors of the night.

But what I faced now were not imaginary creatures taking form from the shadows of the trees blowing in the wind. This was beyond the realms of fantasy, far worse than any nightmarish dream. The breakers that slammed against the bunca confirmed that this was one nightmare I wouldn't wake up from and say, "Thank God, it was only a dream!" This was real. I was locked into this frozen black terror of my own making.

To know I was the cause of my plight simply intensified my anguish. Being so frightened, I was overpowered with the anger I held inside me. I felt like an emotional pressure cooker ready to explode. One emotion kept replacing another, until I was drained beyond the capacity to think or feel. I wished desperately to find an escape, a big hole I could hide inside until this ordeal was over.

It occurred to me my desire may have an obscure significance. Why was I searching for a hole to hide inside? Was I already giving up, accepting my inevitable destiny, digging my own watery grave? In my state of near emotional delirium, paranoid thoughts and images were eroding my hold on sanity. One thought that consistently returned in the medley of grotesque emotions was, *Am I going to die out here tonight? Is my life already over before it's had a chance to begin?* It couldn't be the truth; surely it wasn't possible; I wouldn't let it be! I'd fight to the death!

The Storm

The sky abruptly exploded into sheets of rain which beat down on my naked back mercilessly. I lay sprawled in the slopping water which had filled the bunca to a hazardous level. It required all my will power and energy to force myself to sit up and begin bailing. I was exhausted beyond comprehension. The physical energy I had expended throughout this harrowing day would have been the equivalent of doing a triathalon, not including the mental torture I had endured.

Bailing water and fear had become my constant companions. The sea showed me not an ounce of compassion or respite. I was trapped in a monotonous cycle: The bunca filled up with water almost as fast as I could bail. Not only was I being battered by the sea but now also from the teeming skies and the wind. Would this vigil ever cease? I felt as if I were caught on a subliminal plane between living and existing. A thick blanket of protection had formed across the emotional compartment of my brain, rendering it incapable of reacting any further. I was numb! I was relieved at the ability my mind had to protect itself from what was beyond my enduring; it knew how much I could take, and this disaster was altogether too much.

A loud clap of thunder boomed across the sky, sounding like freight trains smashing into each other head-on. I sat bolt upright, registering the cataclysmic conditions around me. The storm was gathering momentum. For an instant the sky was ablaze with a blinding bolt of lightning. This illumination revealed everything I had tried to avoid acknowledging. Here it was displayed in technicolor, like a 3D movie. The awesome waves lumbering towards me were gigantic. The bunca in comparison was no more than a matchstick being tossed around in the immense ocean. Unbelievable as I found it, this was no movie. The credits wouldn't start rolling; the curtain wouldn't come down; there were no 3D glasses to remove. This was for real!

Clenching my teeth tightly, I waited for the inevitable. It would either worsen or blow over. I clutched the sides of the bunca, as it rocked wildly from side to side. Whatever prevented it from completely flipping over amazed me. In a silent frenzy I began bailing until I had reduced the water to a safe level. I knew it would be only a matter of minutes before I would have to repeat the process. Covering my head with my hands, I squeezed myself back down into the bunca.

I was so tired, so incredibly tired! If only the waves would cease for awhile, just long enough for me to rest. I'd reached the stage where I was beyond caring anymore about what happened to me. I had to rest, no matter what! While a part of me remained alert, the other grabbed hungrily at the few minute's rest I spared. Moments later I was shaken from my dazed stupor, gasping for air. I found my face was submerged in water; I had been blowing bubbles while exhaling.

Somewhere from the corners of my consciousness I was made aware of the need to bail again. As I raised my head from the water, my mind returned from some darkened tunnel. With supreme effort I willed myself to sit up. As I did so I realized I had rested longer than I had imagined. It must have been only a matter of minutes, but the water in the bunca had risen again to a threatening level.

Suddenly the skies opened up again with huge drops of water. The warm tropical rain didn't stop me from shivering uncontrollably from scalp to toes. Every muscle was taut and aching from the continuous spasms that shook my body. A combination of fear, fatigue, and cold caused the tremors to become so intense that the involuntary effort of doing so completely drained me.

The fragile bunca lifted high onto the waves that increased in size as I moved into still deeper water. The bunca rose like the car of a roller coaster with each wave, then teetered for an instant on the crest before plummeting violently down into the next breaker. I held onto the sides in a vise-like grip, determined not to be swept out of the bunca by the savage waves that were thrashing around me. The bunca was now completely filled with water, but I dared not let go of the sides to start bailing. Towering sheets of smashing water slammed against me. My sight was blinded by the salty water that filled my eyes. I was frozen with terror! There was no time to think, feel, or be sick. All I could do was to hold on for dear life and wait for it to end.

Each time I convinced myself the waves couldn't possibly get any bigger, an unfathomable monster, higher than the rest, lifted the bunca skyward. The bunca was completely out of control, being flung in whichever direction the waves tossed it. Again, images of the bunca capsizing flashed unbidden into my mind. What would I do if this happened? Would I be able to find the bunca in the darkness? Even if I did manage to locate it, would I have the strength to hang on to the sides? Or right it? Or would this night end in my death? Would I drown in the churning water now only inches from swallowing me up?

When would this nightmare end? Where was morning? Surely it was near. Time had become distorted in an endless procession of darkness. I lost all perception of time and felt as if I were traveling through a warped black labyrinth. How long would it be before the morning light would release me from this prison of darkness?

The only thought that kept me going was that at first light I knew Mum would have rescue teams out searching for me. I believed I only had to hold on another couple of hours more and my ordeal would be over. Floating slowly back to reality, I noted with enormous relief that the storm had finally abated. The torrential downpour of wind-driven rain had ceased. Looking up into the sky at last I could see the first signs of dawn. Relief washed over me in a tidal wave of emotion. The worst was over! I had survived the night!

"I was so tired, so incredibly tired! If only the waves would cease for awhile, just long enough for me to rest. I'd reached the stage where I was beyond caring anymore about what happened to me."

I resumed my position lying face down in the bottom of the bunca. In the approaching light of morning I noticed a sheltered and dry compartment in the front of the bunca where I had stored my belongings. *What a perfect place to rest my head,* I thought. *At least I will be able to breathe without inhaling water.* Pushing my bag back further to make room, I began to squeeze my head inside.

"Don't put your head in there," the voice I heard before commanded. It was loud and distinctive.

Too exhausted to be surprised, I automatically followed the instruction without hesitation, obeying without reasoning why. In my severe exhaustion my brain tried with much difficulty to fathom who or where this source of information was coming from. With painstakingly slow thought processes, I found I was incapable of making any sense of it. I was shaken and a little apprehensive about delving into the supernatural occurrence. Not understanding why it was given or identifying exactly who had given it, I appreciated the advice nevertheless. Through a foggy mental haze, I still couldn't help wondering why I shouldn't place my head under the stern of the bunca.

The answer instantly popped into my head, *If the boat capsizes, your neck would be snapped in two.*

"Oh, of course," I muttered to myself, nodding my head in agreement. "Why didn't I think of that?" Obviously, my invisible benefactor had realized the danger.

Rolling up my towel I lay my forehead on it. Fatigue and fear had driven itself into every cell of my being. Whirling in a void of unreal thoughts and images I tried desperately to sleep, if only to escape. I willed myself to rest but to remain marginally conscious as I felt my mind spiraling downward into a tunnel of pitch blackness. I continually had to shake myself awake, but eventually exhaustion overtook me.

A vicious blow of water crashed on me, suddenly jerking me awake. My mind leapt into action. I automatically sat up, grabbing the plastic bailer, and began furiously emptying the bunca of the deluge of water that had poured into it. While doing this, nightmarish glances at the sea still raging around me snapped my fuzzy mind back to attention. The storm had abated but only slightly.

The dark and confused landscape I had been trapped in for twelve horrendous hours was being transformed as the sun crept over the horizon. In the golden haze of morning the island of Panay was now barely visible. A heavy mist hung low over the mountainous ranges, blanketing the peaks. I realized with disbelief how very far I had traveled out to sea during the long night. I calculated I must be at least thirty nautical miles from Panay.

How on earth would I ever get back? I no longer possessed the will or energy to face the enormity of this problem. It was too colossal for me to even begin to comprehend. I was devoid of all emotion! I was past caring; exhaustion had robbed me of my will to live and my fight for survival. I retreated back into the safety of the bunca, burying my face in the bottom; my only alternative was to lie down, wait, and pray to be rescued.

No sooner had I lay down when an enormous wall of water crashed on me. I tried to sit up under the weight of the water filling the bunca, but to my horror I saw it was completely swamped. *Oh my God, it's going to sink!* A rush of panic surged through me. In a wild fury, I began bailing. My eyes were riveted on the ocean. Humongous waves in trains were moving towards me at breakneck speed.

I stopped bailing. It was futile! The waves were only a matter of seconds away; now my destiny was inevitable. I braced myself for the worst and uttered a hurried prayer. In a frozen, heart-stopping moment, I turned to see a mammoth wave rearing up in front of me a split second before it struck. This was the end. I was doomed!

The bunca was smashed into with such violent force that it was thrown high into the air like matchwood. I lost contact with the bunca and felt myself free falling as I was hurtled through the air. All I could think of was, *This is it, Michelle. Everything you feared most, the thing you had pleaded and prayed not to happen, is taking place.*

The bunca was gone; I had lost hold of my lifeline. I collided with such a savage force upon the ocean's surface that the sheer impact forced the breath from my lungs. I felt myself spiraling down under the sea, ploughing deeper and deeper into its foreboding depths.

Six

EXTREME REVELATIONS

RACHELLE . . . 6:00 P.M., THURSDAY, MARCH 9, BORACAY ISLAND. The empty space of beach where the bunca should have been was foreboding. It screamed the truth at me. Michelle hadn't come back! The last lingering light of day was diminishing in the shadows of the evening sky. The ocean . . . I couldn't bear to look at it. Was my daughter lost out there, alone and terrified? The dreadful uncertainty of not knowing was slicing into my heart like the blade of a knife.

The sound of David's voice behind me transported me back from the black despairing thoughts. He sat down on the sand beside me, placing a comforting arm around my shoulders.

"Rachelle, I'm sure you'll find that Michelle will turn up. I think you're underestimating her ability to take care of herself. If you want my opinion, she is probably sipping cocktails around the other side of the island," he said again.

Everything inside me rose up, adamantly rejecting his explanation. "No, David," I insisted. "I know Michelle better than that. She would not be so thoughtless."

"Well, you do know her better than I, but it's highly possible she's gotten stuck around the other side of the island with the threat of a storm coming on. Possibly she may have thought it safest to wait until it has blown over."

"I suppose," I said as I tried to imagine the likelihood of this happening. "But sitting here helplessly, doing nothing, is eating away at me. Shouldn't I alert the sea rescue or at least do something? David, it's my daughter who could be out there," I said, desperately trying to retain a degree of control.

"At this time of night there is really not much more anyone can do. It would be hazardous to put the boats out. Let's not panic or jump to conclusions. By tomorrow we will know for sure. Then we can raise the alarm and get a full-scale rescue underway at first light."

Seeing the wildly fearful look in my eyes he added, "I can't explain it, but I feel wherever she is she's okay." He spoke with the impact of complete conviction. "If it will make you feel better, I'll walk up the beach and talk to a few of the local fishermen who may have seen her this afternoon. I'm sure everything will turn out fine. I'll be by early in the morning. Take it easy until then, okay?" David said squeezing my hand.

I watched as his tall muscular body strode purposefully up the beach and disappeared into the shadows of the palm trees. The beach was almost deserted apart from the silhouetted figures of a pair of holiday lovers sauntering along the shore. Tomorrow I would be forced to face the truth head-on, but tonight I needed action to release the spiraling maelstrom of uncertainty. Anything would be preferable to waiting, doing nothing.

My eyes sought the ocean. The moon had paved a shimmering path across the surface of the sea. *Where are you, Michelle? Where are you?*

I was too terrified to cry, for fear I would shatter my fragile defenses. I was aware of the steel-like grip my constricted emotions had wound around my heart, to the point where even breathing had become labored. A whirling mélange of feelings had taken hold of me, and I wanted to escape from them. I wished desperately to divorce myself from this trauma; the consequences were too shocking to contemplate. I found the confusion of uncertainty agonizing. Keeping a vigil in the vacant space where Michelle's bunca should have been held me paralyzed to that spot.

My mind was anchored to sanity by the only saving thought: There was a slim chance that she could still be on the island. Tomorrow would confirm or deny this, but tomorrow was an endless eternity away. How could I pass the hours not knowing until morning? *Sleep! That is my way out. I'll go to sleep.* I desperately needed to block out the reality which had reduced me to powerlessness. My shoulders sagged in relief as I remembered I did have some sleeping pills somewhere in my bag. I found them essential when we traveled; and now, thank God I had the means to escape the anxiety, at least temporarily.

Unbuckling my arms from around my knees which I had been tightly clutching, I stood up on shaky legs, attempted to balance myself, and made my way towards our bungalow. As I moved through the palm trees, the truth assaulted me. Our bungalow was empty—Michelle was not there! I stood reeling in the devastating knowledge that my little girl was gone. In a waking sleepwalk I dragged my leaden feet through the sand towards the bungalow. The intense solitude and unnerving silence that met me sent a fresh wave of shock through me. My first impulse was to run, run far away from the place that taunted me with Michelle's undeniable absence.

Illusions

The scene before me took on a mystical quality. Pools of golden light shone from the lanterns which hung enchantingly from the surrounding bungalows, where the sound of tinkling laughter floated to my ears on the evening breeze. It struck like an arrow in my heart! How could there still be laughter when my daughter might be lost at sea? It seemed as alien as if the sounds were coming from the dark side of the moon. I climbed the two stairs onto our balcony, turned the key in the lock, and with trepidation opened the door.

Michelle's belongings took on grotesque forms in the flickering glow of the lanterns, projecting frightening shadows on the bamboo walls. Her backpack lay open in one corner, clothes lay draped over the edge, spilling over onto the floor where she had hurriedly left them in her excitement to get our day's excursion underway. Her workout equipment had been tossed into a corner, make-up lay scattered on the table, and the hand mirror which had reflected her face that very morning ominously rested face down. A pervading atmosphere of desolation hung in the air.

My strength began to crumble. I was aware how shockingly alone I was. There were no friends to support me, no arms to hold me, and tell me it's all going to be okay. Moving into the bathroom I fumbled with the medicine case; tipping two sleeping pills out of the bottle, I swallowed them quickly. I prayed for them to work and release me from the agony of not knowing where Michelle was. To my right hand lay Michelle's toothbrush and toothpaste squeezed into the imprint her hand had made that morning. *Would she ever get to use them again?* I thought morbidly.

Don't think! To speculate what had happened to Michelle would be to subject myself to further torment and add salt to an already open wound. I reasoned there was absolutely nothing I could do until morning. To torture myself further by picturing her floating somewhere out in the black sea was so excruciatingly painful that I knew for the preservation of my sanity it was a vision I must at all costs avoid.

Staggering toward the bed I drew back the mosquito net and slumped down onto the bed. Instantly, distorted images of Michelle floating in that tiny craft in the pitch blackness of the ocean infiltrated my mind. I cast them out, immediately knowing if I dwelt on these pessimistic images I would crack into a thousand pieces. My sanity depended upon blanketing out these debilitating notions. At present I was rendered impotent! There was nothing I could do but wait out the next few hours until dawn.

The pills were beginning to take effect. I was feeling the wrought-up tenseness of every nerve and muscle unwind the strangle hold they had on me. The iron curtain attitude I had adopted of obliterating my senses was working. I needed to be in control and alert if I was to be useful for the search tomorrow. Any negative, self-pitying, sentimental thoughts or mental pictures of Michelle, I managed to blot out entirely. I felt I was traveling along a thin line, delicately balanced between controlled calmness and hysteria. Over the edge lay a murky pit of swirling emotions. If I crossed the invisible barrier I felt I would fall into a state beyond help. Any time my mind threw up a thought or frightening image, I quickly slammed a trapdoor tightly shut. I could not afford to succumb to its temptation.

I had to keep one last illusion intact, that Michelle was not lost at sea but over on the other side of Boracay Island. Lying outstretched on the bed, encased in the surrounding mosquito net, I felt cocooned by this pristine white shroud. As sleep enveloped me I had the sense of floating on clouds in a surreal dimension.

It seemed bizarre that since this morning the entire atmosphere of the room had altered dramatically. Gone was the bubbly enthusiastic mood, replaced by a sinister fear and foreboding. Outside, the strong tropical winds had whipped up the leafy fonds of the palm trees, slapping them against each other. The sounds of the waves breaking powerfully onto the beach sent a chill of alarm through me. Muffled sounds of people talking and laughing in the distance were all a part of the intermingling patchwork of the night.

The effects of the sleeping pill were only moments away from taking me into the unknown chambers of unconsciousness. My mind had sealed me into a capsule where I was placed beyond reach, prevented by nature from going into shock or emotional delirium. My eyes were dry!

Tears were paralyzed in the ducts, or I would have gladly released them—if, that is, I wasn't terrified of the pain and emotion that lay tethered at the gateway of that first tear. It would be better if they remain frozen. I felt myself slipping further and further in a dark spiraling tunnel of sleep, and I willingly succumbed.

"Instantly distorted images of Michelle floating in that tiny craft in the pitch blackness of the ocean infiltrated my mind."

I drifted into a mystical landscape of fantasy where impressions can be even more frightening than the world of waking hours. I saw Michelle's beautiful blonde hair being splayed out like tentacles, floating rhythmically in the ocean currents. She was face down in the water with her slender arms outstretched on the surface. She looked so peaceful bobbing up and down gently on the waves. A colorful tropical fish swam out from a clump of hair strands, darting in and out, touching the ends of the lengths searching for food. I watched transfixed as several other fish appeared, opening and closing their mouths, playfully weaving through the foreign substance they had mistaken for seaweed. One nibbled at her earlobe while his mate attempted to make a home inside her ear. Michelle was oblivious to these proceedings, unperturbed and free from care, as she drifted with the movement of the swell.

From the top right-hand corner of my mind, a beautiful, ethereal woman came floating in slow motion into the background of the picture. Her lips reflected an unfathomable Mona Lisa smile, as if behind that smile were hidden a significant secret that went beyond my understanding. My attention was riveted and, in a fleeting moment of heightened pleasure, I instantly recognized the angelic woman as my beloved grandmother, Esther Cohen. Empathy and compassion emanated from her countenance as she smiled at me. The compassion from her pale blue eyes penetrated the depths of my soul, balming the frayed edges of my pain. I felt as if under her gaze a sweet healing potion had been poured over me.

Her arms were reaching out, reaching out to someone, calling a name I couldn't quite catch. What did she want? Was it me she was calling? I strained my ears to hear the words of this lovely apparition, who was standing slightly apart from the essence of my picture. Gran's posture still retained its regal bearing, her hair immaculately coiffured as I had remembered it. Behind vaporous wisps I could see she was wearing the dress of peacock blue brocade that had been one of her favorites. I desperately wished I could talk to her and hear what she was saying. Her arm beckoned, *Come, Come,* she appeared to be motioning. I managed to catch a fragment of her dialogue.Was she calling my name? My God, no, it's Michelle she is calling! She's calling for Michelle!

Instantly I turned my eyes back to Michelle, but she had gone! Panic seized me! Why did I take my eyes off her, even for a moment?

"Oh no, my baby, my Michelle," I groaned.

Had she been taken away with Gran and passed over to another dimension of life beyond my reach? Had she gone to heaven? There where Michelle had been was only a broken doll, lying face up in the water, only the torso and head remaining. Where the arms and legs should have been were black gaping holes. My eyes were suddenly held captive by the upturned face. Stark horror struck me with a smashing blow. The doll's eyes were missing! It was just a body. The windows of the soul that registered life were missing, and in their place were two sunken black caverns. Whoever had lived in that body was no longer there; the life force had been extinguished. It was only a body now; the personality of the doll had been retracted, and the soul transported to another realm.

In a distorted confusion I screamed out, "Michelle, where are you? Come back to me! What is happening? Someone, tell me what is happening!"

I had been a witness to these bizarre, unexplainable events, looking into a strange world where conditions as I knew them did not prevail. Turning my focus back to the corner of the picture, I was about to ask my grandmother what on earth was going on for I was sure she would know, but she was gone.

"Don't leave me. Please, don't leave me alone," I called out.

Turning back to face the doll, I was just in time to see the last glimpse as the entire screen went blank as if someone had pulled the plug.

The sound of my own voice screaming instantly released me from this nightmare. I found myself sitting bolt upright in bed, shaking so forcefully I was unable to stop myself. I was bathed in perspiration which seemed to have trickled out every pore. The thudding of my heart pumped vigorously against my chest. Whimpering inconsolably, I tried to shake myself loose from this shocking dream.

It took some time to orient myself and realize where I was. The fleeting moments of disillusionment were shattered. I was back to the present, instantly plugged back into the pain I had tried so desperately to escape. I had been propelled back to consciousness and faced with the alarming truth which was even more bizarre than my nightmare. I turned to look at the side of the bed where Michelle had slept only the night before.

It was empty! In her place, neatly folded at the end of the bed, was her cuddly blanket, which she used as a sheet when traveling. I reached over and took hold of the soft, fleecy folds of fabric, burying my face into the rug as if I could bring her closer to me. Stripped of my defenses, I felt myself crumbling under the crushing weight of the implications of my dream. Rocking back and forth, hugging Michelle's blanket to me, I was ravaged by waves of uncontrollable anguish as the tears fell, breaking through the last bastions of control.

I gave way to the painful truth. My beautiful girl was either lost out at sea or dead—the other shocking alternative that the vivid dream had blatantly suggested. "No, no, it is not true!" I groaned between streams of tears.

I screamed my denial against destiny. Maybe the dream was generated by fear, not a supernatural premonition of the path destiny had taken. Was my deceased grandmother reassuring me that where Michelle had gone there was nothing to fear, that she was in loving hands? No, I could not accept that.

"She is not dead," I cried. "She's not dead. Oh, God, please, don't let her be dead. I could not bear it!"

My pain was as tangible as a knife blade stabbing into me relentlessly. As a volcano spews forth its molten hot innards, raw flashes of frenzied anger erupted in me. But there was no one to console me. I desperately needed human contact, someone to anchor me, a link to reality. *Get a hold of yourself,* I demanded. *This is not getting you anywhere.*

Aloud I spoke the words, "Calm down!" to shock myself back from the edges of emotional collapse.

The air rasped in my throat as I took in a slow, deep, deliberate breath, then another. The rhythm and control of my breathing had the desired calming effect in me, to the point where emotion had begun to give way to thinking. It seemed impossible to comprehend that only yesterday we had spent the evening together in such high spirits. So distorted had time become, that last night remained trapped in a warped maze where nothing seemed real anymore. I let my mind drift back and retrace the memories of just last night when Michelle and I had spent a wonderful time together.

The night air enveloped us like a velvety cloak. The sultry heat seemed to hug the body and stimulate the senses. Tripping through the tropically warm water which lapped gently onto the shore, we sauntered up the beach hand in hand, abandoning ourselves to peals of happy laughter just for the sheer enjoyment of it. Diamond stars lit the ebony sky in a glittering silver trail. The Milky Way was so clear that it appeared translucent, allowing the naked eye to penetrate its depths.

My feet had the impulse to dance to the vibrant, pulsating music which floated toward us from the clubs which lined the foreshore. Multi-colored lights adorned the outdoor cocktail bars, lighting them up like Christmas trees. A throng of casually dressed holiday makers relaxed in this beautiful setting. Small groups of people lounged contentedly at the bamboo tables and chairs placed strategically along the beach outside the Beachcomber. The enchanting surroundings wove a mysterious atmosphere in and around us.

Pure happiness washed over me as I drank in the atmosphere. It was hard to believe that only a matter of days before I was locked into the nine-to-five syndrome in the stressful world of the media. My Sydney office seemed light years away. While ordering a Midori margarita for Michelle and a strawberry dacquiri for me, we saw David sitting at a table with the fun crowd of people we had met the previous night.

As we moved toward their table, we were greeted by a cacophony of exuberant voices. The young intrepid travelers who made up the group were from Sweden, Germany, America, and Australia. Throughout the evening a steady stream of outrageously funny jokes kept us laughing until our sides ached. The mini league of nations present took devilish delight in thinking up even more hilarious jokes, poking good-natured fun at each country represented. Australia certainly received its share of "down under" comments. I felt privileged to experience many cultures, sharing together warm friendship without any obvious barriers between us.

I had surreptitiously watched David and Michelle together. Even though they had only known each other such a short time, the rapport between them was evident. David was typical of many American men that I had met—friendly, open, and instantly at ease with people. He'd naturally taken it upon himself to ensure everyone was comfortable, accepted into the group, and enjoying the evening.

I could understand why these two were attracted to each other. Both saw a reflection of themselves in the other. Michelle possessed a spontaneous sense of humor which she injected into every situation; even in the most melodramatic instances she could always see the funny side. Her uncanny sense of the ridiculous would break the tension when others resorted to worry. David instantly recognized this quality and found an evenly-matched sparring partner. During the course of the evening I came to the conclusion they had each found a compatible companion to enjoy their sundrenched holiday with. I had no doubt we would be seeing a lot more of David.

Later we lay on the bed in our bungalow, giggling together over some of the jokes we managed to remember and the interesting characters we had met. Our chattering began to dwindle as tiredness took over. I reached over and took Michelle's hand, entwining our fingers together.

"You have the softest hands, darling."

"Have I, Mum? Thanks. I've never thought about it. No one has ever said that to me before. But mothers do tend to be a touch biased when it comes to their children, do they not?" she laughed.

"You looked as if you were having a great time tonight."

"I did. It was fantastic! I haven't laughed so much in years. I'm enjoying myself so much, and it is only the beginning. Just think of it, we have weeks left to have fun."

Then I said, seriously, "Thanks for the holiday, I really appreciate it. I love you, Mich!"

"I love you too, Mum!"

"Goodnight, sweetheart. Sweet dreams," I said, squeezing her hand in mine.

That took place only yesterday! Was it possible time could be warped like that? It seemed a lifetime ago when she had lain safely in bed, contemplating the future weeks with anticipation. God, I wanted to see her face again, to take hold of her hand and tell her not to be afraid, that everything would be all right, Mummy's here—just as I did when she was a little girl with a skinned knee or bruised ego. But now she was far from me, lost God knows where. The choking emotion was rising again. I knew I had to get out of bed, place my feet on the floorboards, and make contact with reality.

I knew I had to break this dream like quality I'd slipped into! Standing up in the small room, I began pacing the floor. If Michelle was still alive somewhere out in the ocean, then a plan of action to rescue her would have to be initiated first thing in the morning.

Reality

Suddenly I heard a rumbling in the distant skies. I stood rooted to the spot as I strained to hear further evidence of bad weather. Before I had a chance to think, my fears were confirmed. An earth-shattering clap of thunder pealed almost directly overhead. The throbbing patter of rain began pelting noisily onto the bamboo-thatched roof of the bungalow. The drops fell intermittently at first, but quickly developed into a deluge. Heavy tropical rain fell in huge drops as the heavens opened up. I could hear the wind lashing the palm trees, carrying the sodden rain in its wake. Driven by the wind, the rain smashed against meager bamboo walls which were laced together with flax.

I rushed to the door needing to know if the velocity of the storm was really as bad as it sounded. Opening the door I was physically forced back by a gust of wind which drove the rain into my face. I strained to close the door against the weather. The ferocity of the storm was worse than I could have imagined. Not just rain and wind, my first tropical storm was sudden and savage! This new aspect was of such horrendous proportions that it assaulted my already taut nerves. Drying my face with a towel I paced back and forth on the bare floor, rallying my pitiful voice against the storm that raged around me.

"Not now! Why is this happening?" I shouted at the heavens.

If by some miracle Michelle had managed to stay alive until now, clinging to that minute boat, then surely this storm would be the element of her undoing. I knew if she was still alive, she would be utterly petrified and clinging to life by a delicate thread. The sense of powerlessness plagued me. This cruelty was aimed at the core of my maternal instincts—the thought that Michelle needed me and I was unable to do anything to help her until morning. A futile sense of defeat seeped through my being.

Suddenly the sound of Michelle's voice sounded in my ears. "Mum, help me. I'm so scared. Come and save me, please. I need you. I don't want to die!"

In anguish I could endure no longer. I clapped my hands over my ears and tried to block out her desperate cries. But it was in vain. The cries were coming from the realms of my own fear which raged through me like a devouring beast.

I was torn by two conflicting thoughts, diametrically opposed. A part of me wanted to protect her from the paralyzing fear she would no doubt be experiencing if she was still alive out there in that water. My instincts wanted her to have receded beyond the curtain of terror; I could not bear the thought of her being out in the storm, terrified and struggling for her life. But for that condition to exist ultimately would mean she had to relinquish her hold on life. Only then could she obtain the peace and safety waiting beyond this physical life. Ambivalent as these thoughts were, I desperately prayed she was still alive, but my dominant emotion was that she be free of the pain and excruciating anxiety I knew she must be feeling right now if she were still alive.

"Suddenly I heard a rumbling in the distant skies. I stood rooted to the spot as I strained to hear further evidence of bad weather. Before I had a chance to think, my fears were confirmed. An earth-shattering clap of thunder pealed almost directly overhead."

I began sketching mental scenarios of how it might still be possible for her to have hung on to life. Recalling the events of the previous morning, first I envisioned the bunca. It was not more than seven feet long, looking much like a canoe with no sail and barely wide enough to sit in. I remembered we had to perch on top of a narrow plank of wood that strutted across its width, precariously balanced with nothing to hold on to. The canoe was flanked by two flimsy outriggers, and the extent of the freeboard above the waterline was, at a generous guess, not more than eight inches. Judging by what we experienced yesterday morning, when it was necessary for us to bail water every five minutes in relatively calm waters, I could see in my mind the deluge of water breaking over the rim of the bunca in choppy seas.

Turning over the possibilities in my mind, I didn't see how she would manage to keep afloat under such horrendous conditions. Being shockingly honest with myself, I realized in such conditions the bunca was not seaworthy or even capable of staying afloat. If this had been the case, what were her alternatives? Visualizing the outriggers, though the boat might be submerged under the surface of the water, I felt that conceivably the bunca might not sink entirely. If this actually happened, I wondered what Michelle could do to keep from drowning? Would it be possible for her to curl her legs around the submerged hull, hanging on to the arms of the outriggers for support? This would help her keep her head above water.

Logic told me this was an extremely farfetched theory. With only the strength of her limbs to keep her attached, I reasoned that the first sizable wave would sweep her into the jaws of the sea. I was under no illusion as to the gravity of the situation. The more I rationalized her chances, the more obvious how devastating were the odds stacked against her survival. I knew we needed a miracle.

I desperately needed to believe in the possibility that Michelle was on the island, or at least alive. I held fast to the hope that at any time she would come bursting through the door as large as life, her exuberant nature shedding sunshine on the dark, oppressive cloud of uncertainty that hung over me. I was so relieved when the storm finally began to subside, loosing its murderous intensity. The first signs of dawn were evident in the cloudy morning sky. The time had come to reveal the crucial truth. Was Michelle, in fact, still on the island, or were my real fears going to be verified?

Daylight . . . and Disillusionment

Locking the bungalow door behind me I set out on the trek that would take me around the farthest point of Boracay. The entire length of the beach as far as the eye could see was deserted. As I was striding at an urgent pace along the water's edge, my eyes were held captive by the intense stretch of water. It had never looked so ominous. I felt an icy trickle of dread penetrate the substance of my being, my body reacting involuntarily as goose bumps of fear rose on my arms. With squinted eyes I scanned the ocean in the unrealistic hope that I might see Michelle's boat bobbing out there. There was nothing!

Mounds of wet sand lay in small clumps along the foreshore. I couldn't help but take an inquisitive look. A myriad of tiny crabs had been busy during the night burying themselves beneath the grains of sand. Boracay Island was covered in lush tropical foliage, and I noticed that the rocky perimeter sloping towards the beach was abundantly adorned with banana trees and bamboo groves. Tall, gracious palm trees inclined towards the ocean, swaying in the breeze, heralding the morning light. The peace and tranquility were sharp contradictions to the rigid intensity of my emotions.

Approaching the jagged rocks at the pinnacle, to my dismay I found the high tide had swelled up around the rocks. I would have to climb over. Picking my way over the top, I was alarmed when I realized the edge fell away into the swirling water. To continue my search I would have to jump in and swim around the jutting rock to the next beach.

Taking a deep breath I leapt off the rock, submerging for an instant, then bobbing back up to the surface. With strong strokes I easily swam the ten yards to the shore. Dripping wet, I hauled myself up onto the beach, wiping the salty water from my eyes. The saturated clothing clung to me, although I knew in this heat it would be dry very quickly.

It was the first time I had seen the island from this perspective. Boracay was far more remote and undeveloped than the popular stretch of white beach, where the tourists congregated. I was startled by the rugged, primitive outlook. Powerful waves gathered strength and crashed noisily onto the beach, and the obviously marked difference of this exposed beach astounded me. This stretch of the island was not protected and was exposed to the open sea. The isolated beauty of this wind-swept side had a somewhat breathtaking appeal. My alien presence was magnified against this desolate beach. Gone was the soft white sand and the gentle lap of the turquoise sea.

Noticing figures at the far end of the bay, I hastened my step. Acknowledging the rough water around this side of the island struck me once again as to Michelle's plight. If she had ventured around this point yesterday she would have found herself in vastly different waters. I grimaced at the thought of how very easy it would be for a small boat to be carried out to sea.

I tried to quicken my pace, but my feet sunk into the freshly wet sand. The silhouettes had now taken form; the natives of the island appeared to be preparing for a day's fishing. Their inquisitive faces turned towards me, momentarily distracted from their task of mending their nets. I approached one of them.

"Hello! Have you seen a girl with blonde hair paddling a small bunca around here yesterday?" I pronounced this slowly, pointing to my blonde hair.

Looking dismayed, he simultaneously shrugged his shoulders and shook his head saying, "No English."

Communicating by sign language, he motioned for me to wait, then disappeared over the dunes. Several minutes later he returned with half the village in tow. I could see astounded faces and gaping mouths at this unexpected early morning encounter. Obviously by the number of people who turned out, the sight of this blonde lady wishing to speak to them would no doubt be the highlight of their day. A young native boy, looking decidedly nervous, was pushed to the forefront of the group.

"Hello, ma'am, I speak good English," he said grinning widely, pleased that all those boring lessons had in fact become useful.

"That's good," I said, grateful that the territory I was in was not so alien. "Have you seen a blonde lady paddling a bunca around here yesterday?"

"No, not me," he said after a second's thought.

"Could you please ask the other people for me? Maybe one of the fishermen saw her. It's my daughter. She went out in a bunca yesterday and hasn't come back yet."

In a rushed dialogue he excitedly explained my unexpected presence. I waited with baited breath for their response which could confirm or deny her destiny. The shaking of heads and sympathetic expressions revealed the answer before it was spoken.

"Sorry, nobody has seen a white lady yesterday."

My spirits sagged. Forcing a smile I asked, "How could I get around the next bay?"

"Only by boat. We can take you, okay?" he suggested, enthusiastic at the prospect of this adventure.

"Yes, that is very kind of you. I will pay you. Is one hundred pesos okay?"

Money speaks all languages; even the nonspeaking village elders seemed to comprehend this sentence. As if I had spoken a magic word, ten willing hands were instantly spurred into action to carry a large bunca down to the water's edge. Preparing to enter the water, I bent to roll up the legs on my jeans. A robust young man, instructed no doubt by an elder, indicated that he would piggyback me to the waiting bunca. Peals of high-pitched giggles rose in a chorus from the villagers at this extraordinary spectacle.

"My worst fears had been confirmed. She wasn't sheltering around the other side of the island. She must be out at sea!"

The bunca glided powerfully through the choppy water under the expert control of these two strong young boys. This small band of people who had collected on the beach faded from view as we maneuvered around the point into the next bay. Being back into those treacherous waters yet again started my heart pounding.

I sat in silence, my eyes riveted to the beach for the sight of Michelle's bunca. If it was at all possible, this beach was even more rugged and desolate than the one I had just left. There was absolutely no sign of life there. The farfetched possibility that Michelle had spent the night here was beyond the realms of believable explanations. As the boys rowed further along parallel to the beach, I realized the futility of it all. My worst fears had been confirmed. She wasn't sheltering around the other side of the island. She must be out at sea!

Though I had sensed it all along, I knew I had to eliminate every possibility before sending out a full-scale search party. Silent tears of anguish blinded me at this tragedy, too shocking to contemplate. My lips were quivering as I instructed the boys to turn the boat around and head back. They had a battle steering the boat around as forceful waves battered against the sides. I had never felt so utterly wretched. Paddling through these strange waters with two native boys on a remote island made me feel as if I were acting out a bizarre scene where I had been unwillingly cast as the main character.

Sydney seemed a very long way. It was difficult to comprehend this was actually happening. The only thing real to me was the heart-wrenching pain and fear that had taken up residence within my body.

A small crowd had gathered on the foreshore, inquisitive of the outcome of our search. As I stumbled out of the boat into shallow water, strong arms supported me onto the beach. I felt the gaze of many eyes as if they were trying to understand my thoughts. The voice of a withered, bandylegged native woman reached me.

"You no find daughter?"

The repressed sobs caught in my throat. I was unable to answer. Compassionate understanding and the common bond of motherhood were revealed in a sorrowful expression of empathy in her coffee-colored eyes. From within, something screamed out, *No, not now; don't show me sympathy!* One tender look or display of compassion could disarm my fragile control, rendering me useless for the task that I had ahead of me. If Michelle was still alive and out on that ocean, then she needed me. I knew I had to get back and raise the alarm, arrange a sea search and get the boats out to sea. No, this was no time to fall apart.

With a surge of courage, I smiled weakly and turned away from her gentle eyes. I paid the willing helpers a healthy sum and took off at a run along the beach. The need to be back in civilization and raise the alarm was paramount.

My legs wouldn't carry me quickly enough. The action of running, I found, mildly relieved the snapping tension of the past twelve hours. Inactivity was like a destructive parasite, eating away at the core of my being. At least now I was able to do something positive and constructive to save Michelle.

A plane! That's what I needed. A plane. I remembered Manila had a huge American military base. No doubt there would be rescue planes and helicopters available to help find her. All I needed was to get to a phone and call the Australian Embassy. They should be able to get an air search underway within a few hours.

"Hang on, Michelle! I'm coming to get you. Hold on just a little bit longer," I said into the wind as I ran breathlessly along the beach.

Reaching the rocks that I previously had to swim around, I noticed a trail leading up over the rocky perimeter. I attempted to scale it rather than swim back around the point. The path was fairly hazardous, but I was relieved not to have to swim.

Reaching the top of the hill, the entire splendor of Boracay Island lay stretched out below me. The sun had now risen, shedding its golden haze over the ocean. The resort was deserted apart from a few early morning joggers. It seemed inconceivable that such a magnificent day in paradise could possibly turn out to be the most tragic day of my life. I almost expected the sun not to have risen today and the skies to be raining tears of sorrow, but no! It was the same world as yesterday, continuing on as if the loss of my child went unnoticed in the heavens.

Suddenly, I was tantalized by the thought that maybe Michelle would be home when I got back.

Don't build up unrealistic expectations, I told myself. The disappointment of another false hope was something I could not stand.

Arriving back at the bungalow I barely glanced at the empty space on the beach. Steeling myself, I approached our bungalow; even so I held my breath as it came into view. There was no sign of her! Opening the door, I was bombarded once again with the absence of Michelle. Objects seemed to leap out at me, emphasizing her disappearance. I became claustrophobic as the walls seemed to close in on me. Changing my wet clothes quickly, I was out of there immediately, for I didn't want to spend a second longer in that room so full of painful reminders. For what seemed like the hundredth time, I found myself running up the beach to the main village where I believed a telephone would be available.

Out of the corner of my eye, the sea taunted me. I knew it held a crucial secret, one I desperately needed to know. The sea had captured my beloved child! Now I was about to pit myself against it and retrieve what belonged to me!

SEVEN

DOOMED TO DIE

MICHELLE . . . 6:00 A.M., FRIDAY, MARCH 10TH, CUYO EAST PASSAGE. In one heart-stopping moment I found myself plummeting downward into a current of suffocating foam, buried in a turmoil of furious water. I became trapped in a violent whirlpool, held captive by the powerfully sucking force that was trying to swallow me up. My entire world became white and swirling. The weight of the water held me down, prisoner. Struggling to get to the surface, I clawed at the heavy barricades of water. In a frenzy I fought for control, not knowing which direction was up. It was as if an iron fist had reached out and seized my lungs.

I was instantly panic-stricken. The precious life-giving air my lungs demanded was out of my reach. *Keep calm,* I urged myself, but it was futile to battle instinct. I had to get air! Seconds passed; the acute burning in my chest was magnified until the pain was unbearable. Every time I neared the surface, the waves would break, crashing on me and making it impossible for me to get air.

Please stop! Just for one second, just one breath, I silently begged the sea. My head began feeling light, almost feathery, whereas my body felt like a leaden weight. A numb dizziness took hold of me; my brain began starving for oxygen as I experienced the first assaults of vertigo.

I struggled not to surrender. The desire to give in to it was magnetic, but my primal instincts prevented me. *You musn't succumb.* My will to live snapped me out of the submission that was luring me closer to death with every passing second.

With every shred of willpower I made an upward grapple to the surface, fighting desperately to emerge from this watery grave. After what seemed an interminable struggle, my head finally broke the surface as I thrashed around to stay on top of the violent swells. I greedily sucked in huge gasps of life-giving air. My lungs expanded as I inhaled the oxygen deeply; I thought I would never get enough of it. After only three gasps of air I was forced under again. Choking and coughing up a mouthful of salty water I'd just inhaled, I managed to resurface once more. Time began to move again!

The sea drove me tirelessly, continually breaking upon me, not allowing a minute's recuperation. As if my pleas had been heard, after a short span of trying to dodge a series of slamming waves, they eventually passed, leaving me in relatively calm waters. This gave me a moment to recover before the next sequence of waves formed.

"Grab the Flippers"

Now that the imminent danger of drowning had passed, at least for a moment, I had to find the bunca before the next surge of water came hammering down on me. Sheer terror gripped me at the sudden thought that the bunca may have been swept out beyond my reach or, worse still, sunk. I flayed out my arms, frantically propelling myself around and around scanning the ocean. It was nowhere to be seen! Attempting to thrust myself out of the water to gain some height, I tried to see over the waves. Arrows of paralyzing fear shot through me—what if I couldn't find it?

Blinding salty water stung my eyes, making my task almost impossible. My legs felt like sodden weights, but with sheer determination I commanded them to continue treading water while I searched. A tremendous sense of relief flooded through me as I suddenly caught sight of the bunca about twenty yards away. Oh my God, it looked so far. Would I have the strength to make it?

I had no choice. I began to swim. Despite the exhaustion that pervaded my entire body, being so close to the edge of death gave me a superhuman strength and the rush of adrenalin to make the swim. I felt the thrill of accomplishment as my link to survival came within arm's length. I lurched forward and grasped hold of one of the outriggers. The relief I felt was beyond description. Hoisting myself up onto the overturned hull, I wrapped my arms tightly around it as I would a long-lost friend I thought I'd never see again. My bunca was the thin thread attaching me to life. This fragile instrument stood between me and the gaping jaws of death—my only ally in a ruthless sea and my last remnant of security. To lose the bunca would be certain death; of that I had no illusions.

The relief I experienced at finding the bunca was short-lived, however. I'd barely had time to recover from the horror of the boat capsizing, when I had to deal with the onset of another dilemma. The seconds ticked by as I hung, holding precariously onto the outrigger. I calmly registered the sight of my belongings as they emerged from under the bunca and bobbed to the surface. Detached, I witnessed the scene through the eyes of an impartial observer.

"My bunca was the thin thread attaching me to life. This fragile instrument stood between me and the gaping jaws of death—my only ally in a ruthless sea and my last remnant of security."

I spotted my green sarong swaying to the movement of the ocean. *Should I swim after it? No, I won't need it now anyway,* I thought nonchalantly. I was held captive in a trance-like state by the spectacle of my apricot string bag rupturing the surface, then spewing its contents out into the open sea.

I took a mental inventory of what I did or didn't need. *Mangoes . . . no. Sunscreen . . . I really should try to save that, but I suppose it's not essential,* I thought looking on helplessly as it sunk beneath the water and out of reach.

My plastic bottle of water bobbing to the surface snapped me out of my daze, transporting me back to the grim reality of my situation. *Oh, there's the water. I'd better get that.* Holding onto the outrigger with one hand I leaned over to grasp the bottle but it was out of my grasp. Shock paralyzed my mobility as if I'd been cast into stone; my mind was able to move freely although only in distorted slow motion. Despite the exhaustion that fogged my brain, I realized it was imperative to save the water bottle, but debilitating fear had me in its grips. I found I was too frightened to leave the safety of the bunca to retrieve it. I was powerless to do anything but watch as one by one my possessions disappeared to the bottom of the sea.

"Grab the flippers," a voice forcefully instructed me.

It was not a suggestion but a command: Any vestiges of doubt I had previously held about to whom the voice belonged were immediately squashed. An inner truth stronger than any logic told me it was God. He was with me! Although I had felt all along that I had somehow not been alone in the bunca, God's voice now confirmed to me His presence with complete conviction.

The confusion that had prevailed during the past twenty hours instantly dissolved. I felt as if I was in His hands and would follow in faith any instruction He gave, no matter how illogical or ludicrous it seemed. Doubt surfaced as to why I should save the flippers rather than the life-sustaining water. However, the authority of the voice left me no choice except to obey and not question the logic of it. I swam toward the flippers and retrieved them.

I searched the surrounding water for the bunca. There it was, twenty yards to my right. Hugging both flippers to my chest, I rolled over onto my back and paddled toward it. Reaching out a trembling hand, I once again touched the wooden outrigger of the bunca that had become my lifeline. I had come to think of this as my home base; I was only safe when connected to it. Giving myself a few minutes to rest, I wrapped a rigid arm around the outrigger.

I needed time to think, to look at my options, and work out a strategy for survival. My mind seemed incapable of constructive, logical thought. I had to piece together the sodden mess of tangled emotions and produce a plan of action. *You can't afford to dwell on disjointed, self-pitying thoughts,* I told myself.

The repetitive jabbing of the sharp flipper against my chest reminded me of its presence. Putting the flippers on was job number one right now; besides, I needed to have my arms free if I was to right the bunca. The battering of the waves against me was making it difficult to hold onto the boat and the flippers. I knew if I didn't hurry I would lose hold of one of them. With one arm looped around the outrigger for support, I held one flipper securely under my armpit and struggled with my left hand to put on the other flipper.

What I had imagined would be a relatively simple task turned into the most intensely tiring and frustrating ordeal, which left me totally exhausted, almost driving me to the brink of a complete breakdown. Every part of my mind and body felt as if it were being stretched out on a medieval rack, strained beyond endurance. The relentless pounding of the waves was as if the Inquisition's henchman tightened the winch one more notch, propelling me forcibly toward the invisible line where sanity and raving dementia converge. How much more could I take before I cracked up completely?

I was caught in a vicious cycle of simultaneously battling the sea, holding onto the bunca, and trying to put on the flippers. It was as though some fiendish conspiracy was rallying against me, causing a series of minor disasters of such a magnitude that I could barely withstand the onslaught. Every time I almost succeeded in getting the flipper on, an angry swell of furious water would crash against the bunca wrenching it out of my grip, while the other flipper wedged under my armpit would also escape my clutches and be taken off on the crest of a wave. It seemed I was fighting a losing battle, but with the courage and determination I knew I possessed, I kept on struggling.

I began to retaliate against my enemy, which had ensnared me in this watery death trap. I defiantly shouted at the sea and whoever had power over it. I felt an anger rise up in me so overpowering that it momentarily obliterated my fear. I began to pound my fists, smashing them down into the ocean while screaming aloud, "Now, get this straight. You may have won so far, but I'm not beaten yet." The anger had furnished me with the energy I needed. I spent the next half hour struggling against the perpetual onslaught of waves in my bid to get the flippers on, but I eventually succeeded! The flippers were both on.

My arms were free. I could now turn my attention to righting the bunca. I heaved a sigh of relief. With both flippers securely on my feet, I suddenly felt grateful for the small measure of protection and propulsion they gave me. Although I was tired to the very depths of my soul, I felt an underlying strength beginning to rise in me at the prospect of being back cocooned in the safety of the bunca in just a few short minutes. Every corpuscle in me hungered for the oblivion of sleep, but I needed to right the bunca first and climb inside to circumvent my one-to-one combat with the sea. Thank God, it would be only a matter of minutes before I was safe and able to sleep. All I'd have to do then is wait to be rescued.

A Horrifying Realization

In some far off murky abyss of my mind lay the horrendous possibility of failure to right the bunca. This was one challenge I fervently wished I didn't have to face. My heart began to beat a little faster as the reality of this task sunk in.

It was now or never! I began drawing in a series of extremely large gulps of air, filling my lungs to capacity until I felt like a helium balloon that would fly away if not anchored. I plunged down into a huge swell of water.

It took some moments to focus my eyes in the salty water which I was becoming accustomed to. Immersed in a world that was colorless and impressionless, the sea enveloped me to the point of suffocation. It was densely thick and heavy, surrounding me like the veils of an Arabian shroud. The outline of the hull was only barely visible. Placing myself strategically with arms outstretched I grasped the rim on either side of the upturned hull.

With every ounce of my strength I heaved upward. It didn't budge, not even one inch! It felt as if it were bolted to the sea by a ton of concrete. I was instantly stricken with confusion. My mind was racing. *What on earth was happening? Why wouldn't it move?*

I was running out of air. I would have to resurface and try again. Breathing out the last remnants of shallow breath, my head broke the surface as I gulped greedily at the abundant fresh air. *I can't give up. There must be another way to turn it over,* I wondered.

Steeling myself for another attempt, I thrust myself under the water as deep as I could go, then began an upward surge to try to drive the bunca out of the water by sheer force. I was grateful for the extra power and precision the flippers gave me. My legs thrashed wildly back and forth propelling me towards the surface. I turned my face upward and saw the pale glow of the sun illuminating the water, making the shape of the bunca visible. I was hurtling upward like a torpedo; any fraction of a second now the ramming contact of my body against the bunca would send it toppling over.

Crunch! The force with which I hit the bunca sent me reeling. My body twisted violently under the jamming impact. I felt my wrists crack as they were wrenched backwards. Searing pain shot up my arms like steel darts. My mouth fell open in gasping shock as the air was expelled from my mouth and water rushed in, filling the gap. I felt the stirrings of panic. Air, I needed air!

Choking and retching from the lungful of salty water I had just inhaled, I clawed my way frantically to the surface. What was I going to do? I swallowed hard over the metallic taste of pure terror. The ocean had claimed my bunca, holding it captive in a vacuum deadlock. The delicate thread that held me to life was directly linked to that bunca. The most diabolical circumstance I had continually feared happening had now occurred. Although part of me refused to believe the truth, at my inner core I somehow knew, no matter if I had enlisted twenty iron men to lend their strength, it would still not be enough. I would never be able to turn over the bunca.

I was devastated! Like a leaden weight dropping to the pit of my stomach, I felt a sinking sensation. It was like being thrown onto the set of a science fiction movie, written into the wrong scene, and cast as the wrong character! I wanted to scream at the director, "Hey, you've made a huge mistake. I want you to stop production and write me out of this script. I'm really frightened because this has become too real. I want out!" But this was no movie role. It was a real-life drama, one that was actually happening to me.

My heart was pounding so wildly the deafening echo reverberated through my ears. For the past twenty hours I had been living precariously on the edge of death and had so far survived. But now without the frail protection of the bunca, what hope did I have? All my bravado and belief in my own ability to challenge the sea were pathetically futile. The pure irony of it was almost laughable, but I found I couldn't quite form a smile. At this moment I did not know if I wanted to continue to fight against such hopeless odds.

Oh God, what am I to do? Please tell me, I prayed. My head felt as if it would explode as I was forced to face such an insurmountable ordeal alone. Throwing back my head I let out an animal cry of utter despair. It was lost to the ocean, swallowed up almost as soon as it was uttered. Who would hear me? A terrible truth penetrated my thoughts. Would my mother ever hear the sound of my voice again? The alarming possibility of this struck me with such force that I felt myself cracking like an egg shell. The fragments of hope anchoring me to sanity were crushed under the weight of such overbearing circumstances. I tried to pull myself together, systematically shutting out the mixture of violent emotions that were searing themselves deep into my soul.

Just don't think about it, at least not yet, I commanded myself. As I tried to inject calmness into the core of my jagged nerve center, I slowly absorbed and accepted that the situation was irreversible. With the conviction of truth, there settled over me a strange, icy calm, and in that instant I felt myself turn from china into steel.

The tormented thoughts of death and disaster lost importance as getting warm took precedence. Dragging myself out of the water, I clambered up onto the hull—and immediately slid off the other side. My second attempt was just as futile. The hull of the bunca was covered with a film of slimy green algae, making the surface extremely slippery.

Could I maneuver myself under the hull? The thought of being half submerged beneath the water gave me the impetus to find another alternative. I tried sitting on the bar that connected the outrigger to the hull, with my legs dangling into the water. With one arm pressed firmly against the hull, I gripped the outrigger with the other.

Seconds before contact I swiveled around to see the menace of a towering slope of water heading straight for me. *Oh no, not again!* It was too late to get out of its path. I braced myself, sucked in a large breath, and prayed. The wave had gathered such momentum and height that when I looked for the last time it was a horrifying twelve feet tall. A mountainous deluge of water smashed against my back with such force that it felt as if I had fallen off a ten story building and landed flat onto my back. That pain was replaced by a swirling, tumbling, gyrating feeling, like being a sock in the washing machine, as I was caught up in the hellish thrashing of the ocean. Round and round I went in a fetal position until I was too dizzy to know which way was up.

Oh stop! Give me a break, please. I can't stand this anymore; I have no strength left to fight you, I begged the sea, which had become my enemy. Fighting to rise to the surface yet again, I wiped the salt water from my eyes and located the bunca and swam toward it.

I tried an endless variation of positions until I found one, although extremely uncomfortable, that would anchor me to the bunca and enable me to stay alive. Varying the first position, I found that if I sat with my legs scissored on the bar between the upturned hull and the outrigger, I could manage to hang on despite the weight of the waves crashing over me. At long last I felt marginally secure. I breathed in a great sigh of relief; I was still alive!

It was as much as I could hope for right now. Like the petals of a flower, I opened myself up to the rays of the early morning sun and absorbed like a sponge the healing touch it transmitted. Although the sun seemed rather weak, the warming caresses of heat against my skin began to thaw my frozen body and balm my tortured mind. With the warmth and light from the dawning of a new day I felt my hope and strength returning, and the feeling of complete desolation and morbidness slowly dissolved.

I reevaluated my situation. Piece by piece I formed a realistic picture and made a mental note of my resources and how to utilize these to my advantage. I knew without a doubt that by now people would be out searching for me. My main objective was to hold on to the boat and stay alive until they arrived. As I looked over the infinite stretch of ocean, the island of Panay was now barely visible. Thank God, I could still see it even if it was so very far away, probably about twenty nautical miles. It was now just a shadowy bluish haze on the distant horizon. Heavy mist clung to the mountainous regions of Panay, endowing them with a mystical aura.

It was with utter disbelief that I realized how far I had been carried out. Was there any chance at all I could paddle back? I doubted it. The expanse of water was endless and becoming even greater as the currents rapidly moved me farther away with every passing minute. Between here and there stretched billions of tons of water and hundreds and thousands of waves, all working against me.

Realistically, it was physically impossible for me to paddle all the way back to Panay, but maybe by making an effort I would be moving closer to my rescuers. If I allowed myself to just drift at the alarming

"As I looked over the infinite stretch of ocean, the island of Panay was now barely visible. . . . It was with utter disbelief that I realized how far I had been carried out."

speed I was moving, I would end up so far out to sea that rescue teams wouldn't even consider searching in the vicinity. Besides I couldn't sit here and wallow in destructive self-pity. I had to occupy myself with action, lest phantoms erode my will to live. I believed fighting for my life was better than dying in wait.

Although I desperately longed to sleep and obliterate the traumatic past twenty-two hours, I knew sleep was certain death. I would have to guard myself against slipping into a deadly slumber. With the extra propulsion I gained from the flippers I sat on the outrigger and paddled with gusto. I drove myself tirelessly! Although the series of rushing waves colliding with me made my progress almost ineffective, my stubborn streak of determination willed me to go on.

It was the most intensely painful workout I had ever experienced, but my life was the prize. I was driven by a quiet obsession not to give in to the agonizing cramps that were making a permanent home in my calf muscles. The more I struggled against the pain, the more power I gained. I was imbued with the strength and clarity of a superhuman. Tingles of raw energy and adrenalin throbbed through my veins. I was making ground, conquering the sea and my fear. By keeping active, I didn't have time to be swamped by thoughts too terrible to contemplate. The sheer immensity of the problem, had I stopped to think about it, was overwhelming. I found the easiest thing to do was to not think, because to think rationally would be to admit I was in a duel to the death so outrageously unbalanced, my odds of winning would be a million to one.

I rolled my tongue around the inside of my mouth to summon some saliva. It had become as parched and arid as the Sahara Desert. Bitter salt now stung my cracked lips and seared into my burnt skin like a branding iron. My mind turned to the delicious thought of water, of cooling liquid sliding down my throat. I would soak it up like blotting paper.

Oh, why didn't I save my water bottle instead of the flippers? That would have made more sense, I berated myself.

No, I was more than pleased to have the flippers reassuringly on my feet. Not only did they protect me from any hungry fish that decided I looked like food, but they aided me through the water. Anyway, the instructions from my Guardian's voice didn't tell me to save the water; the flippers were deemed more valuable.

I endured this painstaking feat for an hour or so until a deep form of paralysis set into my legs, wounding me like a polio victim. I was forced to stop. The muscles in my legs were seized by an intense, burning, cramp-like sensation. Tears of pure frustration, helplessness, and agonizing pain welled up in my eyes. I bowed my head in despair. My body was betraying me; maybe it knew better than I how futile my attempt really was. The thought of spending another endless, petrifying night in this watery hell was more than I could stand.

Drift with the Current

A cold sense of defeat began to fill me. It was hopeless! A reality of absolute logic hit me. I couldn't fight the currents and overpower the sea, and I had to face it. The likelihood of my getting back to Panay was crushed by the stark truth. But in finally acknowledging my own limitations, I was seized with a thought: over seven thousand islands made up the Philippines. I reasoned that if I let myself drift with the currents instead of opposing them, surely I would eventually drift to one of them. There seemed little other choice. This last fragment of hope kept the candle of my faith dimly burning.

Maneuvering the bunca around, I looked out into the direction the currents were taking me. I strained my eyes to see the peak of an island on the ocean's landscape. The daunting sight of not a single stretch of land as far as the eye could see sent a cold premonition through me. I had now surrendered myself to the unpredictable nature of the sea. I'd given up my fight! I was at its mercy, heading on a lethal course to nothing and nowhere.

I was filled with a yearning so deep to see my mother that it physically pained me. Like hard blows to my gut, I winced every time I thought of her. Where was she? She should have realized I was missing by now, lost at sea, so where was she? Her maternal instinct must surely alert her that I'm in grave danger, that this is an emergency. She knew me too well; we were too close for her not to know that my day's outing on the ocean had gone terribly wrong. If I had been with anyone else I could understand them not responding immediately, but not my mother.

I fought hard to fathom what had gone wrong at her end. Was there some blockage that she couldn't receive my cry for help? I had been frantically sending telepathic messages, hoping somehow to signal her, to alert the warning button inside her and every mother that her child was in danger. Even though I was an adult now and she was no longer responsible for me, I still believed as a mother her internal button would always be switched on; instinctively she would always be on guard to look out for and protect me. Why then had this link failed at the time I needed her most?

I swayed between feeling helpless and out of control, to being so incredibly angry that the acid it produced was burning a hole in the lining of my stomach. As much as I loved Mum, I couldn't push aside the notion that I had been abandoned, left out here to die. I desperately fought to keep a grip on the cord of reality. No, she was my mother; she wouldn't do that.

Paralyzed thoughts that were so demented overpowered me. I was alone with no help in sight. I was like a caged animal with no way of slipping through the bars. I had been captured by the ocean, held as its prisoner with no escape possible. Physically, I could not paddle to Panay or anywhere. The currents worked directly against me, making everything an impossible task. I had little choice except to allow myself to drift farther out to sea and hope I struck land. What an abysmal option!

The blazing sun was now high in the sky, illuminating my surroundings with no sight of land on any horizon. This realization kept slapping me with ferocity. I had surrendered the fight and allowed myself to be carried to nowhere. I despised this wretched feeling of powerlessness. Why wasn't there something I could do to help myself, to alleviate the anxiety even if to do so would be futile?

Rescue would come; it had to!

How could a foundation of dreams, thoughts, and memories be washed away in a moment of time, never to be recaptured, never to be relived? It didn't seem feasible that my twenty-two years on this earth could be terminated by a killer wave, wiped out like chalk on a blackboard. I had left no legacy, no husband, and no descendants. The only thing to remember me by would be a pile of photos; my poor family wouldn't even have a grave to visit to keep my memory alive. After a time it would seem as if I had never existed. Who was Michelle Hamilton? What did she achieve in this world worthy of remembrance? What sort of person was she? Only a handful of people would be able to say, I knew Michelle!

I had never believed in self-pity before. I believed if there was a problem in your life, whether you caused it or not, you don't whine and feel sorry for yourself. You solve it, and change what you don't like. Some of us may be victims of circumstance, of our childhood, or education—so what? We can't dwell on that forever. Situations aren't always good; parents are not perfect. That isn't an excuse to live our whole lives being martyrs by blaming other people for our misfortunes. Our parents or circumstances may have created the monster inside us, but we individually have the ability to change it and get on with the job of living a good and fruitful life. Shifting the blame onto other people doesn't solve our problems; it only causes self-pity and erodes our ability to take responsibility for our own lives.

Self-pity was something I usually deplored in people because it showed a weakness in one's character, but as of this moment I had enough self-pity to drown myself in. Never had I felt so sorry for myself, and annoyingly I knew it was all of my own making. Sheer stupidity had brought me to this destination of terror, on the crossroads between life and death. I'd been recklessly taunting destiny since I'd been a child, and now I was paying my dues.

"I had little choice except to allow myself to drift farther out to sea and hope I struck land. What an abysmal option!"

The currents and the waves were lethal adversaries. My destiny hung in the balance! Mum was the only person who could tip the scales in my favor; otherwise it was all over for me. I would not allow myself to die easily—my will to live was too intense—but if I was being truly honest with myself, I knew my chances of making it through another day, much less another night, were a million to one.

The sea had abducted me. Who would have the power to set me free?

EIGHT

THE DAY OF PIERCING TORMENT

RACHELLE . . . 8:25 A.M., FRIDAY, MARCH 10, BORACAY ISLAND. The blazing sun had already transformed the island into a gigantic, sizzling hotplate. The torrid storm of last night now seemed illusionary, a by-product of the chaos inside my head. The beach was relatively deserted, except for a huddle of Filipino men setting up their stalls for the day's trading.

"Excuse me, do you know where I can find the Coast Guard?" I asked in deliberately well-pronounced English.

"You must report to Mr. Gonzales, the radio controller. Then he will take you to the Coast Guard. You will find him in the bungalow behind you," one man answered, pointing.

"Thank you," I said, hurrying off in that direction. Feeling hot and out of breath, I staggered up the few steps into the bungalow which was used for a radio room and blurted out, "I want to report a missing person! I need a search party as soon as possible. My daughter went out in a bunca yesterday and hasn't come home yet."

It was official! I had spoken the dreaded words out loud; they had now shifted from speculative thought into concrete reality. The chilling words reverberated through the air, sending stab wounds of pain that lacerated my heart. The inner conflicts of doubt had been eliminated and the feared truth now spoken aloud. My daughter was missing, lost at sea!

"Please come and sit down," a uniformed gentleman offered. "I will need to get some details from you." I sank into the chair proffered.

"What's your daughter's full name and nationality?"

"Michelle Hamilton. She's an Australian citizen."

"How old is she and what was she wearing when last seen?"

"She's twenty-two and had on a blue and white striped bikini and blue shorts."

"Could you describe the boat she was in?"

"It was a small green and red bunca, with outriggers. We rented it from Willy's Beachfront Cottages yesterday morning."

"Ohhh. And when did you realize she was missing?"

"Well, I was very concerned last night when she didn't come home, but by that time it was already dark and I wasn't entirely sure she was missing. There was a possibility that she could have been on the other side of the island and I didn't want to raise the alarm until I was positive. But this morning I went out and searched the island and couldn't find her. It was then I knew for definite," I said, my voice trailing off.

"Where are you staying?"

"Look, I know you have to know these things, but can't you get the search underway? All these questions are wasting valuable time. How many blonde twenty-two-year-olds floating in a bunca will you find out there? Please hurry," I insisted, as I struggled to maintain an outward calm.

"First, I must take you to report to my superior. He's in charge and will know what to do."

"You mean you're not Mr. Gonzales and I've just wasted all this time telling you?" I asked in disbelief. "Please take me immediately to the person who can authorize a search. Time is so precious!"

"Yes, ma'am, I do understand. Please come with me."

Get a Search Underway

Following him along the sandy tracks through the lazy palm trees, I felt as if I had entered the mystical terrain of the world of Alice in Wonderland where everything seemed unreal. In silence I traced his steps winding through a maze. Behind the tourist facade lay a small village, its bamboo bungalows cocooned in lush vegetation. This was a part of the island not usually seen by tourists but inhabited by the locals.

Mothers, squatting in colorful sarongs, bathed bare-bottomed children whose wet skins glistened in the morning sunlight. The village was a hive of buzzing, productive activity. Chickens and ducks ran free over the earth, scratching out morsels of food. We were obliged to move aside as a huge bullock lumbered slowly along the path, fettered to logs of wood destined for new construction. At another time, this spectacle would have been a priceless experience, but in these grave circumstances, I wasn't able to appreciate it. I had only one thought which obliterated all others: to get the search underway as soon as possible.

We climbed the steps of a sparsely furnished bungalow. My eyes were immediately drawn to the radio equipment. Communication! I felt instant relief to have a link with the outside world. Finally, something positive could be done. But the place was deserted!

"Please sit down and I will go and find Mr. Gonzales," said my guide. I mutely obeyed him by sitting down, feeling alienated in the unfamiliar atmosphere. The pent-up frustration I was experiencing bore a crushing weight from which there was no escape. *Why can't they hurry? Where is everybody?* Too anxious to remain seated, I began pacing the room. Back and forth I paced, trying to relieve the unbearable uncertainty and impending doom that had settled over me. Hearing footsteps outside, I moved toward the door.

"Hello, I'm Pedro," a tall man said as he entered. "I'm told your daughter is missing. Please come and sit down over here and tell me exactly what's happened." His professional manner inspired confidence.

"My daughter Michelle went out yesterday in a bunca she hired and hasn't come home yet. I want a rescue team sent out immediately, do you understand?" I pleaded.

"The pent-up frustration I was experiencing bore a crushing weight from which there was no escape. Why can't they hurry? Where is everybody?"

"Yes, ma'am, I do understand your concern, but first I need some information from you."

"But I've already spent ten minutes of valuable time telling the other man everything I could," I said, getting very irritated with their drawn-out procedures.

Speaking at the speed of an express train, I once again related the events of the previous day, giving him all the relevant information.

"Where was she last sighted?" he asked in a methodical voice that made me want to scream.

"I last saw her heading off toward the southernmost tip of Boracay at about 11:30 A.M. yesterday."

"Mmmm," he said, digesting the information. I caught an expression of concern play across his face, which he immediately masked, continuing in his official capacity. "There is a very strong current at this time of year which could have carried the bunca out toward Panay. I think it would be best if we started searching in that general area."

"I'll trust your judgment. You know the territory better than I do. But how long will it take to get the search underway?" I asked him with mounting anxiety.

"Please calm yourself, ma'am. We will do everything as quickly as possible. Now that I have the correct information, we will dispatch the rescue team."

At last the tedious paper work had been completed. I rose with trepidation knowing the burden of responsibility had been transferred to his shoulders. I felt as if I had relinquished control of the situation, this act rendering me virtually impotent. Like a dog following his master, I found myself blindly trudging down the pathway that led towards the beach. My mind was traveling like a runaway roller coaster being propelled from one crazy thought to another while my body obediently followed instructions mechanically like a wind-up doll. The nerves in my stomach were bunched up tightly, giving me a hollow, nauseous feeling.

An opening of palm trees offered an open window to the ocean, and an innocent patch of blue water appeared as we made our way towards the sea. I cast my eyes around and all beauty seemed erased from the scene before me. How could something that usually instilled such peace in me now be the instrument of such anguish and suffering?

As I stepped out from the thick wall of palm trees, the glistening expanse of white shimmering beach burned my eyes. Squinting from the glare, I saw directly in front of us a boat painted with bright red lettering, "Sea Rescue."

"The crew are on their way. Now we should be able to have the rescue underway in about ten minutes," the official voice broke into my silence.

Waiting, waiting—it's all I seemed to do. I turned to confront the ocean. As far as the eye could see was a velvety blanket of blue merged into azure skies on the hazy distant horizon, the two elements blended into one forming a complete blue splendor. The vast watery landscape stretched out forever. Would they ever be able to find her out there? The magnitude of the ocean now seemed horrendous. My eyes stung with unshed tears as the scene before me misted over.

"Excuse me, ma'am, Captain Alfonso would like to speak to you," said a young man.

"Oh, of course" I muttered as the words shattered through into the depth of my abysmal thoughts.

"Mr. Gonzales told me that your daughter is missing, and the last time you saw her was yesterday morning. Is that correct?" Captain Alfonso asked.

"Yes, it was around eleven o'clock. She was heading in the direction of the southernmost tip of the island."

"Can you describe the boat? Were there any distinctive markings?"

"I'm sorry, but all I can remember is it was about seven feet long, painted red and green, with outriggers but no sail."

"Is there anything else you can tell us that would be helpful in the search?"

"No, not that I can think of," I said apologetically, realizing my information was rather sketchy. "Please find her for me, please." I heard my voice quavering. His eyes showed compassion as he patted my hand, reassuring me that he would do all he could.

With that he turned to instruct his crew as a number of men began to drag the boat down to the water's edge. The solemn faces of the crew conveyed a thousand unspoken words. I was bathed in the sympathetic collective gaze they bestowed upon me. I watched in silence, my heart twisting as if it were being wrenched out of its cavity.

Please bring her back to me, I prayed fervently as I watched the men put the boat to sea. I turned away and began walking back to the radio room but suddenly found my legs wouldn't carry me. My limbs crumpled under me as I fell down onto the soft warm sand.

Strong arms were instantly at my side raising me up. With a stumbling gait I was helped back to the office.

"Would you like a cup of tea?" a gentle voice asked. "Yes, please," I heard myself answer.

Feeling slightly revived, and knowing the boats were out, I dug deeply into my reservoir of strength, piecing back together the tattered shreds of my emotions. Mr. Gonzales had left me in the care of the radio operator who was endeavouring to contact Manila to report the incident.

Contact Manila

Staccato beeps and static waves from the radio transmitter filled the room. A pretty young Filipino girl spoke into the mike, repeating the same coded message, earnestly seeking a reply. My raw nerves were pierced by the sounds of the high-pitched frequency. The static was interrupted by the sound of a feeble voice.

A flicker of hope returned as I asked, "Have you managed to contact Manila?"

"No, it's Lotti, who is stationed at our other transmitter."

I was stricken by confusion. "You mean to say Manila hasn't even been contacted yet?"

"No, I'm sorry, but we only have an amateur transmitter which is not powerful enough to reach Manila. As we don't have a direct line, first we must contact Caticlan, the station on Panay island, which will then relay the message through to Manila."

I felt my heart plummet as I realized the painstaking procedure we would have to go through and the loss of time which was so critical.

"How long do you think this will take?" I asked.

"It's hard to say, but Lotti, who is our most experienced operator, has been informed and is already trying to contact the Australian Embassy."

"That's a consolation! But one solitary boat searching out there is just not enough. I want more boats and a plane or helicopter looking for her. I don't care how much it costs! I know there is a large American base in Manila. Surely they must have planes and helicopters at their disposal."

"Your embassy will be more equipped to help you organize that, but I know Lotti has already notified Caticlan, and their fishing fleet has been alerted to look out for her. Also the fishermen have sent out several other boats so there's more than one searching. I know this ordeal must be terrible for you. We are all doing the best we can; I'm sure your daughter will be found," she said, although the reassuring words were of little comfort.

Somewhere outside of myself I was aware of other people milling around, whispering in respectful, sensitive undertones. But my whole being was solely attuned to the radio which represented hope, help, and my only link to the outside world. I felt as if I were adrift on a deserted island, surrounded by a sea of isolation, completely severed from anything familiar, in never-never land. I desperately needed to speak to my

"I desperately needed to speak to my embassy, someone I could relate to, whose authority I could rely on to get a full-scale search operational."

embassy, someone I could relate to, whose authority I could rely on to get a full-scale search operational. Rising from my feelings of helplessness, I naively clung to the belief that one word from the seat of embassy power would command a fleet of helicopters to search the sea and save one of their own.

I was infuriated by the seemingly fruitless conversations between bases, none of which had extended beyond the island. I could feel the pressure building up in me. Like the bubbles in a champagne bottle surging upward to the surface, I felt that if I didn't get out of that room I would explode. The hateful, frustrating inaction was inwardly destroying the fragile self-control I had fought to keep intact.

"Where can I find Lotti? Is she in walking distance from here?" I said, reasoning to myself I may as well speak directly to her, at least that would eliminate one link in the connection to Manila.

"She is not far from here. Sonia will take you there if you like," said the dispatcher. "I'll continue here and try to establish a contact."

Thank God, I thought, as I left the tiny room and headed down that dreaded stretch of beach.

The sun was hidden behind misty clouds; the fact that it wasn't blazing hot was a blessing. I reasoned if Michelle was still afloat at least she wouldn't be getting too burnt. Images of Michelle adrift out there, her bare skin burning under the scorching heat, was a private hell for me. I forcibly denied the visual picture of last night's dream which thrust itself into a clear space in my head. I erased from my mind's eye the image of the doll with no eyes. I would not entertain the idea that this search was all in vain and the attempts of rescue were a futile gesture by men who knew the indeterminable odds. But I had to believe she was still alive, or they would not even bother to mount the search.

The ten-minute walk from one end of the beach to Lotti's house seemed an eternity. The island had sprung to life. A migration of people sauntered toward the sea armed with towels, beach chairs, and other assorted paraphernalia. The ocean was dotted with windsurfers, sailboats, and swimmers. The exuberant holiday atmosphere that I witnessed about me was in sharp contrast to the chaotic activity within me.

We arrived at Lotti Abrams' place where the radio equipment was housed upstairs in a tiny room. Rafel Gelito, daughter of the proprietor of the bungalows and owner of the boat, was also at Lotti's.

"I'm so sorry to hear about Michelle," Rafel said emotionally. "I want you to know that we have sent out several boats from here. My father has gone out as well. He said he will stay out as long as it takes to find her, and he's going to search the outer islands. It's possible she may have drifted out there. Don't give up hope. We are all praying for her safe return. Lotti is upstairs trying to make contact with the mainland for you. Come on, I'll take you up to her."

I nodded mutely, feeling my throat constrict with emotion as I followed her up the narrow wooden stairs. She introduced me to Lotti, who smiled warmly as she continued repeating the S.O.S. message into the radio. As Rafel headed back to the restaurant, she squeezed my hand, imparting understanding. Her lashes were wet with tears of empathy, but there was nothing left that she could do.

Lotti was a wonderfully warm, vivacious young woman and when she stood up she turned toward me wrapping her arms around me. A mutual rapport between us was established. We were linked by the common bond of motherhood, as if by an act of compassion she wanted to absorb some of the anguish I was experiencing.

"I've been on the radio ever since I heard Michelle was missing, but I'm having a lot of trouble getting through," she admitted apologetically. "I think I'll have to go to another base and see if I can get a better reception from there."

"You mean the office where I have just come from?" I asked, not believing what I was hearing.

"Yes, the signal may be clearer from there. This must seem like a terribly inadequate procedure, but we're only amateur radio operators, and there is no official connection to the mainland," she apologized.

"It's not your fault, but it's my daughter out there and all this time being wasted is unbearable. I need to get a plane out looking. If I don't, . . ." A lump rose in my throat and a flood of emotions suddenly overwhelmed me. It could cost Michelle her life.

This time I was unable to withstand the impact. Racking sobs rose up from their forced imprisonment, spilling over like a burst dam. At that moment I did not believe I could go on.

Within minutes we were yet again pacing that well-trodden path. Just two nights ago Michelle and I were carousing down this very track laughing and bursting with happiness. *Don't think of it,* my mind warned. *Blank your mind. It's the only way you'll get through this and remain sane,* I inwardly shouted, trying to drown out my fear.

Suddenly, I was torn by an impulse to take a look at our bungalow. My rational self needed positive confirmation that Michelle was in fact actually gone. The refusal of my intellect to comprehend the full implications of what this meant was overwhelming. But I couldn't deny this was real. These things you read about—they happen to other people; they don't touch your own life, do they?

I felt as if an oppressive weight had descended on me, crushing in on all sides. Merely to breathe became arduous as I fought to keep this unseen element of fear from suffocating me. It took all my resolve not to surrender to the force that was threatening to control my senses. Time had slipped into a warped dimension. My fragile resolve to wait kept me on such a pinnacle of tension that it bordered on physical agony.

Around me I sensed voices were respectfully hushed and sympathetic, but my mind had withdrawn from the present and now resided in a terrain of nebulous unreality. I wanted to hide in a corner, close my eyes and shut out the world. I didn't want to think; I tried to feel nothing. But a persistent inner voice jarred its way into my thoughts, refusing me the escape I desperately sought. Now that the first paralyzing feelings of shock had subsided, I was compelled for Michelle's sake to think rationally and to fight my way out of the stupor in which I was trapped.

The sound of a voice over the transmitter snapped me into the present.

"Boracay, are you receiving me?"

"Yes, go ahead," Lotti answered.

"We have a Mr. George Frazer from the Australian Embassy standing by. He's in the radio office in Manila and wants to confirm where the missing person is from. Is the mother there with you now?"

"Yes, Ms. Hamilton is here with us. She says she's from Sydney, over." She looked at me intently.

I heard the voice of the operator relay what Lotti had said to Mr. Frazer in Manila. My heart leapt into my throat as I heard the unmistakable Australian accent crackle through the transmitter: "Ask Ms. Hamilton if she is okay and if we can be of assistance. Is there anything she needs?"

Leaping from the chair, I took hold of the receiver as relief flowed through me like cool spring water on a searing hot day. Every cell in my body became alert. Everything was finally going to be okay. I had been thrown a life line; someone from home knew of our predicament, could share the burden, and could actively help. I felt confident that with embassy authority, this place would be swarming with rescue equipment within the hour.

Gripping the receiver tightly, I said, "Mr. Frazer, I do need your help. I need a plane or a helicopter over here to search for my daughter. What can you do to help me get them?"

"Boracay, this is Caticlan. Sorry Manila can't hear you direct, but I will relay your message through. Stand by, over."

And I stood there with my heart pounding as I heard the operator repeat my message with none of the desperation with which I had uttered it.

Mr. Frazer's voice came on the line. It was annoying that we could hear him direct, but he could not hear us.

"Tell Ms. Hamilton that we are extremely distressed to hear of the situation but unfortunately we do not have planes or these types of resources at our disposal. There is nothing we could do to help in that regard. Could you please find out what has already been done in the way of a search?" he said, being brutally frank.

My relief and expectations were crushed by his devastating words; each one fell on me as if bearing a great weight. I felt myself sway, a black space inside my head filled with flashing lights. I sensed I was about to faint. I reached for the chair and slumped into it. Taking in a few slow, deep breaths, I fought to overcome the sensation.

Then I responded, with emphasis on each word. "There are only a few boats out looking for her now. Without a plane the chances of finding Michelle are like looking for a needle in a haystack. Tell Mr. Frazer I need a plane today and I don't care what it costs. Can he suggest where I might be able to hire one? Anything will do!" I slumped back, waiting for my message to be relayed.

"You could try Air Pacific. They may be able to assist. They have a small fleet that services the islands and may be willing to let you hire one. At present I can't think of anyone else who may be able to help. However, we have notified the Manila Coast Guard, and all fishing vessels within the area are being alerted. Would you ask if there is anyone in Australia she wishes us to contact for her?" His voice echoed in my ear.

"'Without a plane the chances of finding Michelle are like looking for a needle in a haystack. Tell Mr. Frazer I need a plane today and I don't care what it costs.'"

Lotti removed the transmitter from my lap where I had consciously let it fall, having no further use for it. There seemed no point in prolonging the conversation. If he couldn't help me, what was there left to say? Lotti looked into my eyes, seeking my answer to his question. I heard myself say, "No, there's nobody I want to contact, nobody. . . ."

Distantly, I heard Mr. Frazer say, "Please keep us informed of the situation. We will be standing by, over."

For some minutes I sat immobilized in the chair, unable to think. I felt as if I were suspended, caught in a limbo of unspeakable doom. I centered my thoughts on a clear space in my mind just above the heavy black veils of grief, not being able to absorb this shocking new information.

No plane! It was too appalling to believe. Every atom of hope and faith I owned hung precariously on the premise that getting a plane to search for Michelle was the only real chance she had of being found. However, I couldn't allow myself to become overwhelmed by this latest diabolical news. There was still Michelle to think of and if by some miracle she was still alive, this was not the time to give up. It was the time to fight!

NINE

ANGELIC ENCOUNTER

MICHELLE . . . 6:00 P.M., FRIDAY, MARCH 10, CUYO EAST PASSAGE. Hues of amber and russet bronzed the sky as the sun made its final plunge. Its extraordinary beauty simply intensified my pain. Romantic couples would most probably be sitting on the beaches of Boracay at this very moment, viewing the sunset with appreciation, blissfully unaware that this identical sunset was the cause of such terror and despair to another human being. Darkness would soon fall upon the face of the earth, blanketing me in an inky blackness.

My heart was wrenched with a savage despair as I contemplated how I would physically and mentally get through another night. A decision needed to be made! Would I fight to survive until the last remaining breath was left in my body, or should I give up the struggle now? It was painfully obvious that rescue would not come. I had been abandoned, and knowing that hurt me more than anything else I had experienced. It far surpassed the physical pain that afflicted me. I thought my mind would short-circuit with an explosive brew of highly charged emotions.

No matter what different scenario I imagined or what excuse I made for Mum not coming to rescue me, none of them sufficed. I felt that, as my mother, she had betrayed my trust in the worst way imaginable. The intensity of hurt and anger I felt toward her scared even me. If I were to see her now I would be torn between hugging or strangling her. What possible reason could there be for her not to have come to my rescue by now?

Last night was understandable; I rationalized that she had probably thought me to be on the other side of Boracay Island. By the time she would have realized that this was not the case, it would have been too dark to search for me. So I hung onto life with a vengeance throughout the night because I had no doubt that at first light Mum would have rescue boats out looking for me. I had been sadly mistaken. There was only one thing I now knew with utter certainty and could guarantee would happen: Night would fall and I would be left alone to face another twelve hours of horrendous anguish.

Why? Why? Why was this happening to me? I believed that I had been a good person in my life. Kind and generous, I always went out of my way to help my fellow man. A moral person, I had never intentionally inflicted pain on another human being, either physically or emotionally. So why me? Surely I didn't warrant this kind of treatment. If I were being punished, I would sincerely like to know the reason.

"For what, God? Are You listening to me?" I called out angrily as my last vestige of control evaporated. "If it's You who is handing down this undeserved punishment, then I'll never forgive You. Do You hear me? Never.

"Is that Your idea of justice? Because it's certainly not mine! You know, if I wasn't so terrified of what other hideous surprises You have in store for me, like being eaten by a shark, You can be sure You would be receiving the full brunt of my anger. I feel both You and Mum have betrayed me, almost as if you were conspirators against me. To spite you both I intend to fight to the death. I will not surrender easily. You will have to take my life by force."

My anger quickly turned into iron determination. To live would be my ultimate revenge! I would no longer allow myself to be manipulated by the whim of destiny; I had made a pledge to live and live I would. In that instant I felt my heart turn to solid ice, my anger congealed into cold, bitter hatred for all those who had abandoned me. If I survived, no one would ever be able to melt this heart of mine again. No, as surely as night and day, I would never be the same trusting person again. The innocence and naiveté of my youth had been irretrievably lost. Who had come to my aid in my most desperate hours? Not even the one who had given birth to me! Thus, the battle between me and God continued over the next couple of hours, swaying dangerously between bitter anger and forlorn disillusionment.

Why Me?

The enormous lump in my throat urged me to cry, but I refused to allow its expression. To cry would be a sign of weakness, and I would not give God that satisfaction. A breakdown would destroy my resolve, and then I would have nothing left to cling to. The fury inside me at the total injustice of my predicament was sustaining my life. I was afraid if I allowed it to dissolve into self-pity and tears, I would be powerless to save myself. Besides there would be plenty of time for tears later.

The amber sunset all too quickly turned to indigo as twilight fell. The charcoal blackness of night would soon obliterate any traces of color, so that my surroundings would be totally obscured. I would be left with only my thoughts and fears.

Even though in my anguish I had rejected God, I found myself praying that there would not be another storm. I had miraculously escaped from the ferocious clutches of last night's squall; I may not be so lucky the second time around. No matter how intense my inner strength, I still had the sense of being a hostage of destiny, at God's mercy!

"The charcoal blackness of night would soon obliterate any traces of color, so that my surroundings would be totally obscured. I would be left with only my thoughts and fears."

As I hovered near death I began ironically to question the meaning of life. *Are we ever really in control of our own lives or are we just pawns in a divine plan?* I wondered. I began delving down unexplored avenues of thought, searching for some answers to these age-old mysteries. If our lives are not preordained, then why are we led down certain paths and arrive at destinations that seem in retrospect laced with more than mere coincidences, that seem not of our own making or choice? If there is not a prepared place for our souls to go after our bodies have expired, then what is the purpose of life here on earth? The trials and tribulations we suffer would be in vain, totally meaningless.

As a person, I therefore had to believe that we have been put on this earth for a reason; otherwise nothing made sense. Why would we all have been given a conscience and the discernment to know the difference between right and wrong if there was no consequence to avoid or reward to strive for? There would be no reason to make an effort to be a good and moral person if there were no heaven or hell. It all made perfectly good sense, and yet it didn't. If there was a righteous God in heaven, then why wasn't I being rewarded instead of being persecuted without a legitimate reason?

I had heard the audible voice of God speak to me several times, giving me instructions to prolong my life, but to what end? Wouldn't it be kinder of God to take me now if my time was up instead of letting me linger on in this living hell? Was I going to be the culmination of a supernatural miracle, or would my death just be a senseless loss? If the latter were true, then God's reasoning and wisdom were totally beyond my comprehension. In fact, it appeared to be extreme cruelty and pain for me and those I'd leave behind to mourn my death and forever wonder why.

I had so many questions that now required a response. I had always accepted these unexplainable tragedies as being the way life was, but with my death so imminent I felt a desperate need to have the answers revealed to me. Perhaps these things are only unveiled to us once we die and go to either heaven or hell. I speculated that if I didn't make it through the night, then maybe my questions would be answered sooner than I thought.

Heaven or hell, up or down, which way would I go? I felt sure that I would go to heaven, for presumably I had done nothing deserving of going to hell. I supposed that was at least one consolation for having to leave life at my youthful age.

A few Scriptures I remembered from Sunday school abruptly popped into my mind: "No man cometh unto the Father, but by me" (John 14:6, KJV) and "Verily, verily, I say unto thee, Except a man be born again, he cannot see the kingdom of God" (John 3:3, KJV).

Can that be true? I wondered now, suddenly panicked. Was I to take that verse from the Bible literally, with no exceptions? Many people believe in God but not Jesus; did that mean they went to hell? Surely not! Although from my memory that is what the Scripture conveyed in no uncertain terms.

Perhaps there was a place between heaven and hell where the good but unbelieving people went. Surely I wouldn't be sent to a place with the evil and corrupt people who had lived wretched existences and inflicted pain on innocent people. I began to shake with palpable fear. Icy terror froze the blood in my veins.

"God, You wouldn't send me to hell, would You?" I cried out mortified at the possibility. I was thunderstruck by how very limited my knowledge of spiritual matters was and how very little importance I had placed upon seeking the truth—until now. So absorbed had I been in the frivolity of life that it hadn't for one moment occurred to me that no one knew the hour of their death, and I had been caught completely unaware and totally unprepared. In the exuberance and gaiety of my fun-filled holiday on a tropical paradise, how could I ever have known that death was waiting just around the corner, lurking in the shadows?

As if my inner struggles had been heard, the voice of Mum came rippling through the airways and whispered in my ears the words she had said to me in Singapore, only days before this ordeal had begun. In retrospect, how ironic it had been for her to say words of this religious nature completely out of the blue. Had she had a premonition that I would soon find myself in a situation of utter desperation, my back against a wall with nowhere to turn?

Her voice came back to me with astounding clarity "Michelle, while you were away in Japan I found the truth that I have spent the best part of my life searching for, and it has changed me dramatically. I discovered that while believing in God was satisfying, I still felt unfulfilled and there were a great many things I didn't understand. The ultimate ingredient that was missing in my life was Jesus who I discovered is the key to unlocking the door to true peace and happiness."

I listened to what Mum had said with reservations and doubt, but I didn't believe I had the right to ostracize her newfound religious beliefs. If it was a source of comfort to her, then I was truly happy for her. However, I personally didn't feel I needed a spiritual mentor in my life; I was managing perfectly well without the crutch of religion. I considered myself a strong and independent person. As far as I was concerned, only the weak and dependent of this world needed religion.

Without wishing to offend Mum, I explained my point of view: "I am pleased that you have found the missing piece of the puzzle at this stage of life. Right now it's obviously something you need, and I respect that; but frankly I would appreciate it if you didn't preach your newfound beliefs to me."

Mum had only smiled. "I certainly don't wish to preach to you, but there is something I would like you to know. I feel it is important and would appreciate your hearing me out. One day you may find yourself in circumstances beyond your control, when you need help desperately but don't know where to turn. Please remember this simple scripture, 'Ask and it will be given to you; seek and you will find; knock and the door will be opened to you' (Matthew 7:7, NIV).

"If you find yourself in trouble, know that God is forever waiting for you to call upon Him for help. However, before someone can accept His help, it is sometimes necessary to bring that person to his knees and to break his self-reliance. Then he will surrender his will to the will of God and reach out to Him in the manner of a little child. Jesus said that whoever falls upon Him will be broken (Matthew 21:44); in other words, you must be stripped of your independence and be humbled before God. I hope that life doesn't ever bring you that far down, but if it ever does, remember God always has His arms outstretched to you. He will help you if you ask with a humble heart."

The repetitive words now rung in my ears over and over again, "Sometimes He may have to bring you to your knees, . . . to your knees, . . . submit your will to His will, . . . cry out to Him with a humble heart." How significant these remarks now seemed to me.

Without warning a flash of understanding shone in my mind, illuminating all the darkness and confusion. The truth became transparent, and I could see it as clearly as if it were written on a wall in black and white. I had stumbled upon a reason that I could logically accept for going through this ordeal. I realized that I hadn't been lost at sea and made to suffer such extreme mental and physical torment in vain. God had a purpose in subjecting me to this trial. It was to strip me bare of my defenses, to force me into submission, and to bend my will to His.

100 Percent Faith

Throughout this catastrophe I had relied totally on my personal resilience and resourcefulness. I was convinced that survival depended upon my ingenuity, my physical strength, my courage, my tenacity, but most of all, my defiance at accepting this unjust death sentence. My youth and bravado had sustained me so far, but the lesson I now learned was that these admirable character traits didn't have the power to save my life. I could now see I had to be rendered powerless and brought to my knees before I would genuinely seek God's help and acknowledge my true weakness.

I did not have control over life and death. I was made painfully aware that my total independence had been my own worst enemy. In life-and-death circumstances of this magnitude, my human ego and supreme confidence were nothing more than a pseudocoverup for my true human impotency. Now that all my other options had been eliminated, and I was totally at the mercy of God, I realized how very much I needed Him. Living in the rat race, caught up on the treadmill in the material world, I was unable to see the forest for the trees. Now the veil

---

"I did not have control over life and death. I was made painfully aware that my total independence had been my own worst enemy."

---

that had blinded my eyes had been lifted, and I could see with surprising clarity. It was terrible to think that I had been brought to these extremities before I could accept this simple truth.

A vast silence reigned over the ocean. Looking up into the sky, my eyes strained to penetrate the inky blackness.

With humility I cried aloud to God, "I really need to talk to You. Please be listening to me. I know I have been angry with You and thought and said things that I shouldn't have, but up until now I haven't been able to understand why this tragedy is happening to me. I have doubted Your wisdom, Your logic, and Your reasoning, and I probably don't deserve Your help, but You are my only hope. I'm not asking for You to save my life. I just want You to answer one question."

Hesitantly, in a flat voice that concealed my anxiety and highly strung emotions, I continued, "God, if You are up there and listening to me, I want You to know that I am not afraid of death itself. It's more the uncertainty of not knowing whether I will die and if so, when will it happen? So please tell me the truth, God. Is my number up? Am I going to die?" I waited in trepidation, not really expecting an answer, but at the same time terrified I would hear a yes.

An incredibly powerful voice shattered the night air, extinguishing the heavy desolation that had descended on me. "No, you are not going to die!"

I sat dumbstruck, barely able to believe that of all the people in the world begging for help He had been listening to me, and in answer to my plea, He had responded. His words confirmed to me that He was much more than just an invisible entity. He was truly the living God and cared about me personally.

My human instinct was to immediately doubt what I had heard. In fear that it may not be true, I asked Him to repeat it. Once again I called out, "Did You say I wasn't going to die? Are you sure, God?"

"You will not die!" the same authoritative voice reiterated what He had said. This time the intensity was diminished; nevertheless, the words were formidable and full of conviction.

I sat motionless, not wanting to break the spell of intimacy that had taken place. I found it utterly staggering that the Creator of the universe had just spoken to me personally. I was riveted to the spot as I attempted to absorb the magnitude of what I had just experienced. I knew in many cultures tradition stated that if you saved a person's life, then he was forever in your debt. In essence, your life from that point belonged to another. I imagined that this exchange system would work much the same with God.

I called again, "What do You want from me in return, God?"

Again His imperious voice pierced the night. "I want 100 percent of your faith in Me."

"What?" I said, stupefied. "Is that all?" It seemed impossible to believe that after saving my life this was all He asked of me. I thought the list of conditions would be endless. I was expecting Him to say, "Michelle, you must give up any thought of marriage, enter a convent, become a missionary, and help the poor and needy." What He was asking me seemed all too simple and this disarmed me. Not realizing what the full implications of 100 percent of my faith meant, it made me wonder whether His request was sincere.

And not knowing the mind of God and what He had planned for me this seemed so incredibly easy. Not knowing the true meaning of faith I willingly agreed, saying "Yes, God, You have 100 percent of my faith." I waited confidently half expecting a pat on the back for obediently complying with God's wishes.

The firm reply I received shocked me into submission. In an instant of time He showed me He was not someone to be taken lightly, but Someone to be feared because He had the ability to see into my mind and read my every thought. His stern response shook me to the core of my foundations. He said, "No, not 90 percent. I want 100 percent of your faith."

He knew exactly what I had been thinking and how blasé I was in offering my faith. He had intercepted my thoughts with an opposing inquiry. This for me was absolute proof that God existed and knew my

---

"I knew God's promise was an act of grace; now I would have to rely on Him to perform a miracle, because that's what it would take!"

---

heart and mind intimately. Knowing that the secrets of my heart were not hidden from God, I had the overwhelming desire to unburden myself to Him and make a pledge of obedience and absolute trust in Him—even though I had held off turning to Him until the eleventh hour.

"I want you to understand that these are not the ravings of a desperate person who will make any promise to save her life. Whatever You ask of me in the future I will do it without hesitation. If it takes me an eternity to repay this gift of life that You have given me, then I guarantee that I will."

An airy stillness met my words. God's assurance that I would not die was all He chose to reveal to me. The rest was up to me, to act in faith and wait on His deliverance. I knew God's promise was an act of grace; now I would have to rely on Him to perform a miracle, because that's what it would take!

With ten hours of darkness looming before me, I realized it would be most daunting to remain faithful to my word. The words I spoke so naively of 100 percent faith were about to be put through a monumental test. I would have to learn to trust Him beyond human emotion, rationality, and insurmountable circumstances.

The wind began its eerie howling. Its force had whipped up the ocean to white-capped swells which were illuminated by the light of the stars. The sea had taken on the image of a grotesque monster with its predatory actions of snarling and lashing at me with whip-like swiftness. It was like a medieval dragon whose tongue licked hungrily at the edges of the bunca, trying to swallow us both. My defenseless body, which ached almost beyond my endurance, was a target for its violent onslaught. Although last night's storm had abated, the seas still raged out of control. The gigantic size of the waves had not yet ceased to amaze me. I had never experienced or seen waves of this magnitude.

Wedging myself even more firmly between the upturned hull of the bunca and the arm of the outrigger, I hung on for dear life! I could not escape the ferocity of the squall and its seeming determination to break me. My only choice was to hold fast to God's promise and await the passing of time until morning. Looking at the treacherous conditions I was in, I was amazed at the gargantuan task God would have to perform to keep me alive.

Angels

Without warning, I sensed something near me. Swiveling around in every direction I was confronted with only the dense blackness of the night. Suddenly surrounding me was an aura of magnetic, vibrating forces that electrically charged the air around me, so much so that I could tangibly feel it! Terrified, I tried to shrink into obscurity under the surface of the ocean. Up to my neck in water, with the acid taste of abject fear in my mouth, I waited, instinctively knowing I was about to experience a spiritual encounter.

Suddenly, before my eyes the vibrating energy took form, an effervescent movement massing together like molecules of light and materializing into the visible images of three angels, not more than five feet from my bunca. Absolutely stunned, I was unable to move. I wanted to swim away from these intimidating spiritual beings. Closing my eyes, I tried to eliminate this vision, truly hoping that when I opened my eyes again the angels would be gone and I would realize that this was just an apparition, a figment of my haunted mind.

Opening my eyes again, I was assaulted with the truth: It was no apparition—I was in the presence of three angels. Angels from God, sent from heaven to protect me. I'd heard of people having heavenly visitations before, but I had dismissed these people with having overactive imaginations. Would my friends do the same to me? I experienced an eerie sensation as if the meeting of physical and spiritual beings was forbidden. Pure, blinding white light emanated from these three angels which stood together on the surface of the ocean. Towering above the surface, thet seemed to be about nine feet tall. Coming from the area of their shoulders was the rounded protrusion of clearly defined feathery wings. With my mouth open in awe and fear, I looked on at these angels that stood on the ocean in a very stoic stance until the white aura of light from them diffused and disappeared. After several minutes, the visual sight of the three angels had dissolved; yet I continued to feel surrounded by what I can only describe as an electromagnetic force.

A tingling sensation rippled up and down my back as I felt a fourth angel directly behind me. Like a cloak it spread its wings and wrapped them around my body, totally enveloping me. Looking down I could see the clearly defined, but translucent, wings of the angel, looking very much like that of a enormously large bird. I was completely swathed in a protective covering. The angels were my defensive shield against the murderous ocean. I conciously knew their God-given mission was to keep a vigil throughout the night and guard me from the jaws of death.

Although initially it was a chilling sensation to be in such close proximity to supernatural beings, the eerie feeling soon dissipated, and for the first time since this ordeal began, I felt safe! I felt an overwhelming sense of relief and comfort to know that God was watching over me. The thundering seas continued to pound my body mercilessly and yet I felt cocooned by the angelic covering God had provided. As if encased in a glass screen box, I viewed the stormy tempest around me with a calm instilled in me that went beyond all human comprehension.

A Long Vigil

The ebony blackness enveloped me like a dense fog. It was impossible for me to pierce through the obscurity of darkness. Nothing broke up the monotony of indistinct color; only a smattering of stars shed light on the commotion surrounding me. What most frightened me was that I could unsuspectingly be within a few miles, maybe even yards of land, and pass it by during the night, never knowing. Only the night held the mysterious secrets, and its camouflage of opaque blackness concealed them from my eyes.

I was exhausted to the very depths of my soul! There wasn't a part of me that didn't ache. I desperately longed to lie in a bed, to stretch out and close my eyes, without the fear of banging my head on the bunca, becoming unconscious, and drowning. Despite God's hand upon me, I had to remain awake if I wanted to stay alive.

An uncontrollable shivering had taken possession of my body, shaking it violently like the branches of a birch tree in a savage storm. There seemed no way I could get warmth back into my icy body. The chilling winds gusting over the ocean penetrated me to my innermost core. Although I dreaded the very thought of it, I knew the only way to get out of the bitter wind was to submerge myself under water.

Releasing my hold, I allowed myself to slip beneath the inky depths with only my head bobbing above the ocean surface. Securely sandwiching myself in, with my back pressed hard against the hull of the upturned bunca and with my knees bent, I pushed the soles of my flippered feet firmly against the narrow wooden outrigger. Like two negative forces repelling each other, I created a tension that kept me rigidly wedged in position. It was diabolical to know that I would have to remain in this position all night. There was nothing beneath me except water, and if I relaxed the pressure for even a second, I would fall beneath the depths.

This night was an agonizingly brutal vigil, but one I had no alternative but to endure until the light of morning would release me. It felt like a prison sentence, the worst degree of solitary confinement imaginable. Like captives in a P.O.W. camp, I knew there was no hope of escape, but still I exhausted my mind with the remote possibility of breaking free without bringing about my own death. At this stage I could even see death as an escape in itself. I imagined that like me, many times a P.O.W. would have wanted nothing better than to close his eyes and sleep forever, to be freed of injured and aching flesh, to be rid of tortured thoughts. Yet still, each hung onto life with a tenacity immeasurable.

But why? What for? What is so wonderful about life on this earth that we are willing to endure and suffer any extremities, to do whatever it takes to continue our existence, to hold onto life almost to the point of masochism? Why do we fight so hard to stay alive, preferring the sometimes terrible affliction of living, when death is presumably so peaceful? Why is it that even when we have reached the point of wanting to die, even longing to die, this instinct of self-preservation is so predominant over all other instincts? What would become of me once the umbilical cord attaching me to life was severed? Would my spirit rise out of my bodily shell and ascend to heaven?

My insecurity and fear began dredging up some ghastly scenarios. Perhaps my mind, body, and soul would sink to the bottom of the ocean floor and that would be the end? No afterlife, no eternity—just dead, kaput, finished! Before these black thoughts were allowed to take root, a contradictory shaft of truth beamed into my consciousness—illuminating an inner truth. I could not forget God's presence and the words He had spoken to me. No, I could not logically believe that life ended when my body expired. To believe otherwise would mean my twenty-two years on this planet were meaningless and had no purpose.

The harrowing reality of my miserable predicament and thoughts of what my ultimate outcome would be dominated everything else. A prevailing sense of doom was ever present, hanging over me like a dagger. The night dragged on interminably, holding me hostage in a dark, dank

"It was diabolical to know that I would have to remain in this position all night. There was nothing beneath me except water, and if I relaxed the pressure for even a second, I would fall beneath the depths."

pit. I was cloaked in a canopy of blackness where there was nothing else. It was as if all my senses had been snatched away, leaving only my exterior frame, an inoperative hollow shell to prove that I was still alive. Although my eyes were open it was as if I had been blinded, the world obscured by a charcoal blanket of blackness.

A deathly silence reigned over the ocean. The only sound to be heard was the breaking of the swell and the throbbing of my heart. It was so intensely quiet that the silence resounded in my eardrums like an alarm. There was nothing to relieve the soundlessness of the night. Although the sea was tepid and thus would enhance my chances of survival, still it was cold enough to have numbed my body so completely that I could feel nothing. This night was the culmination of my very worst fears, the most gruesome nightmare I could ever have dreamed. It was unthinkable to accept that it was real and I was living it. *When will it ever end?* I wondered desperately.

Physically I believed I had it in me to survive another few days if nothing drastic happened, but it was the mental trauma that made me realize I wasn't capable of enduring another night. The total isolation and severe loneliness threatened to destroy my well-preserved sanity. The acute sensation was burning my insides, eating away at the essential core of my being like acid on an open wound. There was no mercy to be had. This feeling of being totally alone and abandoned had ingrained itself so deeply within me that it would be with me always.

No one could fill this well of emptiness or bear this pain with me. I realized that we may live our lives with other people, but ultimately we are alone. We can unite with another in friendship, marriage, and parenthood, yet we are still a single entity, and our physical bonds to people are of this earth only.

The flippant human cry of "I am lonely" now bore such a shallow echo of truth. I too had been guilty of uttering the same words, but I had absolutely no comprehension of the words' true meaning until this night. Now I understood what it meant to be lonely in its entirety, so much so that it sickened me; my whole body shuddered in revulsion against its crushing force. Nothing in my life could have prepared me for this! Even if a person is incapacitated and confined to his bed, still there are entertaining pursuits which can stimulate the mind. They can turn on the television and absorb themselves in another world, or tune into the radio and sing along to the familiar songs, or open a book and be captivated into the lives of the characters. They would at least be able to switch on a light and see their surroundings. All these are forms of escapism, where one can be absorbed into the lives of others and have attention diverted from his own troubles.

I felt like an astronaut, who while exploring had become detached from his craft and was now floating aimlessly in space, lost in a black, vast void. I was drifting through a foreign territory, where my enemies abounded and my friends were none. Somehow I alone would have to find a solution to this catastrophe. I found it difficult to imagine a situation more hopeless and incurable than mine.

Holding onto God's promise had become like grasping onto a whisperous vapor and watching it dissolve into nothing at the touch of my hand. As the hours dragged on, His words had become remote, and fear took a stronghold.

I found it impossible to blot out and banish the hideous thoughts that entered my mind. Scenarios of how I would meet my death loomed up before me, each one more gruesome than the last. My imagination had escaped my control, running wildly farther and farther down a path of terror. I was powerless to stop these fears from consuming me and had no alternative but to let them run their course. One nightmarish thought that reoccurred with petrifying reality was the very real threat of man-eating sharks. I was easy prey to any marauding predator. Their keen sense would alert them to my presence in their territorial waters. Seeing my flippered feet dangling in the ocean, they would move in for the kill. Without warning I would feel the shark's segregated teeth sink

" 'Oh God, please let daybreak come soon. I can't stand this,' I pleaded aloud."

into the flesh of my calf, shaking his head from side to side in a feeding frenzy. I would desperately try to hold onto the bunca, but would feel myself being dragged farther under the ocean.

I made a despairing attempt to expel these thoughts from my mind by substituting these imaginings with pleasant mental thoughts. I tried to picture myself running through a field of wild flowers, the sun streaming down on me, warming my body. It was hopeless! This beautiful image faded from my thoughts as quickly as I had conceived it. I could not dispel these ghastly thoughts and fears; they had become entrenched in my mind.

Groping blindly in the dark, I speedily hauled myself up higher onto the bunca, drawing as much of my body as possible out of the water. "Oh God, please let daybreak come soon. I can't stand this," I pleaded aloud.

This night seemed to last forever; twelve hours had stretched out before me like a never-ending road. It was as if the sun had agreed not to rise for a week, as if the culmination of that entire seven days of darkness had been condensed into this very night. Having lost my watch in the storm only made matters worse, more deceptive. Hypothetically speaking, I knew that if I still had my watch and continually looked at it, the minutes would have ticked by like hours and hours like days, but it would at least prove that time was moving forward. Without it I found it difficult to believe time was moving at all. It was as if I were caught in a time warp, held prisoner in a blackened dungeon.

All sense of time had been lost; time had expired and now lay motionless in a stagnating swamp. I hoped this was not true. By all logic I kept believing that at any minute darkness would break its captive grasp on me, and the lightening of the sky would reveal dawn, which would set me free. But that moment never seemed to come! I had no choice but to endure through those endless hours. Surely it would arrive soon!

My stomach began to burn; the acids excreted becsuse of severe anxiety began to scorch my inner organs. The ulcer I had contracted in Japan was ablaze like a raging forest fire, and I had no water to quench it. The accidental mouthfuls of salt water I swallowed only antagonized it further, causing me to clutch hold of my stomach in excruciating agony. I tried to keep calm and suppress my agitation, hoping it would placate my ulcer, but to no avail. Until the sun rose I could not expect to feel a modicum of safety and relief. By dead reckoning, I guessed the time to be around 3 A.M. Only two more insufferable hours left. Would I live to see the sunrise? God seemed to think so!

I jolted my head upwards in alarm. Oh no! I had allowed my eyes to close. I shook my head from side to side to be freed of the hypnotic grasp of exhaustion. In an unguarded instant, I had allowed myself to slip into its deadly clutches. Thank God, I had stopped short of falling into a fatal slumber. Reprimanding myself severely I promised not to let it happen again; to sleep was a self-inflicted death sentence!

Between these early hours of morning and the rising of the sun, there are numerous blank spaces in my memory, periods of mental drifting where my unconscious seemed to leave my body and wander to the far-off realms of the earth. The trauma of my ordeal was too devastating for my mind to bear, so its natural mechanism allowed it to escape reality until it was safe to come back. These passages of time I cannot recall; it was as if I had no thoughts at all. These intervals when I was transported to a type of dreamtime are a total blank, never to be remembered and harnessed. They are gone, lost to me forever.

TEN

INSURMOUNTABLE ODDS

RACHELLE . . . 6:00 P.M., FRIDAY, MARCH 10, BORACAY ISLAND. Two opposing trains of thought had set themselves up to do battle inside my head. They traveled through my mind with the rapidity and crackle of electricity. One part of me was saying, *Why don't you face it? She's dead. You know in your heart she's gone. The undeniable signs are all there in black and white. You can't deny the significance of the dream! It symbolized what had already come to pass, a compassionate fore-warning to soften the blow when confronted with the facts.* Then from a remote part of me a voice rose up in defiance, *No, Michelle can't be dead. I won't accept that! While there is no body or no proof, I'll continue searching for her.*

This second facet of the argument appeared to have little substance; its case was built on faith, hope, and nonacceptance of the cold, hard facts. The other aspect of the argument was based on conclusive evidence. Michelle hadn't come home last night and there had been a violent storm; these were the facts I couldn't deny. The boat she had set out in was minute, with no sail or motor, and the waters she was adrift in were notorious for sharks. The chance of finding such a small vessel in thousands of miles of ocean was almost impossible.

All the overwhelming evidence was stacked against my faith and flew in the face of logical thinking. My hope was being eaten away like a slow cancer, consuming the remnant of optimism. Yet I had to keep on with the search; I would never give up knowing I hadn't done everything humanly possible to find her. My future days would be a torment, and I would never know another day's peace. With this thought, an anger welled up in me, raw and potent with energy. It delivered me from the destructive feelings of self-pity and listlessness. Resolutely I obliterated them from my mind and moved on.

I Need an Air Search

The chill of the sunset settled into every fiber of my being as I sat on the balcony of our bungalow. How nightmarish the events of this afternoon had been!

"Lotti, I want to hire a plane. I don't care how much it costs. Who's this company Air Pacific that Mr. Frazer mentioned? Could you please try to contact them for me?"

"Sure I can. I've already got the number here. I'll try it for you right now."

The next half an hour was spent trying to contact the right people who could authorize a plane for the rescue. I sat immobilized, turning myself into granite, as angry, frustrated emotions savagely wrecked havoc on my senses. I sat motionless, experiencing them without acknowledging their potential to demolish me in a brief, unguarded moment. I had retreated into a remote corner of my mind when the hum of Lotti's voice reached me as if it had traveled down a long distant corridor. I was drawn back into the moment by Lotti's triumphant voice shouting, "They've got a plane available, Rachelle."

My sagging spirits were instantly revived, as I found myself transported once again down the river of hope. The hours of frustration and disappointment dissolved; faith now reigned. I was aware of the wild mood swings each and every fresh piece of information brought with it, but this new dimension of the search bore the most positive aspect to date. An aerial search could do in half an hour what ten boats could do in an entire day.

"Lotti, that's fantastic! What do we have to do? How soon can they be here?" I exclaimed.

"I haven't asked them yet; unfortunately, it's a matter of finances. They require twelve hundred U.S. dollars cash, paid in advance, before they will proceed with the arrangements. Have you got that much with you?" she asked, somewhat embarrassed at having to ask me such a personal question.

"No, I haven't," I groaned. "Michelle has all the money and travelers' checks in her money belt, which she has on her. But I would be able to pay them once I contacted my bank."

"Sorry, Rachelle, they want the money up front. They said they've been caught before. Once the search is over, people won't pay up. That's their regulations."

"Oh no, where could I get that amount of money? I don't know anyone on the island that well. Look, tell them I'll call them back in fifteen minutes and I'll see if I can raise the money somehow."

"An aerial search could do in half an hour what ten boats could do in an entire day."

A shudder of panic ran down my spine; the thought of not being able to get the plane and thus jeopardizing Michelle's chances of being rescued—over money—was appalling. My mind was spurred into action! Seeking out a solution, I now had a challenge with a deadline to meet; the prize, my daughter's life. I felt my blood run cold, the possibility of rejection was all too evident.

I took off from that office like a woman possessed, running down the length of the well-worn beachfront path. *David, David, David,* I breathed with every step. He was my only hope! Thoughts whirled frantically around inside my head. Did he have that much money on him? Even if he did, would he lend it to me? I felt positively ill with trepidation, and it was now only moments before I would have the answer. My nerves were stretched to breaking.

"Do you know where David is?" I asked, panting breathlessly, when I reached his bungalow.

"He went down to Rafel's. I think you will find him there," said a maid.

"Thanks," I said, barely stopping for a moment. As I neared the restaurant, I saw Rafel outside speaking to a group of men. She looked up as I neared and came forward to meet me.

"Are you okay?"

"Yes, I'm all right. I'm looking for David. Have you seen him?"

"Yes, he's over at the far table. He's been trying to organize several fishermen to join the search in their own boats."

"Oh, that's good. The more people out there the better." I moved unseeing through the throng of people, knowing all eyes were upon me and voices hushed when I approached.

David appeared to sense a change in the atmosphere and looked up from the group. "Rachelle, what's up? Is there any news?"

"No, they still haven't found her, but I've managed to organize a plane to search for her. But they want twelve hundred dollars up front before they will even consider going ahead with the operation. I haven't got that kind of money on me. Michelle's got it all in her money belt. I know it's a lot to ask of you, but have you got enough money that you could lend me?"

I held his gaze with the utter pleading in my eyes. I shivered suddenly as if being touched by an iceberg, I was so terrified of his reply.

He jumped up.

"Yes, I have and it's yours. Come with me and I'll get it for you. It's locked up in Rafel's safe."

I unclenched my fists and breathed in deeply; a feeling of intense relief sped through me like anesthetic. I watched as David retrieved his wallet from the safe and opened it up.

"Are you sure twelve hundred is enough?" he asked with no more emphasis than if he were loaning me pocket money.

"Yes, that's all they said they need in cash. Rafel said we can use her as a guarantor for anything else they may require. Thanks so much, David, this money could very well save Michelle's life."

"Look, take it. The money's nothing. Just find Michelle, okay?"

The money was thrust into my hand, and I sensed his emotions straining behind a thin veneer of control. In one heart-stopping moment I knew this transaction would bond me to this man forever; regardless of the outcome I would always be indebted to him. Our eyes held for an instant, revealing the unspoken anxiety we were both experiencing. David's voice broke into the depth of the moment as if a pebble had been dropped into a pond.

"Everyone on the island has heard about Michelle. We have been organizing local boats to go out looking for her. You're not alone, just know that."

"Thanks a lot, David," I said and hurriedly retraced my steps to the transmitter room clutching those precious dollars which now represented Michelle's life.

A plane! I ran like the wind, dodging people, dogs, children, and chickens as I made my way toward my destination. People stared at me openly; probably nobody was ever seen running on this lackadaisical island. I must have looked absurd to the locals, but I had only one obsessive thought on my mind: To get back and get the rescue operation underway. David's kindness and generosity cut through my armor. His sincere empathy had the ability to touch me in a way that penetrated the walls of my defenses, the invisible adhesive which was holding me together, but I rebelled against the sentimentality for fear of its reducing me to rubble.

I burst into the room shouting, "I've got the money, Lotti, most of it anyway. Rafel is willing to be guarantor for the balance. Please call Air Pacific and confirm the flight."

Lotti reached excitedly for the receiver and after some minutes made the connection to Caticlan. With nerve-racking trepidation I waited, barely daring to breathe lest I break the spell. The atmosphere was tense as if the air had been electrically charged. The time was now 3 P.M.! A voice responded as it came through the receiver and hung in the air, reverberating over and over in my ears.

"I'm sorry, Boracay. Air Pacific has said it's too late at this hour to send out the plane. By the time they authorize the search, plus the one hour flight time between Manila to Boracay, it will be dark. They would have to allow at least two hours for the search, and it's just not possible to be able to complete the search in the hours of daylight left. They said they would have the plane ready at Caticlan by first light tomorrow. Would you please confirm those arrangements, over?"

My world stopped turning! I felt as if a dagger of ice had been plunged into my heart, and with every word she uttered the icy dread bore deeper. A loud humming sounded inside my head, and I felt my chest hammering as if by its force it would tear through the flesh.

"No! No!" I heard myself scream hysterically, "I must have that plane today."

Lotti was at my side in an instant trying to reassure me. Such a mixture of violent emotions were churning in me that I fought to regain control. I couldn't fall apart now.

"Lotti, I can't accept that decision. Don't they understand tomorrow could be too late? Michelle could still be alive now, but another night at sea might very well mean her death. Please beg them. We have to look for her today. There's still time! Make them understand my daughter's life is at stake."

Lotti picked up the receiver, and once again I heard her pleading my case. It was futile! The decision had been made; they were responsible for the safety and lives of the rescuers and their equipment. There was absolutely nothing I could do! I felt myself plummeting down as if I had been flung off a cliff and was free falling into an abyss. I felt a scream rise to my throat, and I knew I had to get out of that room before I unleashed the cauldron of seething emotions.

"Thanks, Lotti, for trying for me. Tell them to be here in the morning. I've got to get out of here. I'll see you later."

"Are you sure you'll be all right? I can go with you if you like."

"No, it's okay. I need to be alone." And I hurried out the door.

"Please take care," she said with a look of utter desolation.

Fleeing the confines of the office I broke into a run, hoping by sheer propulsion I could leave behind the torment in me. I needed to find solitude where I could release this fiendish pain and anger which had transformed my insides into a snake pit. I craved a padded room where I could release the intensity of what I was feeling, scream out my anger where nobody would be offended.

I looked for a place to retreat but there was no escape. I carried the intolerable grief within me. Tomorrow! I had to wait until tomorrow. It seemed an eternity away! Endless hours stretched out before me, each one reduced to minutes and seconds which I had to live through, experience, and endure. My little girl, what hope had she now? I'd let her down. If she were alive, what terrors was she going through? The thought that she would have to suffer another horrible night in the cold dark of night, lost and alone in the ocean, was too much for me to withstand.

The anxiety I felt for her almost made me wish she were dead; at least she would be beyond the paralyzing fear she would be experiencing. I knew if she were still alive she would be crying out for me, praying for me to come and rescue her, and here I was, utterly powerless to lift a finger to save her life. This knowledge bore a crushing blow to the protective maternal instincts in me. There was nothing I could do to help my child. I had been reduced to an ineffectual bystander, floundering in my own human vulnerability and impotence. I came face to face with my powerlessness, and though I thrashed and rallied against it, I recognized my inability to control life, mine or my child's. I wanted the earth to swallow me up. I needed an escape hatch, but the life beating in me denied me a release.

I had no other alternative; I had to wait it out. I was lost in a swirl of debilitating emotions, yet my eyes couldn't deny the abundant force of life that surrounded me—people, birds, animals, trees, and plants. Until this moment I had taken these for granted, the essence of life. I very rarely thought about it until now, when it was possible I could lose something very precious to me.

The pervading feelings of imminent loss draped themselves over me like a blanket. Suddenly, I needed to go back to the bungalow. It was the only place on the island I could identify as home, although the shocking thought of being there alone surrounded by recent memories was intolerable. But where else did I have to go?

Our bungalow came into view, nestled peacefully among the flowing palms, bathed in the glow of the setting sun. I couldn't face going inside; instead I sat on the patio and watched the burnished sun cast its last flaming light over the sea.

Was Michelle out there somewhere, also witnessing it disappear? The implications of the sun's departure for her would be horrendous. I felt a crying ache, a desire to transmit to her hope and the knowledge that we would be out looking for her tomorrow. I yearned to fortify her with the strength to hang in there and not to give up hope. My heart was breaking in two, knowing there was so little I could do. I wanted to pray but couldn't. There was still too much fight in me. I felt any show of weakness could have the power to reduce me to uncontrollable hysteria, and this I couldn't afford. No medication on the island could possibly help me cope; it was vital to keep myself from being completely incapacitated by the ordeal. The balance of my sanity hung by tenuous threads.

Do I Trust Him?

How long I sat on the balcony I wasn't sure. I moved through a warped passage of time that became a blur. On some level I was absently aware what was taking place around me, but my heart had receded into a safety zone for self-preservation. I was abruptly jarred back from my sanctuary by David stepping onto the balcony.

"Rachelle, are you okay? I heard about the plane not being able to be here till tomorrow. I'm really sorry."

As I was being sucked back to awareness, I tried to escape the pain I knew awaited me the instant I made contact. I heard David's words, muted as if they had been spoken under water, and I experienced only the vibration. It took a few seconds before I focused on him and realized he was actually standing in front of me.

"Rachelle, are you sure you're okay?" he said, touching my shoulder gently.

I was almost too choked up to speak, but I said, "I don't know, David. I don't know if I'm all right. Sometimes I think I'm handling it, and then the next minute I'm drowning and there's no way for me to escape from it. Worse is the uncertainty which erodes all my strength and hope. I just don't know where she is. It's a living nightmare not knowing."

"I don't think it's a good idea for you to be by yourself," he murmured. "Rachelle, you need support right now, not isolation. Come down to the Beachcomber Bar and have a drink with me. It will make you feel a little better. There's absolutely nothing you can do until morning and you shouldn't be here all night on your own. Come on, what do you say? Will you come with me? I'll look after you. We have an extra room at the house. You must stay with us tonight. You really shouldn't be alone."

I looked into David's pleading eyes and knew what he said made sense. To be alienated at such a time as this was an added torture I didn't need. I longed for human contact to uphold my spirit. All of a sudden I felt an overwhelming desire to be encompassed by humanity, an ache for human warmth and conversation. It seemed to me a lifetime ago since I'd known happiness.

"I think you're right. I do need to be with people, but I look so awful. How can I face anyone looking like this?"

"You look just fine to me. Everyone knows what you've been through today. They won't be judging you. They understand."

Momentarily I contemplated going inside, changing my clothes and running a brush through my hair but no sooner had I thought of this, than I was assaulted with an anxiety so intense I knew I wasn't capable of entering the bungalow for any reason. With David's comforting arm around me, we made our way to the Beachcomber. I felt as if I had been rescued from the jaws of a devouring beast who was waiting to swallow me up. Thankfully, David had momentarily saved me from this destiny.

As we walked into the bar I felt all eyes turn to look at me and then respectfully look away. The events of the past two days had cast me as an oddity, a conversation piece, an object of sympathy. I sensed people were uncomfortable in my presence; they were unsure what to say to me. Should they mention Michelle or ignore the subject completely? Maybe it was best to avoid me altogether. This peculiarity in human nature identifies our inability to face death or any other loss. Mind you, I didn't blame them. I also wanted to lose myself in the crowded room.

David found a table for us in a secluded corner where I could retreat into insignificance and not be bothered by the patrons' inquisitive stares. The first few cocktails I drank without even realizing it. After several more had been gulped down in much the same way, a numbing effect began to seep through me like an anesthetic, putting space between me and what I knew I would have to face in the morning. The raw situation confronting me had been diluted as the alcohol dulled my senses. As it fused with my blood, it warmed to life the chill within me.

The night air was cloaked in a velvety stillness which only a tropical climate could create. We strolled down to the water's edge where the luminous evening silence was broken only by the ocean gently stroking the shore. Lying down on the blanket of soft sand, we gazed skyward, awed by the global planetarium. The evening sky was domed by a blazing galaxy of a trillion glittering stars, each one so well-defined that I felt as if I could reach out and touch them. The sultry heat of the day still lingered in the air, caressing my skin, hugging me with its invisible touch. Time ceased to have meaning; there remained only the echoes of the night, the incessant chattering of crickets, the fluttering of birds' wings as they flew among the palm trees, and the sound of the perpetually stirring ocean—all illuminated by the canopy of starlight.

"I wonder if Michelle can see the stars tonight from wherever she is?" I said wistfully, speaking more to myself than to David.

"I'm sure she can, and we'll make sure this is the last night she has to spend alone—because tomorrow we'll find her!" David said with believable conviction. I nodded in agreement although I had no confidence in what he was saying.

"I don't think I have ever seen the sky quite so clear as it is tonight. Look at the Milky Way," he said, pointing skyward. "You can see right into its depths. It certainly makes you feel insignificant, doesn't it?" he said, attempting to divert the conversation away from Michelle's disappearance.

"When my daughters were small, my husband Brett, the girls, and I would occasionally go outside, spread a blanket on the back lawn and all lie down for hours at a time and gaze out into the mystical universe. We'd point out to the children orbiting satellites and shooting stars. whispering to each other in soft tones, not wanting to shatter the mesmerizing effect a tranquil night created. The girls would often ask questions so profound that we were unable to answer them. As they say, out of the mouths of the innocent are often declared great truths. 'Why don't the stars fall out of the sky?' 'Where does God live?' were some of the questions we struggled to explain.

"They were special moments I'll always treasure. It's all gone now; time has eroded everything I once valued so much. My home, my marriage, my husband, all those precious moments have been tainted by life's harsh realities and lost through the march of time. Now even Michelle is lost; she's fallen prey to the atrophy of living. It feels as if I'm being stripped of everything I love and hold dear. I sometimes wish time would stand still and allow me to hold on to the things I cherish, but it's impossible, isn't it? Life's just not designed that way.

"I suppose I'm sounding dreadfully morbid, but this catastrophe has made me realize even more so, that the only stability we have in life is God. He is eternally the same and never changes.

"I've exhausted all my options; I feel as if I've come to the end of the road. It seems there is only one path left open to me and that is to throw myself on God's mercy and beg for compassion for myself and my child. I know I must place my trust and faith in Him and believe that in His wisdom He knows what He is doing and take comfort in His words that 'all things work together for good'" (Romans 8:28).

My attention was captured by a group of young holiday makers strolling along the beach behind us. How I envied their carefree attitude, lost in the enchantment of the evening. They displayed an exuberant energy, the evidence of thriving life blatantly obvious in these young people. They exuded an expectancy, knowing their future was full of promise. Like ripe fruit it was hanging on the tree of life, just waiting to be plucked at will. A little less then three days ago, Michelle would have been numbered among these fortunate young people.

Then without warning, her abundant life had been literally swept out from under her at the height of the harvest. How could this be possible? Memories of Michelle flooded back into my mind—the baby, the child, the adolescent, all the stages of experience which had made up the woman she had grown into.

"Hey, you've gone quiet. What are you thinking about?" David said, breaking into my thoughts.

" 'It feels as if I'm being stripped of everything I love and hold dear. I sometimes wish time would stand still and allow me to hold on to the things I cherish, but it's impossible, isn't it?' "

"Oh, I was just remembering when Michelle and her sisters were younger and how much easier it was then to keep them protected and safe. Now that they've grown up, they do what they want. I'm not able to shield them the same. Like all mothers I have had to set them free, to let them make their own decisions, and pray they will be safe. It's not easy being a mother; in fact it must be one of the most difficult jobs on earth."

"I can imagine! I'm not a parent as yet so I don't have firsthand experience, though from what I've observed it appears to be a daunting task. I think I'll postpone the responsibility for a few years yet."

"You're quite wise to do just that. I suggest you be aware of exactly what you're getting into before you take the plunge because it is a lifetime commitment. I never did! I entered into marriage with a blindfold on. I realize when I look back to those days how very naive I was. I got married, gave birth to Michelle, and was divorced before I was twenty-two years old. I didn't know what had hit me. Then I married my second husband when Michelle was four years old. That lasted sixteen years, and we broke up only three years ago."

"Oh, I am sorry. It's so common these days, but divorce seems to have reached epidemic proportions," he said sympathetically. "I've noticed that Michelle is so devoted to you and her sisters. She must have been great support to you during the family breakup. When she told me about her sisters Angeline and Natalie, it was obvious how much she loved them. I saw her eyes light up immediately when she spoke about them."

"Really, you noticed that? What did she say about them?" I asked, wishing to know more intimately Michelle's last words, every one of which had now become so precious.

"She told me that although there was quite a significant age difference between her and her sisters, they were close. She said she felt like a second mother to them."

"Yes, that's very true. Michelle was about eight years old when I had the girls, so she naturally took on that role. You can imagine how difficult the situation must have been for her. First, she had to learn to adjust to having Brett around. Then with the arrival of these two little red-faced strangers, she had to share me, although it was not in her nature to be jealous. Even though Brett was besotted by the two new arrivals, it made little difference to her. She still adored her sisters and did everything to help me with them."

"It takes a certain strength of character to overcome sibling rivalry and determine your own behavior and reactions. I believe it's what makes the difference between winners and losers in this world. Michelle obviously adopted this winner's attitude early in life. That's why she has become the person she is today, a survivor."

"That's for sure," I said, wondering what earthly use this was to her, lost out in the middle of the ocean, but I refrained from commenting.

"Even when Michelle was small, she was such an extroverted child, very intelligent and full of mischief," I said, wistfully delving into my memories. "Michelle was always a leader and had many followers. If any child didn't obey her, they would be banished from her 'court' and would have to placate her with candy if they wished to return to her good graces. Sometimes I used to worry about her. She was petite as a child, but what she lacked in size she certainly made up for in willpower and determination. I suppose she felt like a vulnerable pawn in the adult world of authority that surrounded her, so she took control of life from her perspective and crowned herself queen of the tiny tots. She always knew what was best, and the other children seemed to agree with her."

"I can imagine Michelle being like that. She's got an authoritative presence about her as if she knows exactly what she wants and how to get it. I'd only known her a day when already we were hotly debating an issue. I remember calling her feisty, and she laughed at me with such an air of confidence. She's got real charisma and I like that in a woman. Not to mention how easy she is to talk to," he said.

"Yes, she's a very special person. It's probably that determined streak in her that's the root cause of getting her into this disaster in the first place."

And with that remark we lapsed into silence. But David wouldn't let me hold on to my frustration.

He began, "I sense Michelle wouldn't be the type of person who could easily be swayed once her mind was made up. She was determined to paddle that bunca around the island and no one could have persuaded her otherwise. No one is to blame! How could she have known the wind would suddenly come up as quickly as it did that day?"

"No, I suppose not, just a cruel twist of destiny or maybe a divine appointment."

"Perhaps, but don't dwell on that. You will only upset yourself again. Tell me about Michelle and what life is like in Australia. I'd love to hear about it."

Without knowing it, David provided me with an outlet. He had opened the door and offered me the opportunity to share a part of Michelle's life with him, to release a portion of the pressure of the past few days. He encouraged me to talk about Michelle and remember her. What a welcome relief after having to bear this burden all alone.

"Michelle was thirteen years old when we moved to Perth in western Australia. She was in essence basically a loner, even though she was surrounded by people. She enjoyed their company but didn't need them for her happiness or well-being. Moving wasn't that much of an upheaval for her. She disliked the school system because the teachers tried to mold her into what they expected students should be. Teachers and pupils pressure you to conform to a certain set of ideas and modes of behavior. They churn out people who graduate in mediocrity; Michelle was determined not to be one of them."

"Yes, I noticed that she displayed her individuality clearly. She's a very unique person."

"That's my Michelle all right. I know she's high-spirited and impulsive, but she has such a generous heart. She would help anyone in need."

"I only wish we had a chance to get to know each other better. You know, if anyone could survive out there it would be her."

"David, waves don't bow down to human will, even I know that."

"Maybe not," he shot back, "but she's tenacious, fit, and by what little I've seen has an iron determination. It's those qualities which will be a great asset to her out there."

"I appreciate what you're saying, and I know she is mentally and physically fit. But we both know it will take nothing short of a miracle for her to survive. I don't deny her practical attributes; she's had to learn at an early age how to stand on her own two feet. Michelle was only ten months old when I was divorced from her father so we both had to toughen up pretty quickly."

"It must have been very difficult at such a young age to be a single parent, but I believe it's those very same trials we all go through that produce independence and a depth to our characters. I think it can sometimes be beneficial to go through some rough times. It forces us to exercise our strengths and become aware of our capabilities. These tests are like muscles that strengthen our character; if our character doesn't get worked, then it becomes weakened and useless."

"I've never heard it described quite that way before, but I do agree that human struggles produce an inner strength, and we have certainly had our fair share of those. Michelle has been such a strong influence on her sisters; they adore her and look to her for guidance. The loss, if she is not found, will be devastating to all of us. I cannot even begin to imagine the irreparable damage this will do to our already broken family," my voice broke.

"She's not dead yet, Rachelle. You're giving up too early. She's only been gone two days. People have been known to survive for weeks, even months out at sea. Remember, people are still out searching. You musn't give up hope!"

"I try not to, but you didn't see the size of the flimsy boat she went out in. It wouldn't have withstood the slightest battering let alone a raging storm. I keep trying to imagine a possible way in which she might have survived, but in the face of such overwhelming odds stacked against her, it seems truly futile. I feel so frightened. I can't imagine what our lives would be like without her."

"Well, let's hope you never have to find out." Attempting to divert our grim discussion on to a more positive note, David said, "Rachelle, you still haven't finished telling me your story of Australia yet."

"Well," I said, trying to place myself back into my reminiscent narrative, "when my second marriage broke up after sixteen years it was so traumatic for everyone involved. The girls and I closed ranks and nursed each other through the heartbreak. Michelle's commitment to our family was invaluable. She bolstered us with her positive attitude and had long sisterly talks to help the girls come to terms with the family breakdown. She made us laugh again with her spontaneous sense of humor.

"Michelle has a special ability to put things into perspective. We knitted our family together in a protective cocoon with love, friendship, and support. After Brett and I split up, the task of trying to pick up the pieces a second time around was so formidable that I felt I needed an

---

"As I sat on this foreign Filipino beach in the darkened night, I questioned what God was doing in my life. Michelle was lost at sea, and I had no idea if she would ever be returned to me. Was I being put to the test?"

---

entirely new environment to begin life once again as a single parent. Since Brett and I lived in such close proximity after our separation, every memory was a painful reminder of all I had lost. Leaving the house became a detestable experience; would I inadvertently see his car drive by, bump into him at the local supermarket, or worse still would I see him at an intimate restaurant with another woman? This was like an ominous black cloud which hung over me, making me feel impotent to start off my new life. I was always looking over my shoulder!"

"What an awful situation to have to be in," David said sympathetically.

"Yes, it was. When Michelle was eighteen, she went on a holiday to Sydney and decided to live there. She encouraged us to join her, and after six months her sisters and I followed suit. It was such an enormous relief. She had offered me an escape route out of this distressing situation. Michelle dreaded the thought of splitting up the remnants of what was left of our family, so the girls and I moved to Sydney to be together. They were hard days because we arrived there, knowing no one, but we pulled through because we had each other. The thought that Michelle could be taken from us now after all we have been through together is the cruelest blow imaginable."

"I think it's wonderful that you all look out for one another, that's how a family should be. You're lucky to have a daughter like Michelle!"

"Yes, I know. I've been blessed to have three lovely daughters, it makes up for a lot."

As I sat on this foreign Filipino beach in the darkened night, I questioned what God was doing in my life. Michelle was lost at sea, and I had no idea if she would ever be returned to me. Was I being put to the test? I remembered reading that God tests His children in the same way gold is tested. It is put through the fire to evaluate its worth. Was it only through trial that God could test my faith, loyalty, and obedience to Him, thereby deeming me of value and worthy to be a precious child of His?

This trial demanded I trust Him beyond reason and human logic. I was unsure if my assumptions were correct or not, but I knew my faith was immovable. I knew I must endure, but where was God now when my daughter was lost at sea?

On that beach I made a decision that whatever the outcome I would remain faithful, just as Abraham trusted God when he was asked to surrender his beloved first-born son Isaac. I felt compelled to surrender my daughter to Him if that be His will. She belonged to God and was His child, and I realized the truth was she had only been lent to me as a cherished gift from the Lord. God gives life and God takes life. We are all in His hands!

A sudden gust of wind blew off the ocean and brought me out of my thoughts. Tomorrow the search for Michelle would continue, and I would know how faithful my God was. Hopefully the wretched pain of uncertainty would be brought to an end.

Tomorrow . . . my future happiness rested there!

ELEVEN

A LETHAL ADVERSARY

MICHELLE . . . 5:00 A.M., SATURDAY, MARCH 11, CUYO EAST PASSAGE. The first faint streaks of pale yellow emerged on the eastern horizon. Dawn had finally shown itself, lighting up the sky. The twelve insufferable hours of darkness lifted like the curtain on a stage. I had been freed from my private hell by the light of morning. I had waited in acute anxiety for what seemed like an eternity for this glorious moment of reprieve.

I was alive! I had survived yet another night on this hauntingly lonely ocean. The relief I experienced at this moment was tangible. It washed over me like the balm of ointment on an open wound. A pleasurable sensation of buoyant hope was restored to my soul. Every atom and molecule in my body celebrated in victory that I was alive; my skin tingled as if thousands of effervescent bubbles had risen to the surface. Surprisingly, my feeling of relief was not so much that I was alive, but that I had been freed from the interminable hours of darkness and solitude. Now that the blackness and the battle of night had passed, my shoulders slumped forward as I allowed myself a moment's respite. The unbearable waiting for sunrise was over.

It was still too dark to see anything as yet. I strained my eyes to pierce through the obscurity of pre-dawn darkness. What would the light of the new day reveal? Would it bring renewed disappointment? Although I desperately wanted to know, I wished I could postpone the moment of truth. I didn't know how I would cope if the daylight revealed yet again an endless stretch of water with no sight of land. For two days of heartbreaking and unrelenting tension my mind balanced precariously on a tightrope between staying sane and completely breaking down. The intensely lonely vigil I'd sustained had all been in the hope and faith that I'd eventually be rescued or would find land. I prayed it would happen today.

Physically, I guessed I could probably last another two, maybe three days, presuming that nothing disastrous happened. To put a time limit on how long I thought I could survive was futile; I could only guess. I didn't think I was being negative, only realistic. I knew time was running out, and fast.

The hellish storm on the first night and incessant battering of the waves against the bunca had wrenched the right outrigger from the hull. I had no choice but to let it simply float away. This was devastating enough in itself, but now I noticed the remaining outrigger had cracked and was beginning to break away on the other side of the hull. Each time a wave crashed over the bunca, I heard a groaning creak as it broke away a fraction more. I felt an icy terror clutch my guts; I was powerless to stop the boat from breaking into pieces. Once the remaining outrigger broke off, there would be nothing whatsoever for me to hold on to. The chances for survival, then, would be minimal.

Although I would never let go of that bunca while there was still a chance of survival, it now seemed it would let go of me first. My solid rock, my chunk of stability, my lifeline would simply float away. I considered if this happened I could float on my back for awhile and hold on to the side of the bunca, but I knew that the slimy green fungus would make staying on impossible. If only I'd been able to right the bunca! All the speculation was futile; once the outrigger broke off it was just a matter of time. I was playing a waiting game until the gaping jaws of death swallowed me.

I realized that not only the loss of the outrigger, but one powerful wave, one bump to the head, or one moment's lack of concentration could extinguish my life as quickly as blowing out the flame of a candle. I just prayed if it happened, death would come quickly. I dreaded the very thought of drowning. The idea of struggling and thrashing against the ocean, trying to reach to the surface while the force of the waves and the pressure of the water held me prisoner, pushing me deeper and deeper to my death, was hideous.

My lungs would gasp for air until they burned with pain. In the ravaging throes of death I'd continue to struggle upward, only to be repeatedly stopped by a heavy blanket of water blocking my way—then finally the inevitable. My lungs would fill with water as the last remnants of air were expelled from them. I'd feel my eyes bulging as I began to lose consciousness and with it the desire and will to live. Finally yielding to my ultimate destiny, I'd let myself drift downward to my oceanic grave.

I was brought back from my morbid thoughts of drowning by the sound of my heart pounding like a ferocious drumbeat. No, I couldn't bear to die that way; in fact, I could not bear the thought of dying at all.

"I strained my eyes to pierce through the obscurity of pre-dawn darkness. What would the light of the new day reveal? Would it bring renewed disappointment?"

Although I had constantly faced death these last two days, it still seemed so totally alien to me. Inconceivable, that's what it was! I consoled myself, *Why am I worrying? I'm not going to die. God has promised me that.* If I listened to my heart and not my head, I would realize that what He said was the truth. These thoughts were spurred on by my fear and fear alone.

Since God had spoken to me last night and assured me I would not die, my faith in Him and in being rescued shone inside me like a precious jewel. Faith kept me going, the reason I sustained this will to fight. He didn't tell me when He would perform my rescue, but in His infinite wisdom I presumed He knew I couldn't last much longer. Would it be today? Would Mum be here today to rescue me? I could only pray this would be so. It was an indescribable comfort and reassurance to know that God was on my side, that He was with me, protecting me and wanting me to live. I thanked and praised Him continually for that.

The strange thing was that I felt completely natural in trusting Him. Before this experience I was not religious-minded at all. In fact, God was quite unreal to me—an entity up in the sky, sitting on His throne, watching us. God forgive me, I'd only been to church a few times in my life and that had been only to a local Sunday school. This was strange in itself considering I was Jewish, but my dad had been a Catholic, so I had gone to church with my sisters. Mum often talked about God, but until I'd seen her in Singapore she seemed very confused about her beliefs. Hence, I'd never grown up with traditional religion. I don't remember ever seeing a Bible in the house, and if there was, I never saw anybody reading it.

However, this lack of religion never prevented me from talking to God. I always had a sense that I was special to Him, somehow distinctly apart. The sensation is difficult to describe, but from a very early age I always could feel His presence near me, as if Someone were watching over me. It was a tangible feeling, unlike any I'd experienced, and I felt it more intensely these past days than in the accumulation of my entire life. I never before believed in angels, but since last night, when God had spoken to me, I suddenly sensed them surrounding me. Although thoughts of death hung over me constantly, I knew no harm would come to me, for God was with me.

Admittedly I was sick with terror at the prospect of what the light of day would unveil, but I was fortified with a strange courage. Until now I'd kept going on adrenalin, raw nerves, hope, and fear. While I was out here in this frightening and unpredictable ocean, I could at least be assured that I would never lose these emotions.

The Light of Day

Slowly the rounded orb of the sun began to crawl out of the ocean, shedding a pale orange glow over the surroundings. Straining my eyes which had become like two fireballs inside my sockets, I searched across the infinite expanse of water for anything at all. What I saw sent a long dormant charge of electricity through me, sharpening all my senses and energizing me totally.

My heart began to palpitate wildly! Far away, maybe fifteen nautical miles, three humps appeared on the horizon, protruding from the ocean. These looked very much like islands, although I was terrified to allow myself to get too excited in case my eyes were deceiving me. Shutting them, I shook my head a couple of times then re-opened them. There was no doubt about it; the three mounds were still there but they were so far away they were indefinable.

My immediate emotion was that of doubt. *Are those really islands I'm seeing, or just figments of my imagination?* Was starvation, dehydration, and exhaustion showing its face? No, I definitely saw them. But objects from such great distances are often not what they appear when you reach them. I felt my heart plummet! Could my eyes really be playing a cruel trick on me? No, they had to be real. I was scared to allow

MARCH

Sunday

5

Yesterday, Mum and I arrived on beautiful Boracay Island.

Monday

6

Today Mum and I spent a relaxing day on the beach. (Rachelle on beach)

Tuesday

7

Wednesday

8

Thursday

9

Friday

10

Saturday

11

MARCH

Sunday
5

Monday
6

Tuesday
7
Today Mum discovered the "joy" of Horseback riding!

Wednesday
8
March 8th
Enjoying the view of Panay Island from John's launch. Easy to smile today but tomorrow I am lost at sea!

Thursday
9

Friday
10

Saturday
11

MARCH

Su[nday]

5

Mon[day]

6

Tuesday

7

Wednesday

8

Thursday

9

Friday

10

Saturday

11

WILLY'S PLACE
COTTAGES & RESTAURANT
The best place to stay in the nicest Beach and in the most beautiful site of the island.

Rachelle,
I contacted the coastguards in Boracay and Caticlan. One boat from Willy's Place is already searching around. Were waiting for the coastguard to go with us in the yacht. I think we better use the yacht for the rescue. She might be in the nearby islands. I was on the radio. If possible you come down. I was on the radio when you came earlier.

From Willy's Pl[ace]
Rafel

When I realized I was in trouble, I used "The Floating Restaurant" as a marker—trying desperately to get back. But I couldn't...

Our "paradise" proved quite primative as Mum desperately tried to organize a search.

MARCH

Sunday

M

6

Tue

7

Wedne

8

Thursda

9

Friday

10

Saturday

11

THE HUMP

A Cottage Resort

MR. Choto Angara
Protocol Offices
Dept. of Foreign Affairs
TEL 832-030

Dear Choto,

Mrs. R. Hamilton is a friend of ours in Boracay who came here with her daughter for a vacation. Last thursday, March 9, her daughter went by herself on a paddle boat — she has not been seen since then. From what help the Australian Embassy has shown — has, I would say, been very minimal. Maybe with a little encouragement from your office, the Australian Embassy could do more and ask assistance from our government to help on this matter.

Any help would be appreciated. Thank you,

Regards,
Rey

Boracay Island, Malay Aklan Mailing Address: The Hump, P.O. Box 28 Kalibo, Aklan Telex: 5513
: Manila Associate Tel. 825124 Telex 2204

God blessed Mum with new "friends" like Ray who did all they could do to help her find me.

MARCH

Sunday
12

Monday
13

Tuesday
14

Wednesday
15

Thursday
16

Friday
17

Saturday
18

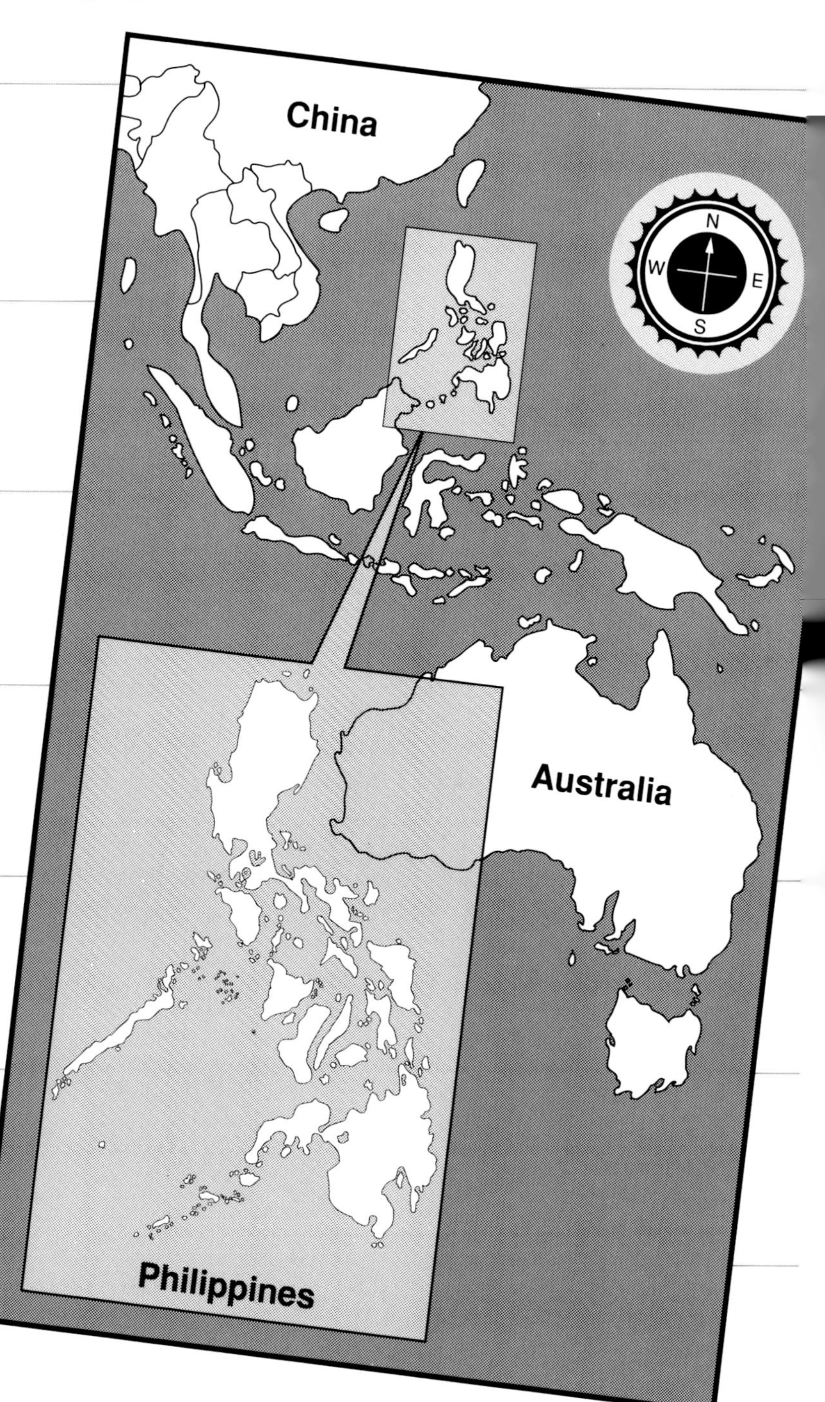

MARCH

Sunday
12

Monday
13

Tuesday
14

Wednesday
15

Thursday
16

Friday
17

Saturday
18

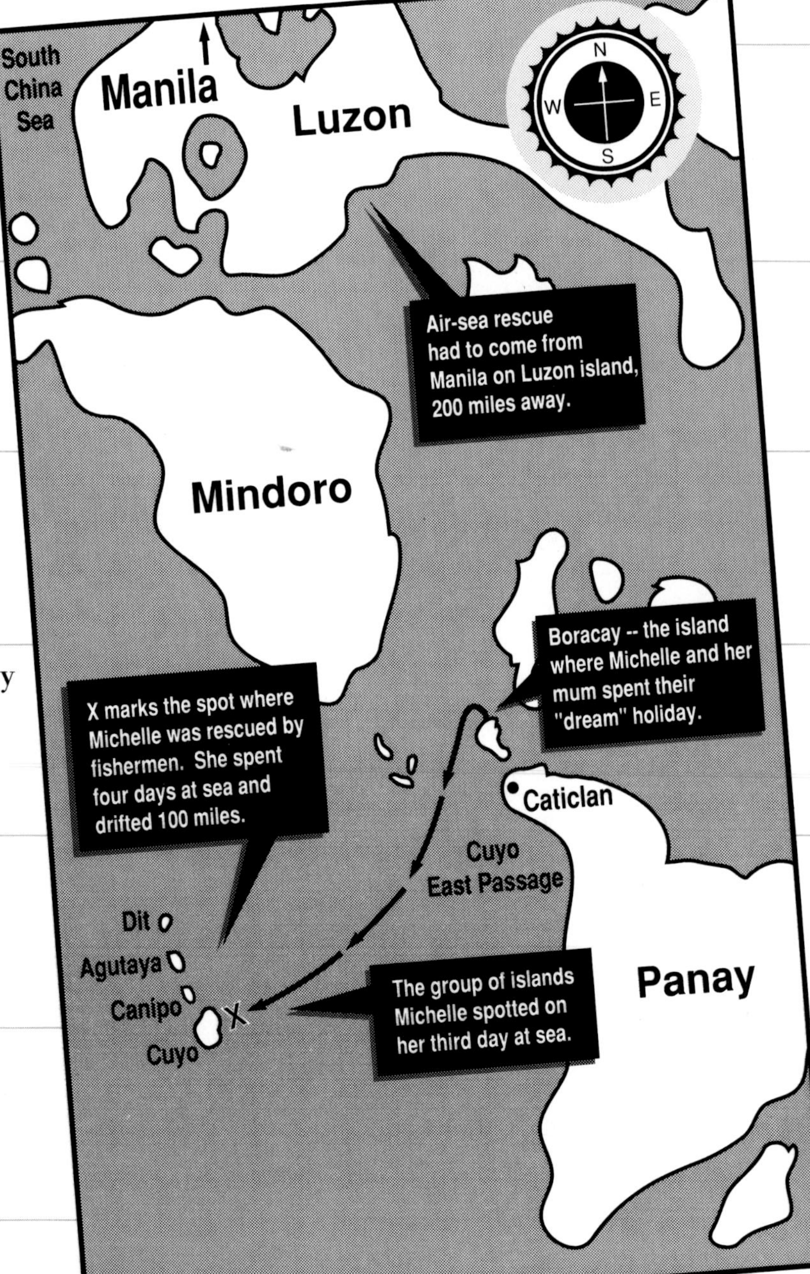

MARCH

Sunday

12

Monday

13

Tuesday

14

Wednesday

15

Thursday

16

Friday

17

Saturday

18

This is the original dispatch of my rescue and a picture of the linoleum-covered concrete bunk I used for the 24 hour voyage to Manila

INCOMING DISPATCH
CGS MLA

DE SULL MSG NR 61-P-121712H MAR 89

FM: SC CGS MLA

TO: C1CGD

INFO: CPCG/C6CGD/CGS ROXAS

DRAFTED BY: LTJG F R DEL ROSARIO PN (SGD)
APPROVED BY: LCDR R V VELASCO PN (SGD)
RELEASED BY: LT B C GANZN PN (SGD)

BT...UNCLAS x CITE CGSM-0389-61 x O/A 121600H MAR 89 CMM CGSS NAVOTAS TURNED OVER TO THIS STN TARNIA MICHELLE HAMILTON CMM AUSTRALIAN CMM 22 YRS OLD OF 14/27 TOR RD. CMM DEE WHY CMM SYDNEY CMM AUSTRALIAN 2099 WITH PASSPORT NR J0086673 CMM WHO WAS RESCUED BY F/B ALICE STAR SKIPERED BY BAUDELIO O PACTAO AND OWNED/ OPERATED BY IRMA FISHING AND TRADING CORPORATION OF MALABON CMM MANILA.

2. INVEST REVEALS SUBJ PERSON WAS RESCUED ON 111420H MAR 89 AT EAST QUINULUBAN ISL CMM CUYO ISL GROUP CMM PALAWAN x SUBJ PERSON CAME INTO ISLAND COUNTRY ON 04 MAR 89 AND CHECKED IN AT WILLY'S BUNGALOW IN BORACAY ISLAND ON SAME DAY x SHE WENT PADDLING ON 08 MAR 89 ABD ALFA BOAT BUT WAS DRIFTED TO SEA UNTIL SHE WAS RESCUED ON 111420H MAR 89

3. NEAREST OF KIN DASH RACHELLE HAMILTON WHO CAME INTO THE COUNTRY WITH HER AND ALSO CHECKED IN AT WILLY'S BUNGALOW IN BORACAY ISL x THIS UNIT ASSISTING SUBJ TO CONTACT HER MOTHER AT BORACAY

4. FOR INFO

BT....

A CERTIFIED TRUE COPY:
HCGSM/RVV/FRDR/aedr-18 AUG 89
LTJG FERNANDO R DEL ROSARIO PN
Admin/Pers Offr, CGS Manila

Michelle,
Above is message sent to Commander, First Coast Guard District by Coast Guard Station Manila
Fernando

MARCH

COVER STORY

"I found God when I got lost at sea"

By Betty Go-Belmonte

4 STARWEEK/The Sunday Magazine of the Philippine Star/April 15,

Sunday

12

Monday

13

Monday, March 13th
Thank you Lord — I am found!

Tuesday

14

Tuesday, March 14th
My "adventure" is front page news around the world.

Wednesday

15

Daily Mirror

Tuesday, March 14, 1989

SYDNEY 'MERMAID' AMAZING RESCUE

SURVIVOR: Michelle Hamilton, 22-year-old blonde "mermaid" who is recovering today from her four-day sea ordeal

FOUR DAYS LOST IN SEA

By JIM POLLARD

A YOUNG Sydney woman today told of her miraculous rescue off the Philippines by local fishermen — who thought they had found a mermaid.

In an exclusive interview from her hotel room today, she told the Mirror: "The fishermen thought they'd picked up a mermaid!

Thursday

16

Friday

17

Saturday

18

MARCH

Sun

Mo

1

Tuesd

14

Wednesda

15

Thursday

16

Friday

17

Saturday

18

'Mermaid' rescued by RP fishers

By ALEX RAMOS

For four days and three nights, Ternia Michelle Hamilton, a 22-year-old tourist from Wellington, New Zealand, drifted at sea before she was rescued off the coast of Palawan by fishermen who thought she was a mermaid.

Michelle, who was reported lost four days ago after going out to sea alone on a boat off the shore of Boracay island, was picked up yesterday by the fishing vessel F/B Alice Star of Irma Shipping and Trading Corp. of Malabon.

"I'm glad there are no sharks in the Philippines," the girl said.

She was just lucky, said Lt. Edward del Rosario of the Philippine Coast Guard Station Manila. According to him, the area where Michelle was found happened to be shark-infested.

"I'm not a religious person but I learned how to pray to God," Michelle said of her ordeal.

Michelle arrived in Boracay with her mother last March 4 for a two-week vacation. In the afternoon of March 8 the two decided to go on boat around the island, but when it became windy the mother asked to be returned to shore. The intrepid Michelle resumed boating on her own for a few more hours.

She said that while rowing back to shore, the wind

Turn to Page 10

MONDAY, MARCH 13, 1989

'Mermaid' survives sea ordeal

MELBOURNE: An Australian woman has survived three days without food or water drifting on an over-turned rowboat in the Philippines.

Michelle Hamilton, 22, of Sydney, floated 100km holding on to the hull of the two-metre boat before being picked up by Filipino fishermen who at first thought she was a mermaid.

Her mother — who was holidaying with her on the resort island of Boracay, 350km south of Manila — had given her daughter up for dead and held a memorial service.

"I don't know how I am alive," Miss Hamilton said from Manila last night.

"I had nothing to eat or drink and I didn't sleep at all because every 10 minutes or so the waves would wash me off the boat."

Miss Hamilton's terrifying ordeal began last Wednesday when she was swept out to sea while paddling the boat off the island.

For two days she saw nothing but water, the horizon — and two sharks.

"On the first day the winds were so strong that the boat capsized," she said.

"The sharks were about 20 metres from me. I couldn't get out of the water into the boat, so I just kept still."

On the third day she said she started hallucinating.

"I kept hearing helicopters and seeing other things," she said.

But on that third day she had just sighted a couple of islands when she saw the fishing boat.

"It was very big and actually went past me," she said.

"The guys at the back of the boat spotted me and they came back.

"They were the nicest people. One man washed my hair, cleaned my teeth and spoon-fed me mangoes.

"Apparently they thought I was a mermaid. They never see anyone in those seas so I don't think they were expecting a woman with long blonde hair to appear from nowhere."

She said her reunion with her mother was something she would never forget.

"She's very happy but I can't stop her crying," she said.

MARCH

Mum flew to Manilla to seek help from our Embassy, after she arrived and faced the truth that I might not be found word came of my rescue.

Twenty-four hours after my rescue Mum and I are finally reunited. It was a moment we will never forget!

Sunday

12

Monday

13

Tuesday

14

Wednesday

15

Thursday

16

Friday

17

Saturday

18

MARCH 14, 1989

THE PHILIPPINE STAR
TRUTH SHALL PREVAIL

Pass the ...

Dolphy quitting RPN-9
Teletalk • 16

Mother calls 'mermaid's' rescue a 'miracle'

By LIZA LACSON

"I asked for a miracle, and He gave us one," said Rachelle Hamilton, mother of 22-year-old Ternia Michelle, the Australian tourist mistaken by Filipino fishermen for a mermaid when they rescued her Sunday from the shark-infested waters off Palawan Island.

"At one time I thought she was dead. . . but I said to myself, my daughter would just walk in and everything would turn out to be just a bad dream," Mrs. Hamilton related how she hang on to the hope of seeing her eldest daughter again after she was lost at sea.

Michelle went sailing in a small boat (canoe) Wednesday in Boracay, some 200 miles south of Manila, when strong winds and currents towed her away from the island. She held on to her capsized boat and floated for three days until the fishing boat Alice Star came near her. The fishermen on the boat, who mistook her for a mermaid, picked her.

Mrs. Hamilton said she was with Michelle at the start of the sail "on that beautiful day," but when she got tired she asked to be brought back ashore.

"When Michelle failed t[o] return to the hut that afte[r]noon, I thought she mu[st] have been brought [to] another island by strong currents and r...

Turn to Pa...

Rachelle Hamilton and her daughter Michelle, their faces alight with joy, recount their experience.

STAR Photo by JUN ESTRADA

MARCH

Sunday
12

Monday *My heros! The crew who saved me and the ship F/V Alyss Star.*
13

Tuesday *Having survived the sea with me, my water-stained passport helped the fishermen identify me after I fainted.*
14

Wednesday
15

Thursday
16

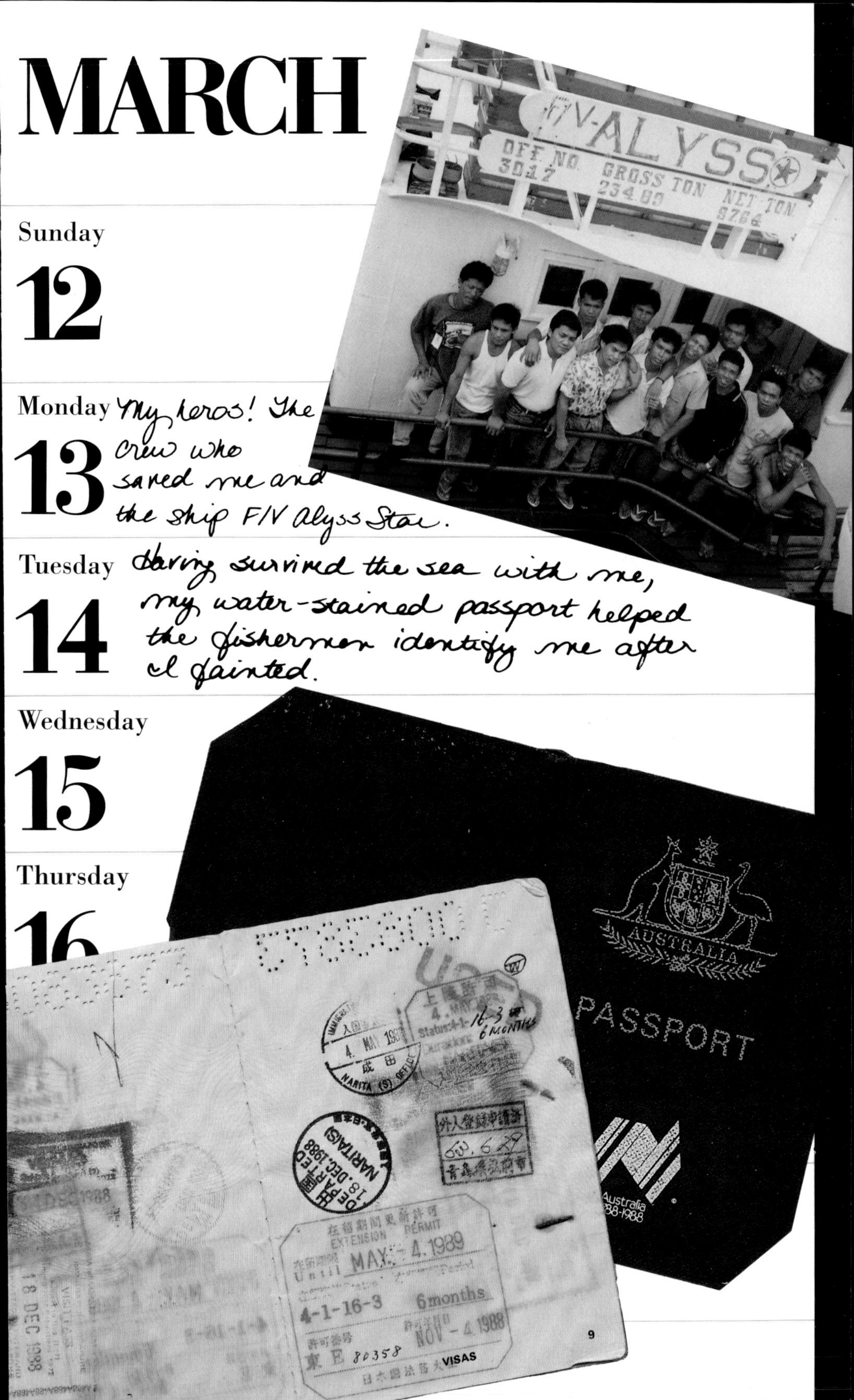

MARCH

Sunday
12

Relating my ordeal to Mum was both thrilling and painful.

Monday
13

Tuesday
14

Wednesday
1

Still in a daze from my ordeal, we drove to Channel 9 TV for the satellite interview.

Thur
16

Friday
17

Saturday
18

MARCH

The Lord shall bless us with prosperity all the days of our lives.

EVENING STAR

Grateful 'mermaid'

By ALEX RAMOS

The Australian tourist community today commended the valiant efforts of the crew of *F/B Alice Star* who also elicited praise for their honesty from Ms. Tarnia Michelle Hamilton whom they rescued Sunday.

"I would like to show our appreciation to the Filipino people by giving them a commendation for bravery and honesty during my rescue Sunday by the crew members of Alice Star," Ms. Hamilton said.

Michelle said all her personal belongings and money remained intact even after she had passed out when rescued.

Michelle who arrived in the country last March 4 for a vacation, Michelle was carried away by the strong currents off Boracay in Aklan, while she was out boating

• Page 2

Grateful...

From Page 1

with a group of friends.

The crew of F/B Alice Star espied her floating beside her capsized banca, Michelle having clung to it for four days.

During her four-day ordeal, Michelle said, she learned how to pray and call for God's help to spare from her from sharks.

She had drifted to the China Sea near Quinoloban Island, some 60 nautical miles from Boracay, when rescued.

Bobby del Rosario (center), representing Irma Shipping and Trading Corp., owner of *F/V Alice Star*, receives a citation from Philippine Coast Guard Commandant Pio Garrido (left) for the rescue by the ship's crew of Australian tourist Tarnia Michelle Hamilton (right) Sunday off the coast of Palawan after a four-day ordeal in the open sea. The crew mistook Tarnia for a mermaid.

STAR photo by ED TAPAN

I was honored to present the commendation for bravery to the crew of the Alyss Star.

Sun

Tue

14

Wednes

15

Thursday

16

Friday

17

Saturday

18

Mum and I just 5 days after I was plucked from the sea.

MARCH

Sunday

12

Captain Pio Garrido, the Coast Guard Commondant was so kind, as were all my rescuers.

Monday

13

Tuesday

14

Woman saved after days in shark seas

MANILA, Mar 13. — A 22-year-old New Zealand-born Australian woman was rescued after drifting more than three days in shark-infested waters in the central Philippines, the Australian Embassy said today.

Australian diplomats said Michelle Tarnia Hamilton of Sydney was picked up yesterday by fishing boat crew off Palawan island. Her rescuers thought she was a mermaid. She was brought to Manila.

Her mother, Rachelle, said she had given up her daughter for dead and had held a memorial service for her on the resort island of Boracay, where they were vacationing.

"I'm not a religious person," Miss Hamilton said. "But someone kept saying to me that my time was not up.

Miss Hamilton, who was born in Wellington and holds dual citizenship, said she went sailing in a small boat on Wednesday at Boracay, about 320km south of Manila.

But strong winds and currents prevented her from getting back to shore.

"The wind took me off really, really fast."

Early on Thursday, the boat capsized off Panay island but she said she was able to hold on to the wreckage.

"The first thing I did was grab my flippers, but everything else, including my Sony Walkman, just floated away.

Miss Hamilton said she kept her wits because she expected search boats and aircraft to come looking for her.

But communications to Boracay are primitive, and the island lacks adequate facilities to report missing boaters or call for help.

She said she saw fins of two sharks about 30 metres from her on two occasions but they never approached.

"I really can't believe I still have two arms and two legs."

"Finally, I saw this island. I was about 5 km from the island, but I thought there were headhunters there and I'd be sacrificed.

Instead, the fishing boat Alice Star appeared.

It passed her but then returned, tossed her a rope and the crew dragged her aboard.

The fishing boat's skipper, Baudelio Pactao, told the Philippine Daily Star newspaper that the crew thought the young woman "was a mermaid."

"They fed me mangoes and gave me water.

The Alice Star brought Miss Hamilton to Manila yesterday, where her mother had flown to seek help from the Australian Embassy in organising a rescue operation.

"I was there only five minutes when someone called to say your daughter is alive," Mrs Hamilton said.

"There are no words to express how I felt." — NZPA-AP

Wednesday

15

Thursday

16

My interview with Shelia Walsh on the 700 Club has been a highlight.

Friday

17

Saturday

18

MARCH

My story made the front cover of Australia's leading Christian magazine.

We

15

Thurs

16

Friday

17

It feels good to hug my warm, soft friend again.

Saturday

18

MARCH

Sunday

13

Th

16

Friday

17

Months later my sisters, Natalie and Angeline, with Mum and myself get a chance to relax and talk together. I hope they don't want to go out in that boat!

Saturday

18

myself to become hopeful, only to be brutally stabbed by the truth of reality yet again. However, emotions are difficult to suppress and even harder to control; without meaning to do so I became excited at the prospect of ending this terrifying ordeal. I had blatantly stoked the forbidden fire. Now I would have to pay the price of bitter disappointment if I were wrong.

I was scarcely able to move my bruised and battered body, though nothing held me down. To move might break the spell and suddenly what I had surely seen would instantly disappear before my eyes, confirming my fear that this was just a figment of my desperate mind. The intense mixture of excitement and fear transformed me onto a level of being I never before experienced. It was as if I had moved into another dimension, my mind and body suspended in limbo, where the seconds ticked by like hours. It was a strange but exquisite sensation, one I wanted to continue, but nature wasn't that kind!

A cold spray of water against my cheek brought me back to reality. This time I was determined to find out whether they were islands or not, no more guesswork. A thought flashed through my mind, *Is this God's promise to me?* Instead of being rescued, would I be saved myself by finding land? I was on the brink of a discovery absolutely vital to my survival, and for once the sea was my ally, not my enemy. A multitude of waves seemed to join in unison to help me. Catching the next large swell, I drove the bunca up onto its peak, riding the wave with the help of my flippers propelling me for a good few seconds. In the space of those five heartbeats, God's promise was revealed to me in a blazing glory of truth that shone upon me like a brilliant star. In a fleeting but unmistakable glimpse, I knew those three formations were islands!

After being surrounded by only water on every horizon for as far as I could see and contemplating death every minute, this was the most beautiful sight I'd ever laid eyes on. I felt as if I'd just woken up on Christmas morning to the best present I could ever hope to receive. I was delirious with relief and happiness, as if a potent drug was intoxicating my body and sending a warm glow through me.

"Oh thank You, thank You, thank You, God!" I called aloud to the heavens. "I knew You would keep Your promise, and my gift back to You is to keep mine."

This flame of hope brought on the most amazing powers of recovery. No longer did I care that my thirst raged like an inferno, that my body felt empty and fragile with only a skeleton structure supporting it.

No longer did the hideous thoughts of death swamp my mind. My fears, self-pity, and despair were all forgotten as my first chance of life and escape appeared. Encompassed in those strips of land was every ounce of hope. I didn't know how I would make it or what awaited me there, but this all seemed irrelevant in the face of hope!

Although the currents were moving toward the islands and would doubtlessly carry me there without any additional effort from me, I wasn't taking any chances! Three days ago when I had presumed the bunca would be caught by the safety net of Panay's Island, I had been proven wrong. I couldn't make the dire mistake of assuming anything again. The stakes were too high! I ascertained that I had about twelve hours to get there before nightfall. Guessing, I imagined it would take me about seven hours. However, a miscalculation on my part could be fatal; if I didn't get to the islands before nightfall, I could easily slip by them in the dark. If I blew this opportunity, I was history. The bitter irony of missing my only chance for survival was unthinkable; I just wouldn't let that happen. I'd come too far and waited too long to be beaten now.

Positioning myself on the remaining outrigger with my legs scissored and the bar in between, I stretched my arms outward, one holding onto the upturned hull and the other on the outrigger, I began paddling furiously. The maximum effectiveness achieved from these flippers was invaluable. When God had instructed me to grab them, I had not fully realized how beneficial they would be. Although they had given me an enormous amount of protection and security, the propulsion they endowed me with would help me more than anything else in getting to the islands.

I propelled my legs similar to riding a bike, which enabled me to move faster by riding the waves effectively. With this physical action totally absorbing me I could feel my fighting spirit return, rising from some reservoir of energy I thought no longer existed. The wild pumping of my adrenal system as the blood throbbed through my veins was a unique feeling. The raw physical exercise of driving myself up onto these swells, then paddling furiously to ride them as long as possible, was a rush.

Strange as it may seem, even considering my daunting predicament, this challenge gave me a curious thrill. I was once again in the driver's seat, in control of my own destiny. With every stroke I came closer to my destination. The taste of achievement and satisfaction was so incredibly sweet. The prize wasn't a monthly bonus check; it was my life and the chance to live it, and that was worth fighting for. A goal couldn't be higher than that, and in my situation it couldn't be more difficult to attain.

Reflections

My entire body felt invigorated from head to toe. I concentrated on each movement, closing my mind to everything except the rhythm of my legs. It felt as if every cell, atom, and muscle were working in conjunction to save my life; every organ moved according to what my brain instructed. Although I had been functioning that way for every second of my twenty-two years, over the past three days I had become acutely more aware of it. The interaction of mind and body was a fantastic spectacle.

I'd never thought of the body as a machine before, but after observing it intimately, I could see that it was exactly that, only infinitely more sophisticated, not to mention clothed in a softer and more beautiful covering. I was absolutely astounded at my body's ability to adapt to its natural environment. It seemed fitter, stronger, and ran on no fuel whatsoever except that which was stored.

Usually after just a few minutes in the ocean my eyes stung for hours, but by now they had completely adapted and I was now able to see underwater for several minutes without their stinging. During my ordeal I'd never once felt seasickness which I occasionally suffered from in rough conditions. From my normal intake of around ten glasses of water a day to not a drop in three days, my body had still managed to function quite normally. From a minimum of eight hours sleep a day to not a wink in three days under extremely exhausting circumstances, my body still coped; my mind operated with all faculties intact. At times of extreme physical exertion, I was often scared my heart would just stop. Even now, though palpitating hard and fast, it just kept going, following the instructions my brain sent it. My skeletal and muscular systems worked together in complete harmony, perfectly integrating with one another to allow me locomotion. I knew, however, that no amount of physical well-being could have sustained me for this ordeal. God was preserving my life as He was my mind.

Moreover, my brain, the most supreme part of human anatomy, never once missed a cue! A masterful system—supervising and instructing every bodily function that took place with 100 percent accuracy, all simultaneously. Incredible! I remember reading somewhere that the brain consists of more than twenty-five billion cells, and the wisdom of just one of these cells is said to exceed all the accumulated knowledge of the human race to date. Inconceivable! All I had to do now was live long enough so I'd be able to use this fantastic body of mine a lot longer and appreciate it more than I ever had before!

Nevertheless, I could endure only so much pain without a resting period, and although I was determined and had every intention of continuing, my body would not obey. I had to rest! Sheer force of will had driven me like a bloodhound in pursuit of its quarry to get to those islands. But after two hours of unrelenting struggle, I was exhausted. Riding up onto the crest of a wave then trying to thrust myself and the bunca out of the way in a split second to avoid a collision, was like moving through a haphazard sort of obstacle course. I was continually brought into brutal contact with the pounding waves and forced against the wooden hull of the bunca. I felt as if I'd been pummelled to the bone with a meat tenderizer; I ached all over with an intense burning. I desperately wanted to continue paddling, but my legs were removed from the control of my brain. I had no choice but to stop and rest for a while.

I lay back against the hull of the bunca, basking in the warm rays of the sun. The heat was thawing and bringing relief to my partially numb body. The physical exertion I'd expended had cooked my internal organs, but the outer layers remained chilled. Opening myself up to the sun like a flower, I absorbed its healing powers. The sensation of rest was so exquisite that it conquered all other considerations for the moment. I started trying to think of what I would do when I got to the islands, but severe exhaustion was clouding my brain. All I could think of was how much pain I was in and how long it would take before it eased off. Swamped with the weight of half-recollected thoughts, I decided to quit thinking and just relax and enjoy the few minutes' rest I had been forced to take.

The brilliant tropical sun had now risen, bathing my surroundings in a haze of gold. The light of the sun had transformed the midnight blue water to a lovely sapphire hue, but its beauty no longer held the same charm for me as it had previously. Before this incident, I loved the sea unconditionally, fearlessly, maybe even recklessly, but now I knew its unpredictable moods and awesome power. I had been humbled by a force to be respected. Once I reached the island and was free from danger, I would be able to gaze out at the ocean once again to appreciate its infinite splendor. For right now I was still its prisoner and it my possible executioner.

The azure sky, now brazen and cloudless, I held in greater esteem. No obstruction would hamper my rescuers searching for me in either a plane or helicopter. However, the prospect of that was at this stage fairly unlikely. If they were going to rescue me I believed it would have been in the first two days, not now. As disconcerting as it was to accept, I knew they had probably resigned themselves to the overwhelming evidence. After the velocity of the storm on the first night, they most probably would have presumed that the boat capsized and I'd drowned. Understandably, they must have all underestimated my resourcefulness and will to hold on to life. Three days without sighting a plane or helicopter—I hadn't even seen a bird—proved to me I had been nowhere near land until now. It was frighteningly obvious that if my rescuers were still searching, they had absolutely no clue as to my location, or more likely they had given up searching all together by now.

Besides, I suddenly realized even if Mum believed I was alive and wanted to search for me, she had absolutely no money. I had everything in my moneybelt! All our cash, travellers' checks, passports, plane tickets, and documents would be ruined after three days in the water. And in the Philippines as in many impoverished countries, no cash meant no help. No exceptions! So how would she have managed to get a plane or the money to hire one? She couldn't even have borrowed the money from someone; everyone we knew was traveling on a shoestring budget. No one just had a spare thousand dollars or however much it would cost to hire a plane.

It really demonstrated to me the truth about money and its absolute worthlessness. It wouldn't have made a difference if I had a platinum American Express card in my moneybelt, or if I was the daughter of a famous celebrity or the heiress to a family fortune, my life was beyond the control of worldly things. In my case it wouldn't be money that saved my life but my own strength and ingenuity, and above all, my faith in God and His grace. No amount of money or power would stop the wheels of destiny from turning. Life and death are predestined by God—of that I was sure. There's no such thing as an accident or being lucky; it was what God decided for us a long time ago.

By not relying on anyone else except my faith in God, I'd learned the limits of my own strength. In these last three days I'd learned more about myself than if I'd spent another sixty years soul searching. My essential self had been opened to me like a book, laying bare all the truths, however painful they may have been for me to face.

I had experienced every emotion known to human beings, and the way I had come to terms with and accepted them filled me with a whole new sense of self-respect. I had precariously hung on to the thread of life for every second during these three days, never knowing when it was going to break. The possibility of existence being snuffed out in a matter of minutes was truly unnerving. It taught me humility. Being face to face with death so intensely for such an enormous length of time, until it becomes a part of you—an added appendage—truly teaches one astounding humility. Having death as my constant companion had magnified a million times the gift of being part of life. In God's wisdom and grace He had seen fit to allow me to enjoy the gift of living a little longer, but I had no illusions that He could have snuffed out my life like extinguishing the flame of a candle if that had been His will.

I had perceived the phrase in its entirety: Every breath you take could be your last. When we're caught up in an everyday existence and not confronting any life-threatening dangers, we just don't think about it; life's taken for granted. When I fully realized the implications of the great gift of life, I honestly felt blessed with every breath that was granted me.

As far as I was concerned, life for me hadn't even started yet. It wasn't that I was so young—I was twenty-two years old and had experienced more than many others of my age I knew. Having traveled extensively throughout Asia for eighteen months, I had learned a lot, grown as a person. But in truth I felt I had far from reached my pinnacle in life. I wanted to achieve so much.

I was positive of one thing: if I survived this ordeal, and I most surely believed I would now that I had seen the island, the simplicity of my carefree youth could never be recaptured. Every detail of these days had been engraved on my soul. I would never be the same again! How could I? Instead of being a victim of circumstance, when I got back to civilization I would use this experience to create something positive, to share my perceptions of what life is really about with others. How I'd do this, I didn't yet know.

I would see the world through different eyes. Things that I had taken for granted before would be viewed with a new perspective. A deeper love and respect for the world and everything it contained had been born within me. It was as if my eyes were really open for the first time, all my senses heightened and fully in tune. I could see what an ungrateful person I'd been before this trial. Now I knew how lucky I was to be alive; I realized I'd really only been existing before. Like a long-dormant volcano, I awoke to the real meaning of life—having a personal relationship with God!

"In these last three days I'd learned more about myself than if I'd spent another sixty years soul searching."

Planning for Landfall

An enormous wave lifted the bunca high onto the peak of a wave, enabling me to see something that caused the adrenalin to rush into my veins. It happened for such an instant in time that afterwards I wondered whether I had really seen it. A brilliant beam of golden light shot out from behind a slither of white cloud, luminating the presence of yet another island about five nautical miles from the cluster of three I had previously spotted. Situated to my right, nevertheless, the island was parallel to the other three.

I was stunned that I hadn't noticed it before. It was quite a large island, at least double the size of the others. The reason I hadn't noticed it before was that I was so overwhelmed at seeing the other three that I didn't think to look any further, feeling so scared that if I took my eyes off them for even a second, they might disappear altogether. They were my sole focus! Now observing the other island, I noticed how mountainous it appeared, not flat like Boracay. It was difficult from such a great distance to gauge how desolate the islands were. I wasn't close enough to see a strip of beach as yet; however, they all appeared to be covered in dense foliage, which reinforced my sneaking suspicion that they were uninhabited.

This was a daunting possibility! How on earth would I survive on a deserted island, alone, isolated from the rest of the world without any resources whatsoever? The islands being uninhabited had occurred to me when I had first seen them this morning, but I hadn't realized that this was something I would have to seriously think about and work out a plan. Being mentally unprepared for disappointments could inflict the greatest harm, I knew, so I must gear myself for the possibility of just such an event. No matter how much I prepared myself, I would probably encounter some cruel surprises. That was inevitable; nevertheless, by bracing myself for these, the devastation would not be so fierce. One thought did however strike me with conviction, eliminating all others: Anything and anywhere was better than being in this ocean!

Now that I had made a definite decision about risking whatever lurking dangers there may be on the island to remove myself from the clutches of the ocean, a strategy for survival on one of these islands had to be formulated. I had to be calculating and rational; it would be stupid to lose my head so close to reaching land. Scrambling through my mind I recalled what I had seen on television and read in books about people who had been shipwrecked on deserted islands. How did they survive? What are the do's and don't's about staying alive?

My mind was racing! I could feel my brain sifting through the stored data, sorting out and processing the relevant information to send me. The movies *Swiss Family Robinson* and *The Blue Lagoon* came to the forefront of my mind. How did those people survive? Snippets of the films floated back to me. In a methodical manner so I wouldn't forget once I arrived on the island, I listed the things to do. My main objective was to get to the islands before nightfall; all other strategies would be useless if I failed to do this. But I wouldn't fail; my determination was too great. Besides what choice was there? If I missed these islands, there would be no second chances, ever! I had no illusions about that. While I paddled furiously towards the islands I made my plans.

Okay, start at the start, Michelle, I said to myself. *What's the second most important thing to do?* I musn't fall asleep on the beach in the hot sun when I arrive on the island, no matter how exhausted I am. I have to find shelter and also remember to pull the bunca high up onto the beach, even tie it to something if necessary. I didn't want to wake up and find that high tide had taken the bunca on a little journey of its own. Actually as soon as I got an opportunity I decided that somehow I'd mend the bunca. If the island was uninhabited, one thing I wouldn't be short of was time.

So many thoughts now crowded my mind, I felt like I was going into overload, ready to blow a fuse at any moment. Breathing deeply for a minute I managed to calm myself and get back to the task at hand. It was wonderful to have something productive to think about. It made me forget about monotonous paddling, the burning feeling in my calves, and the hot sun beating down on my scorched face.

Being a logical person, I was relatively calm considering the circumstances. These facets of my personality had been invaluable in these last three days. If I had been a person who gave up easily or had a weak

---

"My main objective was to get to the islands before nightfall; all other strategies would be useless if I failed to do this."

---

will, I doubt I would have made it past the first day. I realized that the instinct of survival is in all of us, but that alone is not enough to keep us alive. We have to utilize our ingenuity, strength of character, endurance, and above all 100 percent faith. My will to survive had only been part of the reason I had defied death till now; all aspects of my personality, the bedrock of my character, had sustained me so far.

Which is precisely the reason I was being so intent on details. It would be utterly stupid to have struggled so hard to survive, only to reach land, eat some poisonous berries, and die. I knew I must keep my wits about me, not take any chances, especially with food unless I was 100 percent sure. I decided I would rather go hungry. I didn't have a medicine kit with me, so becoming ill could be fatal. But if the primitive people living in the jungle could make medicine and healing potions out of simple herbs and plants, then so could I!

Actually the very thought of eating made me feel ill. If I was completely honest with myself I wasn't even hungry; in fact in the three days I don't remember having a single hunger pang. The imminent danger of dying was constantly on my mind, suppressing my hunger for food. My stomach was such a mass of nerves that I couldn't even contemplate the thought of food.

I did crave a cool drink, preferably a Victorian Bitter Beer. The thought of freezing cold, golden liquid slipping down my throat was pure ecstasy, if only it wasn't just wishful thinking. Although I wasn't hungry, being thirsty was another matter entirely. Water was the elixir my body needed. Every pore craved the pure liquid. My swollen mouth was in dire need of the life-replenishing liquid. But again, when I arrive on the island I must be careful; I musn't let my thirst overshadow logic. The water must be fresh, not from a rancid swamp or anything like that.

Maybe I could catch some mice and test any food substances or water on them. I wasn't in biology class anymore, but the idea did have some merit to it, and it could even save my life. I reasoned I could probably last for another week possibly even longer without food, but I doubted whether I would last another three days without water. It was crucial I scour the island first thing tomorrow morning before dehydration completely took over, debilitating all my senses. So far I had been fortunate that all my faculties were still functioning properly and the lack of water hadn't yet seemed to affect my mind. I intended to keep it that way. I definitely didn't want to end up a raving lunatic running around the island. I imagined dying from dehydration would be a painful way to go, maybe even worse than drowning!

Then a horrible thought struck me: What if there wasn't any water on the island? Oh well, I wouldn't dwell on that right now, best to stay positive. Besides I knew there were other ways to get water other than a running stream. The syrup from sugar cane was liquid; it also contained glucose which would give me energy—that's of course presuming there's some on the island. I wasn't even sure whether it grew in the Philippines. However one food and water source I could practically guarantee being on the island—coconuts! They could sustain me indefinitely. I could drink the delicious coconut milk and eat the flesh, a meal in itself.

A knife would be an invaluable thing too, but as I didn't have one I would devise another implement to do the job. Necessity is the mother of invention so they say, and I fell firmly into the category of needy. I'd watched how the Thai people opened a coconut, and there was nothing to it, or had they just made it look easy? First, I'd have to screw a hole in the top and drink the milk, then split the shell on a sharp pointed rock. I could even use the shells for bowls or to collect rain water in. As yet, I couldn't see myself scouring up a twenty-foot tree to get them, though!

As for food, there were lots of things that were edible, like mangoes, bananas, possibly some wild vegetables. I could eat bird's eggs, small animals like frogs, etc., even rodents if I had to. I wasn't petty when it came to saving my own life. I'd just pop it into my mouth and pretend it was lobster mornay; only my tastebuds would know the difference and what have they got to do with it anyway! I had occasionally eaten Mum's cooking and managed to survive, I laughed, so the risk factor was no longer so enormous. Seafood, if I could catch it, would be my most important and safe source of protein to keep me strong. On an island, being surrounded by water, I presumed there would be no shortage of variety.

How fortunate I was to find not just one island but four. If one was lacking in something, I could take a trip over to the other one. Peculiar as it was, I was almost looking forward to this challenge. Pitting myself against the elements gave me a thrilling sensation. Hadn't I learned anything from my ordeal yet? I guessed not. That was a part of me—the desire for challenge—mentally and physically. It was what made me who I was, I supposed. But to be looking forward to conquering such difficult obstacles does seem a little bizarre. Anyway, who wanted to be normal? I'd always strived to rise above the level of mediocrity.

If I really wanted to catch seafood, I would have to make a spear. Using bamboo or some other sort of wood for the shaft, I could file down a very sharp stone into a point and then tie the two together with rattan or some other strong fiber. It would be a tiring, maybe even an unsuccessful process, but I would give it a try anyway. In the meantime I could make a net out of flax and catch all sorts of shellfish, crabs, and mussels. How weird to imagine myself spear fishing. It was an art form passed down from the generations, and I didn't have a clue, except you had to keep very still, have excellent timing, and good coordination. All things can be learned with patience and perseverance, and those two qualities I had, especially time; it certainly seemed I would have a lot of time once I reached the islands.

The other essential element was fire. I needed a fire to keep warm, although I was in the tropics and the temperatures were warm all year round and that would be a strong factor in my survival. Also fire would be an excellent S.O.S. for passing ships. I would organize that later.

There was one major disadvantage about the warm climate: Heat usually meant mosquitos, and mosquitos meant malaria. I hoped the malaria tablets that I'd been taking for several months now would remain in my system and continue protecting me at least until I could find another solution. Oh God, there was so much to do!

I felt sure there still could be some of my belongings in the bunca, the ones I had stuffed into the far end of the hull before it capsized, and which I may be able to retrieve later. One item I was positive was in there was my pair of Nike track shoes which I had pushed into the compact corner of the bunca when I'd put my flippers on. It was almost too much to hope for! Shoes would be an invaluable asset, one I didn't know quite how I would do without. My snorkeling gear was also a bonus that I hoped had escaped the clutches of the sea. I consoled myself that I at least had my flippers.

It was a weird feeling but again in spite of myself I had to admit I was looking forward to this venture with unexplainable enthusiasm. I didn't even know if I wanted to be rescued anymore; to do so would thwart all my creative ideas for my life on a deserted island. My only regret would be that Mum would worry. I wondered whether the message in the bottle trick had ever really worked. I imagined the press finding me a couple of years from now, with long, blonde, matted hair, darkly-tanned skin, the sinewy body of an athlete and the predator instincts of a mountain lion, running around in a loincloth. What a scoop of a story that would be!

Robinson Crusoe

I guessed now it was around 11 A.M. The burnished sun was pouring its blistering rays on me unheeded. I longed to stop paddling, just to rest my aching bones, but I couldn't afford to. Instead of allowing the pain to encumber me, it was the force that drove me on. The accelerated thudding of my heart echoed in my body. Looking down at my chest, then stomach and legs, I noticed every inch of me was pulsating. I felt like one giant heartbeat! The raw vitality and boundless energy I had possessed this morning had long since departed, but I was under a spell, hypnotized by the monotonous movement of my legs powering through the water.

Every stroke was now accompanied by an unbearable stab of pain that went shooting up my thighs. There was not a part of my body that escaped the torturous agony; every square inch was afflicted with a burning intensity which had lodged itself deep within my muscles. My head throbbed mercilessly with the worst headache imaginable, as if I'd been struck by a baseball bat while recovering from a severe hangover. My head was a heavy-leaden weight that my neck could barely support. My mouth was as parched and dry as the Sahara Desert, my thirst raging with the intensity of a inferno. Barely encased in my mouth was my tongue which was so swollen and dehydrated it lolled out of my bleeding lips like that of a dog's on a hot day.

The tropical sun had beaten down on my unprotected skin for three days burning it severely, to what degree, I wasn't sure. My face had taken the most punishment, the layers of skin feeling as if they had been scalded with acid. It was possible I would have permanent scarring, but right now I would have to save my life before I worried about literally saving my skin.

"There was not a part of my body that escaped the torturous agony; every square inch was afflicted with a burning intensity which had lodged itself deep within my muscles."

Frighteningly, for the two days I had already been exposed and sizzled so ferociously, the sky had been relatively overcast. In that respect I had been fortunate. Today, however, was a scorcher! The cloudless sky and searing heat were sucking the very juices out of me, evaporating what little strength I still possessed. This acknowledgment confirmed for me even more the absolute necessity of getting to the islands as quickly as possible, before I contracted a severe dose of sunstroke and fell unconscious. There was no time now to nurse my aching body; there would be plenty of that when I reached the island. There was fortunately one thing in my favor: at least my body temperature was being kept down by the continual drenching of waves breaking over my head.

Miraculously, even with all these daunting problems hanging over me, I still felt within me an indestructible strength, a sheer defiance against being defeated, which over the course of the day would stir me to feats of incredible courage and endurance I never believed possible. Being exhausted, thirsty, and in pain were not considerations: the facts were simple, straightforward. I couldn't stop paddling until I reached my destination. I would only cease my struggle when I had two feet planted steadfastly on dry ground. I made a promise to myself: I would not give up, nor surrender to exhaustion. However, throughout the day I found myself literally dying to renege on the deal and the agonizing goal I'd set. My need was too great and I wasn't superwoman, although at times I liked to think I was. As a mere mortal, my body could only take so much punishment before collapsing from exhaustion, exposure, and dehydration. With this horrible realization in mind, I decided to grant myself ten minutes rest every hour. Even without my watch, by now I knew how to gauge time quite well!

Maybe it seems rather trivial, but my instincts kept whispering to me that making the right choice of islands was of paramount importance. I felt my whole life was literally geared to making the right decision. But why? Land was land—what did it matter which island I went to? I didn't understand the urgency. My choices were either the cluster of three islands directly in front of me, which the current was naturally taking me to, or the larger island that was approximately two miles parallel to the others.

Going to one of the three islands situated together would be infinitely easier because the currents were moving in that direction. I would make my decision on exactly which one was the best when I got nearer and could observe the islands closely. If they all looked relatively the same, I would choose the one in the middle so that if I had to change to one of the others it would be easier and more accessible. On the other hand, if I decided to go to the large island, it would mean traveling not directly against the currents but moving along sideways. I would have to travel in an arc about 180 degrees to get to the point where the currents would carry me in naturally. If I went in too soon, I might miss the island altogether.

My main problem was time. I had only a small allocation of this before nightfall. Traveling at the rate I was going, I ascertained I would arrive at one of the three islands in approximately three hours. If I tried to get to the larger island I guessed it would take me approximately five hours. That would mean if I guessed the time to be 11:30 A.M. that I wouldn't arrive until 4:30 P.M. No, I couldn't risk it, that was cutting it too close. As the larger island was significantly farther away, my prediction of how long it would take to get there might be inaccurate. Trying to evaluate nautical miles within a time allocation could be very deceptive, and I knew it would be foolhardy of me to take even the slightest element of risk.

One thing, however, was in the favor of the large island: because it was so much bigger, there was a good chance it was inhabited. But inhabited by whom? Cannibals? Headhunters? The truth suddenly dawned on me. I was willing to take my chances with even that possibility. I would more than likely live longer on an island, no matter what the obstacles, than survive another day in the ocean. Instinct told me to go to the big island, but logic prevented me.

Instead I made the safest decision to go to the three islands. I had the gut feeling I'd made the wrong choice, but I wasn't going to risk my life on an instinct. My so-called instincts had gotten me into enough trouble already without adding fuel to the fire. However, it was a poignant warning, one I disregarded. In my mind I had made the most sensible decision; anything else was sheer stupidity.

"My choices were either the cluster of three islands directly in front of me, which the current was naturally taking me to, or the larger island that was approximately two miles parallel to the others."

Although getting out of the water was the thing that mattered most, now that there was the very real possibility of cannibals, I shuddered with fear. Do they still have cannibals in the world practicing their ancient rituals, I wondered? This was conceivable, especially in the Philippines, where there were still pirates. And I was not exactly in the middle of a metropolis. I was way off the beaten track in the middle of nowhere. Of course I was presuming I was still in the Philippines. I imagined those islands to be my shelter, but in retrospect they could be something entirely different. Perhaps even the death of me.

I felt a heavy cloak of fear descend on me, so oppressive I could not escape. I was held transfixed, forced to acknowledge all these hideous possibilities. The morbid thoughts of "what if" consumed my thoughts until they felt suffused into my brain. The most terrifying thing was that they were not exaggerations of a paranoid mind but indeed a very feasible prospect. My eyes sought the islands as I tried desperately to fathom what destiny awaited me there.

In my mind's eye I could see it all. After the most grueling and torturous experience of my life, miraculously I arrive at the shores of the central island in the cluster of the three. Dragging the bunca up the beach, I finally collapse near it. Sometime later when it's still light, my raging thirst wakes me up. I have to find water. My urgent need to find it is more intense than my desire to sleep. Wandering through the dense jungle foliage I search for any signs of life. There appear to be none!

The crunch of a dry twig under my foot captures my attention. I quickly turn around. I can't see anything, but I suddenly have the eerie feeling of being followed. *I'm just paranoid,* I reassure myself, although I'm not convinced. Are my real fears about the islands becoming facts? It's a beautiful island and much larger than I had expected. Already I notice a myriad of bird and plant life; I won't go hungry here.

Without warning I come into a clearing where many primitive huts stand. An enormous structure squats in the middle of the clearing that I imagine is used as a meetinghouse, a type of communal area. *Oh no,* I gasp, *I've stumbled on a village.* My trembling knees buckle under me as I stagger forward. Leaning against a tree trunk, I steady myself. But where are the tribespeople? Maybe they have gone to stay on one of the other islands. I wonder when they will be back. Maybe I can make friends with them. In the meantime, what an extraordinary piece of luck to stumble upon them! My problem of shelter and protection is already solved; I can use theirs.

I begin to feel giddy with relief and happiness. How lucky I am! However, in my exuberance, I forget to be wary. Excited at the prospect of discovery, I quickly stride toward the huts to see what else I can find of use. Upon entering the hut an instinctual chill shudders up my spine, lodging itself between my shoulder blades. These huts haven't been deserted, but recently used. Somebody lives here! Where are they? Hiding?

Turning around, I bolt out of the hut, but stop, dead in my tracks! A score of men greet me dressed in tribal warfare with heavily painted faces, grass skirts, razor sharp spears, and in a fighting stance, ready to do battle. They are not smiling! The sheer terror of them takes my breath away. I am completely spellbound! A multitude of petrifying thoughts flood my mind. Shall I make a run for it? No, then I won't look friendly. I'll prove I am just an intruder. Shall I try to speak to them or use body language to prove to them that I'm a friend and mean no harm, or shall I just stay silent?

I decide my best option is to look vulnerable, harmless. I begin shrinking to look like a defenseless creature in their presence by sliding to the ground and huddling myself into a ball. Abruptly, they start talking to one another in some primeval language that I've never heard before. From the way they are pointing at me I can only guess what they have in store for me. The thought of it chills me to the very marrow of my bones.

There are only three possibilities. They are going to invite me to dinner, have me as dinner, or worse still, push me back out to sea. A thought strikes me with clarity! They have followed me from the beach so they know that I am alone and have been lost at sea. I assume that they will then deduce that I am not here to harm them.

The chorus of voices grows louder, and they seem to be disagreeing about something. My eyes ablaze, I peek at them. Oh, they are a fearsome bunch! I don't like my chances. No matter how defenseless I appear to them, I am still a threat and I know that by the tone of their voices. If only I had a gift to give them, a sort of peace offering. My shorts maybe? No, that won't suffice. My Nike shoes in the bunca might please them. By the looks of their feet they really don't need shoes, but it may prove a novelty.

If only I'd made an effort to retrieve my walkman, it might have saved my life. They would be totally intrigued. *Oh,* I thought, remembering something quite tragic. When I saw the walkman floating along in the water, the earphones were no longer attached. If I gave the chief the walkman without the earphones it may have made him ten times more angry because he can't understand the use of the machine.

Now I am doomed, they will surely kill me! The beating of a tribal drum unexpectedly fills the air, capturing my attention. Simultaneous chanting from the warriors begin. With my eyes glued to the scene, my heart in my mouth, I watch them form a circle and begin performing what is obviously their tribal dance. Although the sound is terribly frightening and makes my blood curdle, I feel myself becoming caught up in the beat of the drum and the chanting, until I can't tear my eyes away. I sit there totally mesmerized, the atmosphere intoxicating me until I feel giddy.

I can't believe this is happening. It is like something I'd seen on television on ancient tribes and their beliefs and rituals. Are they doing this dance as part of a welcome celebration for me, or are these barbarians preparing to celebrate a feast—me? Through the dancing legs that stamp around me, I can see a fire at the other end of the clearing, being prepared by women and children.

Oh no, they are really going to go through with it; they are going to sacrifice me! A serpent of fear slithers over me, seeping into the core of my being. The fear will consume me if I succumb to it. I have to make a run for it, get to the bunca, and push myself back out to sea. At least there is a chance of rescue in the ocean. If I stay on this island I won't live to see midnight, of that there is no doubt.

My heart pounds with a wild ferocity as loud as the beating drum. I slowly stand up. Turning around, I begin running toward the beach as fast as my legs can carry me. I only go a matter of yards when something incredibly hard and sharp pierces the skin of my back, the force pushing itself through my back, lodging between my shoulder blades. In unbearable agony, I collapse to the ground. The rough hands of a tribesman bind my legs with rope and then my arms. Then I am being lifted off the ground, carried by many people far above their heads, toward the fire. . . . I am going to be cooked, roasted like a pig on a spit. *No, no,* I scream. *Stop . . . !*

TWELVE

APPOINTED TIME

RACHELLE . . . 6:00 A.M., SATURDAY, MARCH 11, BORACAY ISLAND AND CATICLAN. I felt myself stirring to consciousness from the depths of sleep. As soon as I'd opened my eyes, I instantly plugged into what this day held for me—foreboding yet fused with a flicker of hope and promise. Morning had finally arrived, the hour I had waited for. At last the aerial search for Michelle could begin; I was desperate to get it underway as soon as possible. Hurriedly, I washed and dressed, preparing in David's spare room for what would undoubtedly be one of the most emotionally charged days of my life. Rafel had arranged a boat to take me to Caticlan at 7:30 A.M.

The scenery outside our bungalow looked as crisp and defined as if a master's brushstroke had painted it to perfection. I was instantly stung by the feelings of desolation, of how very far from home I was. Keeping a tight reign on my emotions, I tried to avoid certain channels of thought: happy times spent with Michelle, thoughts of the unknown future, agonizing over the what if's, how different choices on that ill-fated day might have avoided this disastrous situation.

I relived the scene when we were together in the bunca. If only I had managed to convince her to call it a day and come in when I had, this would never have happened. But this had not been the case and dwelling on the what if's would only crush me further. Thoughts of my two daughters in Sydney and how we would go on with our lives if Michelle were never found were too dangerous to pursue if I was to hold myself together through this living nightmare.

So where did that leave me? I couldn't bear to think about the past; I didn't dare dwell on the future; I couldn't think of Michelle clinging to the bunca, gasping for air, struggling to stay alive while the ocean tried to claim her forever. And what about the possibility of never finding her and wondering in what horrific circumstances she spent her last moments? My mind had been reduced to a very narrow corridor of thought, where the task at hand was all I could contend with. I had to cautiously walk myself through this harrowing ordeal minute by minute.

I noted the sky above me was clear! Good conditions for the search, although I detected quite a strong breeze blowing. I had become delicately attuned to waiting, having woken long before anyone else. I sat down in a bamboo chair on the balcony, tentatively waiting until a respectable hour when I could meet David. My mind turned to the search, although not to the result. There was no way I could foresee what the outcome of today would be. If we found Michelle or if we didn't seemed to be veiled behind a distant horizon, where the truth was hidden from me. My only task was to carry out the plane search; I could not think beyond that.

In this tranquil moment at daybreak, as the sun rose over this exotic island paradise, I was overwhelmed by the glorious natural beauty that surrounded me. I was suddenly awash with unsolicited contradictions. How could I justify the splendid, seemingly unaltered world outside myself and relate it to the chaos within me?

Don't Think About the Future

I realized that up until now I hadn't been able to pray except out of desperation. The serenity of nature this morning captured my spirit and instilled me with a calm conducive to rational thought. Up until this moment I hadn't been in a state of mind to formulate structured, heartfelt prayers, but had only garbled words of pleading more likened to wild ramblings uttered in despair. As yet, I hadn't been stripped down to the bare bone, revealing my own futility. I still had the measure of confidence in my ability to save Michelle by human means. I wasn't ready to relinquish control, abandon my own strength, and throw myself on God's mercy—to beg, plead, and cry out for Him to supernaturally reach down and rescue my child. To me this act of submission, in some profound way, would symbolize defeat.

Although I wasn't aware of it at the time, I was subconsciously saving God as my final trump card if all else failed. I was scared to waste this option prematurely and squander the only powerful asset I felt I had left. I was still unwilling to submit myself to God's compassion and judgment, because His verdict may be a death sentence, and I wasn't willing to accept this yet. I focused all hope on the aerial search being successful. The next few hours would unearth either intense joy or utter despair.

By 7 A.M. my patience was exhausted. I could not wait any longer and made my way to David's bungalow. As I approached his bungalow, I saw David emerge from his room, rubbing his eyes as he encountered the brilliant light of day.

"My mind had been reduced to a very narrow corridor of thought, where the task at hand was all I could contend with."

"Good morning. Have you been up long?" David asked, squinting his eyes from the brightness.

"For about an hour. I've been sitting alone on my balcony trying to make sense of this. I was questioning whether disasters befall people at random or is there a logical reason that we just don't yet understand? Needless to say, my questions are still unanswered. I think there are some things we are just not meant to know," I admitted. "For the moment all I want is the courage to get me through the hours ahead. By the way, David, thanks for being there for me last night. It really helped me to talk to you about Michelle. It was a way of making her feel close to me."

"I'm pleased I was able to be of help in some way. I feel very frustrated at not being able to do more. Anyway, it was great talking to you. I know Michelle a lot better now, and I feel closer to both of you. One day maybe I'll visit Australia and meet your other daughters, Angeline and Natalie. Who knows what the future holds?" he said with a grin. Then changing the subject, he asked, "What time will we have to leave here to reach the airstrip in Caticlan?"

"Rafel has arranged for the boat at 7:30 A.M. It will take about half an hour to get to the island, then ten minutes by jeep to the airport.

"David, I'm so nervous!" I continued. "My stomach's squirmish as if there's a million worms inside me. I have a sense that time is propelling me towards the moment when I'll know the truth about what happened to Michelle, and I'm powerless to stop the process. A part of me can't wait to get up in that plane and begin searching, yet at the same time I'm dreading it. You can't imagine how terrified I feel."

"I understand what you are saying, Rachelle, but I couldn't begin to imagine what it would be like to lose a child, especially one you have such a strong bond with. You know I was astounded when I first found out you were mother and daughter. You behaved more like best friends. The closeness of your relationship struck me as being special even before I knew you."

"That's what makes it all the more tragic, because I wouldn't only be losing a daughter, but also my best friend," I whispered.

"You're being very brave, Rachelle. Just keep on top of it. Let's hope today will put an end to the uncertainty, and you will find Michelle," David responded.

"I'm almost too frightened to think about it. All I can do is point myself in the right direction, place one foot in front of the other, and hope my prayers for Michelle will be answered."

"I hope so too. I'll make us a cup of coffee and then we had better get going," David suggested.

"Thanks. But first I have to go back to my bungalow to get a few things I'll need for the day. Would you mind coming with me?" I asked. "I can't stand being there by myself."

"Of course not. While you're drinking your coffee I'll take a shower and we can go together."

David made coffee, then disappeared for about ten minutes while he got ready. I sat on the balcony once again, alone with my thoughts. Complex, diverse emotions charged through me, as foreboding impressions kept resurfacing. Was this search all in vain? Was Michelle already dead? It seemed almost impossible to believe she wasn't. But still I couldn't allow myself to believe she was dead until I had proof, or until all viable avenues for her survival had been exhausted, and the sheer passage of time proved her existence improbable.

Suddenly I wanted to cry, but I stoically gritted my teeth and held back the tears. I couldn't allow these morbid thoughts to take root in me and shatter my fragile defense. Although I emphatically tried to deny the damning evidence, it kept returning to my mind, disarming me of any remaining faith I had in her survival. What the search would uncover I could only guess; each outcome I envisioned seemed even more hideous than the last. We could find her upturned canoe floating in the ocean with no sign of life on it, or we could sight planks of loose wreckage from the bunca floating in the ocean, or worse still we find the bunca with Michelle's lifeless body in it.

Is there any real chance that we will find Michelle alive, still clinging to the boat? I asked myself with brutal honesty. The odds were so minute, but I had to continue harboring that secret hope in my heart. My other alternative was too grim a reality!

David reappeared some ten minutes later, and we made our way back to my bungalow. With each step I fortified myself with determination. I was going to walk inside the bungalow, do what I had to do, and not give way to emotionalism. My defense was like granite!

By the time we had reached my bungalow, I unlocked the door and entered without hesitation. Despite my resolve, I was instantly confronted with the essence of Michelle. Her very presence seemed to permeate the air, filling the room. *Michelle . . . Michelle, where are you?* my aching heart cried. *Don't you dare crumble now,* the warrior within me shouted back. I obeyed! The entire procedure took less than three minutes. With lightning speed I bolted out of there.

All of a sudden I realized what the search would entail: Frantic eyes intensely scrutinizing the surface of the ocean for any sign of Michelle or the bunca. What if the search all came to nothing and I had to come back to Boracay never knowing what happened to my daughter? Would I ever have any peace of mind again if this tragedy went unresolved? *No, don't think about the outcome or anything in the future. Just put one foot in front of the other and don't think,* I told myself.

Journey to Panay

We reached the beach. The bone-white sand glittered in the morning sunlight. The fine grains of sand squeaked underfoot as we walked. At any other time I would have relished a breathtaking morning such as this. This enchanting island was unparalleled by any place on earth I'd ever seen before. The intoxicating charm of this island had captivated my soul! A part of me would always remain here on Boracay Island.

David and I sat down on the beach, while a hugging swell of emotion wrapped itself around us. As we sat in silence, each absorbed in our own thoughts, the only sound was the sea lapping gently at the shore. A small crowd of people had followed us to the beachfront, but they stood a respectable distance away, awaiting the drama to commence. Eventually the boat was fueled and ready to leave.

Rafel appeared with several young men who would accompany me on the flight and assist in the search. Shakily standing to my feet, I was amazed my legs could support me; they felt like spaghetti! At the water's edge I prepared to roll up the bottoms of my jeans when a willing young man stepped forward offering to lift me out to the boat. I momentarily hesitated, then yielded to his offer, not having the energy to disagree.

David gave me a brief hug, his eyes expressing everything that words could never say. Calls of "good luck" and "God be with you" filled my ears.

On the boat I averted my attention from the sense of panic rising in me and concentrated on watching some boys pull up the anchor and others push the boat out into deeper water. I heard the motor leap into life as it slowly moved away from the shore. I watched the assembly of people on the shoreline becoming smaller and smaller. Soon their warm words and well wishes were drowned out by the noise of the outboard motor.

My existence had been reduced to the whirring machinery around me and the heavy ache inside my heart. David's plan was to stay on Boracay and organize several more fishing boats to join the search. I felt lost and abandoned without his presence, which I had relied on the past days. Of course, it was now only an hour before we could begin effectively searching for Michelle, but my optimism had been eroded by the continual delays. Yesterday the hope of finding her alive had been a valid possibility; . . . today I wasn't sure of anything. When I examined my feelings regarding the search they fluctuated between breathless expectation and heart-stopping dread.

Boracay Island looked magnificent from the vantage point of the sea; I wondered how it had looked to Michelle.

The journey passed quickly! One minute we were leaving Boracay, then it seemed in no time we were arriving at Caticlan, a small portside village on the island of Panay. The wheels of destiny were propelling me forward to the appointed hour when I'd learn the truth. A part of me desired to remain on the boat and float away, avoiding taking action or having to follow this path. However, circumstances had set me on a course which I had no alternative but to see through.

Reaching the jeep, I sat up in the front seat, relieved to be doing something. The jeep was an ancient relic from a bygone age, and I was amazed it was still operational. When I heard the throbbing sound of the motor, however, I was sure that the vehicle still ran on all cylinders. Several Filipinos suddenly materialized and clambered onto the moving vehicle, aptly named in Tagalog a *jeepney*. People hazardously grabbed onto every available handhold; people were even perched on the roof. As we moved along the dusty pot-holed road, animated conversations in Tagalog traveled to and fro like current of electricity. I was doubtful the driver could see anything through the dust-caked windshield.

"Boracay Island looked magnificent from the vantage point of the sea; I wondered how it had looked to Michelle."

At one time I fully braced myself, being convinced he was going to hit a suckling pig scurrying across the center of the road, carelessly daring to cross the narrow track. Obviously this Filipino-bred pig understood that the onus was for it to get out of the way fast, and it did, especially considering that the driver's hand was on the horn at least a good ten seconds longer than necessary.

The momentum of the jeepney seemed to alleviate some of the tension and anxiety that had built up in me over the past days. We trundled past a tiny village where natives sat outside chatting idly. Naked toddlers sat on the dusty ground, giggling at play, unperturbed by our presence. Even at this early hour, women sat pounding their washing, achieving a cleanliness that was their pride to display. Yoked bullocks were at work in the field, laboriously trudging back and forth, tilling the soil. For a brief respite my thoughts were free to take pleasure in the marvels of this peaceful native environment. For a time I was captivated by the harmonious interaction of these people.

Sadly, the airfield came into sight, and I was reminded of the real purpose for my being here. The pleasure I had experienced so briefly was swept away and replaced with a sense of impending doom. The jeepney ground to a halt in a cloud of dust. Filipinos jumped from the roof of the vehicle and poured out from every possible exit. I was flabbergasted! There must have been fifteen people clinging precariously to the outside of the jeepney. Under such a burden, no wonder the motor had groaned!

Fredrico, my escort and driver, took charge. He escorted me to a modest wooden building where the airport office was housed. The makeshift terminal was fairly basic, but adequate. The airfield was little more than a cleared strip of land among the lush vegetation.

An airport official greeted me. "Ms. Hamilton, I would like to express to you how distressed we are to hear about your situation. I assure you we will do everything possible to locate your daughter. Unfortunately, however, there is a slight delay. We expect the flight will probably be detained for half an hour."

A groan escaped my lips, but I said nothing. I resigned myself to the fact that they were doing the best they could with the limited resources available to them. I had to remind myself that this was not Australia and they didn't have search-and-rescue teams at their immediate disposal. I was powerless to fight against the circumstances, so I listened numbly without reacting. I had to conceal my agitation and remember that this wasn't his fault. I handed him the money which David had given me. Sitting idly with nothing to occupy myself, my mind flung open the doors to a ravaging fear that I had managed to keep in abeyance—until now.

I told them I wanted to be alone for a while and was going for a short walk. I explained to my willing helpers not to worry, that I would be back as soon as I heard the plane coming. Feeling very much as if I'd slipped into a hypnotic state, I ambled along the dirt track that ran parallel to the runway. I retreated to the sanctuary of my inner fortress, protecting myself from the destructive emotions which were always waiting, like predators, to devour me the moment I allowed a crack to appear in my armor.

THIRTEEN

DESTINATION OF TERROR

MICHELLE . . . 11:30 A.M., SATURDAY, MARCH 11, CUYO ISLANDS. "No!" I heard myself screaming aloud, seconds before a massive curtain of water hit me like a solid wall, taking my breath away. I felt myself being wrenched from the grip my legs had around the outrigger. Suddenly I was hurtled through the air like a rag doll, then flung into the ocean depths. Clambering upward, my head broke the surface, only to receive the full brunt of a descending torrent. Frantically I dogpaddled to keep my head above water as armies of waves attacked me. From my perspective the waves looked gigantic, how would I ever be able to see over them to find my bunca?

The living nightmare of being sacrificed by the cannibals was momentarily eradicated from my mind as the very real threat that I could drown if I didn't find my bunca was thrust upon me. For a faltering second I had to remind myself I was out of the jungle and away from the fearsome natives of my vivid imagination; however, I'd been transported to a more imminent danger: Not the illusionary clutches of the tribesman but the very real deathtrap of the ocean. My legs felt like leaden weights as I had the sensation of being dragged down. I knew if I didn't find the bunca in the next few minutes I would sink to my death; I was just too exhausted.

I positioned myself to take advantage of the next large wave. Picked up by the motion of the wave, I rode along on its crest scanning the ocean. With indescribable relief I sighted the bunca not five yards away in the next trough. It looked so feeble in the vastness of the ocean; nevertheless this chunk of wood was the mediator between me and death, my island in the stormy sea that raged around me. I frantically battled against the waves to swim to it. Lurching forward, I grasped hold of the arm of the outrigger.

The touch of something solid in this liquid hell filled me with a sensation of utter relief. Hauling myself up onto the arms of the outrigger, I leaned back against the hull of the bunca resting my brutally weary body. Its solid structure upholding and supporting me was immensely reassuring. After taking a brief rest to recover from my ordeal, I resumed paddling, knowing I had no other choice if I wanted to get to the island before nightfall. Paddling toward the islands that soon would become my home, as much as I tried not to, I couldn't help reliving the scene of the gruesome cannibals carrying me towards the sacrificial fire, bound and tied with no means of escape. *Thank God, it is only a dream,* I assured myself.

I wondered if these thoughts were just triggered by fear and anxiety, or were they in fact very real possibilities, something I should worry about? I didn't have an answer. I was unsure if primitive tribes of the world still practiced cannibalism. Nevertheless, if the island I arrived on was inhabited by a tribe of people who weren't savages, I still worried about how I would be received by them. Would I be a threat to them, an unwanted visitor? Or would I be welcomed with open arms, an object of enormous fascination and a source of entertainment? *Oh, what choice do I have,* I realized. *I can't stay here in the water, so I'll have to take my chances, whatever the consequences may be, and paddle toward one of those islands.*

The very notion of my welcoming party on the island turning out to be a bunch of very unfriendly headhunters filled me with dread. I could feel the hysteria rising in my throat, the panic surging through me. I had to slam the door shut on these thoughts before they destroyed my grip on reality. The urgency to escape my hideous visions compelled me to paddle even harder, to push myself to the brink, until the only thing that filled my mind was the agonizing pain shooting up my legs as I drove myself tirelessly almost beyond endurance under the torrid midday sun.

Where He Directs

A deeply-rooted weariness had lodged itself into every crevice, tissue and muscle of my body, sucking the very life force out of me. The only thing that kept me battling on was the sight of the island looming up ahead, bringing me that much nearer with every thrust of my aching legs. I was now only two or three miles from my destination, only hours away from being relieved of my exhausting struggle.

What a relief it would be to stand with solid ground beneath my feet! To close my eyes and sleep safely—knowing I wouldn't be wakened by cascades of water thundering over me or the possibility of hitting my head on the bunca, falling unconscious and drowning—

"My freedom, that's what I wanted back. To be able to stand on dry ground and call a truce, ending my one-to-one combat with the sea."

seemed a marvel almost beyond my comprehension. The first smile in what seemed liked years curved the corners of my mouth at the delightful thought of reaching land. My freedom, that's what I wanted back. To be able to stand on dry ground and call a truce, ending my one-to-one combat with the sea.

I had to remind myself God was with me, protecting and leading me to safety. I again had to reprimand myself for forgetting God's promise of life to me. He would have hardly allowed me to exist this long and reach the shores of safety only to be killed by savages; I couldn't imagine God would be that cruel. I salved my conscience by remembering His words and believing in Him. God's words and His promise were the only thing I had left, the only remnant of hope I could cling to. I had been forced to realize how truly powerless I was to save myself and how futile my battle would have been without His grace.

In the eleventh hour when all else had failed, I admitted to Him how helpless I was to save my life. I submitted my will to Him and became as a trusting child, begging His forgiveness and entrusting my life into His hands. Most of all I knew that He had the power to grant me my life, because I had come to realize that without 100 percent faith in Him and willingness to submit to His will, the prayers uttered were just words! It now made sense to me why the many other times when I was in need and called out to God to help me, He hadn't answered—my words were without real faith, just empty and meaningless. I realized now that it was with this essential ingredient that prayers were answered.

All of a sudden I heard in my ear the clearly defined words, "Turn the boat around and head toward the largest island."

Why would He want me to go to the farthest island which I doubted I would reach before nightfall? I didn't want to argue with the conviction of this voice, the one I'd heard on other occasions throughout this ordeal. The instructions whispered in my ear were not loud but very definite. Telling me paths I should take and vital decisions I should make, actions I should or shouldn't do—the voice was also the voice of reassurance.

This voice was distinctly different from the commanding audible voice that boomed down from the sky, the one that I instinctively knew to be God's. God's voice, the sound of which I would never forget, was impossible to accurately describe but it was etched into my memory. It was like loud thunder when He spoke. So, if this being true, then whose voice was it that was now telling me to turn the boat around and head to the farthest island?

I searched my mind for the embarrassingly limited amount of religious knowledge I remembered from the few scriptures I'd heard. Could this other voice belong to Jesus? Was it He that was talking to me? It seemed a feasible possibility. Although I was raised Jewish, my Dad had grown up a Catholic and on the occasional times I had as a child attended Sunday school, I'd heard the story of Jesus' life. I didn't find this inconceivable to believe because Jesus was Jewish and born into the same faith as I. He was the Son of God, sent down from heaven as a man on earth to be crucified for the atonement of man's sins. He was given dominion over the earth, to be a mediator between man and God, or so in my minimal knowledge I understood His purpose on earth to be.

Or could it be one of God's angels that was instructing me? One thing I knew beyond a shadow of a doubt: I was being instructed and aided by the supernatural force of spiritual beings that were ordained by God. The instruction to turn the boat around and head towards the farthermost island went completely against all logic and the limits of what I thought I could endure. I didn't have the strength to make it that far, especially considering that the cluster of three islands in front of me was a matter of only two hours away. The risk I would be exposing myself to, by attempting to get to the other island by nightfall, and the likelihood of not making it, were horrendous.

Looking into the sun directly overhead I estimated the time to be shortly after noon. Even if I paddled nonstop, I guessed it would take me a minimum of four hours to get there. So, if everything went according to plan, I would arrive around five o'clock. During that time a multitude of things could go wrong. I could collapse from heat stroke, my legs could seize up with cramps, or I could be overcome with extreme exhaustion. Taking into account the odds against me, to enter into this course of action would in my mind be absolute foolishness. If I didn't make it to land before nightfall, I would undoubtedly be doomed to a certain death.

I was torn in half, wrenched by two distinctly opposing forces: my own rational thinking and the wisdom of God. I didn't want to doubt Him, but what He was instructing me to do went far beyond the realm of logic. How could I be sure God knew what was best, fully understood what was at stake, the terrible risk and the fatal consequences? It was so overwhelmingly difficult for me to trust again, to put my trust in someone other than myself, especially something as nebulous as God, even if I felt close to Him.

For the past two days I had all my faith wrapped up in trusting that Mum was going to rescue me. As the minutes turned into hours and the hours into days, my hope and trust in others had been eaten away until there was nothing left. The disappointment I felt was devastating! Every hour that passed without rescue was like a knife that cut out pieces of my heart. It seemed to confirm the impossible, that Mum didn't love me enough to save me. I had been abandoned with no one to trust, no one to rely on. The only thing I had left to cling to was my will to live and my tenacious nature.

I had made a promise to myself not to look back to my past for a refuge, to only look ahead to the immediate future of getting through the next hour, to no longer think of Mum and her ability to rescue me. No, I was on my own; self preservation was the name of the game. Looking after number one was the top priority! I couldn't allow any weaknesses to enter into my mind. Any self-pity or yearning for Mum to rescue me so my trust in her could be restored was debilitating. I knew that to indulge myself in these thoughts could be my undoing.

But last night my resolve had crumbled; my resistance disintegrated. I was forced to confront my own human frailty and the ineffectual struggle for my life. In my hour of desperation, realizing my hopelessness, I reached out for the hand of God and He responded. I asked for the truth, what the final outcome would be, and I received not only an answer but a promise. From that moment forth I had learned to trust again, to put faith in something other than myself, something intangible but nevertheless real. My faith had restored my life to me. Dare I tempt destiny further by ignoring this command?

What a dilemma I had been forced into. Again I had been pushed into a corner with my back up against the wall, compelled to make another life-threatening decision. My numerous escapes from the clutches of death had been nothing short of miraculous, but I was living on a razor edge, slicing it perilously close. One misguided judgment, one bungled calculation, and it was all over. I couldn't let that happen. I hadn't fought these harrowing days to lose my life now because of a foolish decision.

"I'm sorry, God," I whispered, "but I have to do this my way. It's too irrational to try to make it to the farthermost island when right in front of me there's a group of them. The idea just seems too ridiculous to comprehend. The truth is, God, I'm just too scared to fail, too scared to risk dying after all. I truly am sorry, God, and hope You will find it in Your heart to understand my reasonings."

I had made the decision to stick to my original plan and make my destination one of the three islands; still the dilemma went on inside my mind. A confrontation of wills, mine and God's, had set itself up inside my head to engage in battle. I resolved not to give in to the pressure; I would not allow my equilibrium to be eroded by acknowledging the prompting of the insistent voice.

Before I could be swayed to change my mind by sheer guilt and the mental turmoil of disobeying God, a physical feat that could only be described as a supernatural miracle occurred. It shocked the life out of me!

Without warning a monsterous wall of water about eight feet high came from behind me. Instinctively I turned around to see what I felt was coming, but I was blinded by the brilliance of the torrid sun. Dazzled by its burning whiteness through a blurry veil I experienced something that will forever be engraved on my mind. The towering wave swept under the bunca, lifting it skyward. The wave gathered momentum and height, climactically reaching its pinnacle.

Poised in midair, the wave seemed to stop as the bunca suddenly swiveled around 180 degrees in the air, then came back down on the wave's crest. As the wave slid from under the bunca, it dispersed into a cauldron of white foaming surf. Without warning I was propelled in the direction of the farthermost island, the one where I had been instructed by God to go. As if I were being driven along by an imaginary motor, the bunca traveled along for at least fifty feet directly against the currents.

I watched on incredulously as the bunca plowed through the oncoming waves, unaided by my flippers or the motion of the waves. How could I comprehend this supernatural feat that I had witnessed with my own two eyes? This was most assuredly a sign from God. He was obvi-

---

"One misguided judgment, one bungled calculation and it was all over. I couldn't let that happen. I hadn't fought these harrowing days to lose my life now because of a foolish decision."

---

ously adamant in showing me that I must head for the farthest island. Why? I was still at a complete loss to know His reasoning. However, what His words had not conveyed strongly enough, His actions surely had. This time I dared not disobey the wisdom of God, no matter how illogical it seemed to me.

A Human Presence

Summoning up all the strength and courage I had within me, I prepared myself for the next four hours of backbreaking, hard labor in my frantic effort to reach the island before nightfall. I took a furtive glance at the three islands that I was turning my back on. Oh, they looked so invitingly close. Gazing off into the distance at the large island I was now heading for, an ominous foreboding descended over me, congealing the fear that ran through my veins. The notion of doing this seemed like pure, unadulterated insanity to me.

Oh God, what is it You could possibly have planned for me? Because of its size, will this island have more variety of food on it? Or is it more likely to be inhabited? I was so very tired with a weariness and confusion that filled the depths of my soul. God's reasoning and logic made no sense to me, but I had to trust Him. I remember when He told me to grab the flippers instead of the water bottle and how confused I'd been at His choice. He had certainly proved to me over the past days how invaluable the flippers were. In fact if not for them, I probably would not have the means of reaching any island at all. Trust and faith—I would live on these now; they would be my sustenance.

If I had any illusions that this was not going to be too difficult, they were shattered within the first few minutes. If I'd thought paddling with the currents was strenuous, paddling sideways against the currents was horrendous. The entire ocean came rolling towards me, opposing every yard I fought to gain with only the feeble use of my legs propelling me forward. At least when I was heading for the cluster of islands, I had the motion of the waves coming from behind, assisting my passage. Now each wave that collided with the right side of my body steered me off course. With every brutal wave that pounded against me and each vicious lash of surf against my face I found myself vehemently regretting my decision.

Agonizing over the correctness of my resolution inflicted a mental anxiety so intense that it almost matched the physical pain I was experiencing. Every muscle in my body was numb with the multitude of blows it had received. The relentless surging and pounding of the waves against me had made the tissues of skin feel acutely tender, as if I had been pulverized by a meat tenderizer. The pain was all consuming, ravaging every square inch of me. However, to stop paddling and rest now could possibly mean losing the few extra minutes of light I needed to get to the island before night fell. I couldn't afford to risk those vital minutes that would otherwise leave me paddling in darkness. I would have plenty of time to rest once I was safe on the island, which in my estimation was now only five miles away. As I looked up at the sun to gauge the time by its position, I guessed it to be around 1:30 P.M.

Briefly gazing over the endless stretch of ocean, for a lingering instant I thought my eyes were deceiving me, but they were not. What loomed ahead of me was real! Approximately five nautical miles to the northeast, shimmering on the distant horizon, was without a doubt *a ship.*

I froze with the leap of my pulse. I was finally going to be rescued. My whole being ignited with excitement and confidence at the thought of being rescued. Finally someone had come to save me. *Is it you, Mum, at last? Oh, I knew deep in my heart you wouldn't give up on me, Mum. Your maternal instincts must have assured you that I was still alive.* Mothers always have that inner knowledge when their children are in danger and especially if they are no longer alive. My faith in her had been revived!

Suddenly a startling thought came to me as I scrutinized the ship. It didn't look like a rescue boat; in fact it looked more like a fishing vessel. Considering I had all the money, it was quite feasible to assume that Mum had to employ the aid of a fishing vessel to search for me. Painted a soft pink color, it also had a lookout tower. If they were looking in this direction with binoculars then I was sure they would see me.

"What could I possibly do to prevent my only hope of rescue in three days from passing me by?"

Speedily I untied the knot of my T-shirt, ripped it off, and began furiously waving it high above my head, desperately trying to capture their attention. *Mum. I'm here,* I wanted to call out, but the distance between us was still too far to be heard. *Surely they can see me? Why aren't they changing course? Oh, God, please let them see me. Please let them be looking in this direction.*

What could I possibly do to prevent my only hope of rescue in three days from passing me by? I felt myself being enveloped by a cloak of dread as I realized I was powerless to do anything but keep waving my T-shirt and pray they saw me. My confidence in rescue shattered as the ship made no indication of altering its course but continued to plow through the water without acknowledging my awful plight.

If only they knew how close they'd come to finding me. If only they knew how close to death I was and their power to save me. *Why, oh why, God, is this happening?* The futility of my situation bit into me with the savageness of a frustrated cobra.

It would have been better for me if I hadn't seen the boat at all. It was as if candy were being dangled in front of me but out of my reach. With the horror of disbelief I stopped waving my T-shirt and watched helplessly as the possibility of rescue and the comfort of human presence glided past, ignoring my perilous predicament.

With a sickening thud in the pit of my stomach, I was forced to accept the worst—the occupants of that ship hadn't and wouldn't see me. I realized then it was not a rescue boat, just a passing ship. Instead of torturing myself over the mental anguish of why this cruel blow had happened, I resigned myself to the fact that this was not meant to be. I had learned enough by now to realize that you cannot change the course of destiny. It must run its path. You either go along for the ride, accepting all the sudden ups and downs and sharp turns, or you surely live a life of disappointment and disillusionment. I'd lived my life by this rule. Even now, in this catastrophe, I had to accept what I didn't understand.

Arch Enemies

An eerie sensation rippled through me, instinctively urging me to look at the ocean surrounding me. Half expecting to see another ship in the distance, what met my eyes instead immobilized me as if I had been cast into stone. For a moment I thought it was an apparition, an illusion created by my brain that felt as if it had been cooked from three days under the scorching tropical sun.

In shock, I realized it wasn't an illusion! No less than fifteen yards away from me, slicing through the surface of the sea like razors, were the clearly defined fins of two man-eating sharks. I gasped, my breath catching in my throat, as a pocket of air lodged itself in my windpipe. For an instant I was unable to move, gripped by a fear so acute I felt as if the blood running through my veins had turned into ice. Holding my breath I felt too terrified to expel the air in my lungs and break the silence, alerting them of my presence. A sudden involuntary shudder vibrated through my body. Was this to be my end?

To my horror, the theme from *Jaws* began to play in my mind. *Shut up! Shut up!* I said to the music in my head. I thought I could descend no further down the corridors of terror in this petrifying ordeal, but what I was experiencing now was a whole new dimension in the realms of fear. One of mankind's worst nightmares had now become reality for me.

Some seconds after the first shock impact had passed, my survival instincts returned. I suddenly remembered my naked legs dangling in the water. I wondered what they would look like under the water from a shark's perspective. Maybe the flippers would scare them. Thank God, I had them on! Not that they would be much protection from a hungry shark, but I did feel grateful for the sense of security that they gave me.

I had imagined this scenario a hundred times in the past three days and it was always the same. A sudden thrashing in the water alerts my attention. The moon illuminates the spray of water that cascades down in the night sky. For a split second the fin of a shark is also revealed, but when I look again it is gone, melted into the pitch darkness ahead. Horrified, I look to the spot in the ocean where the fin has appeared, to confirm what I saw. Straining my eyes to see through the coal blackness, there appears to be nothing.

Without warning the menacing face of the shark materializes, thrusting itself out of the water toward me. The multiple rows of segregated triangle teeth housed in the jaws of this primeval predator are exposed to me seconds before the gaping jaws clamp shut on my bare leg. I feel the

"In shock, I realized it wasn't an illusion! No less than fifteen yards away from me, slicing through the surface of the sea like razors, were the clearly defined fins of two man-eating sharks."

razor-sharp teeth sinking into my flesh right through to the bone. The sound of bones snapping inside my flesh is like the branches of a tree in a hurricane.

Transfixed with the pure horror of what is happening, I watch, helpless to remove my leg from his vice-like grip. In a feeding frenzy, he savagely shakes his head from side to side to sever the leg. I frantically kick the shark in the face with the free leg. I feel the last shreds of flesh being torn away as the ferocious shark disappears into the glittering depths of the ocean with his prey.

Was my horrific dream now to become a reality? Groping for the hull of the bunca I hauled myself up onto it, compelled to put as much distance as I could between myself and that water, ensuring that every bodily part was removed. Clambering up onto the slimy hull, lying lengthways on my stomach, with outstretched arms I managed to balance precariously by gripping onto the arms of the outriggers. The slippery algae beneath me made me wonder how long I could hold on.

The hideous fins of the sharks continued to cut a path through the water, seemingly unaware of my presence. With abundant relief I noted that they had not changed course or shown any indication that they knew I was there. Thank God, they hadn't changed direction and begun swimming toward me. The thought of them encircling the bunca, then nudging it viciously with their noses causing me to slip off into the water and into their open jaws was hideous. My attention riveted on them, I didn't dare take my eyes from them for a second. Never, even in my worst nightmares, had I experienced the raw, all-consuming fear that I now had.

Suddenly and unexpectedly, an unfathomable calm came over me. It was as if a cloak of assurance had descended on me. Instantly the fear dissolved and was replaced by the knowledge that the sharks wouldn't hurt me. As if to confirm this, the familiar voice whispered in my ear, "Don't worry. They won't harm you." Again I had the tangible sensation of angels surrounding me, as they constructed an invisible cocoon around me, stronger than any earthly fortress. Exactly as last night, I sensed a forcefield of protection encircle me, guarding me from the elements and the enemy.

Seconds before, I had been traumatized by the threat of being attacked and eaten alive; now these fears had been miraculously eliminated. I felt immune to the presence of these frightening predators. Although when I thought about it, it wasn't so strange. If God was the creator of all things, then surely He would have the power to control them.

Just as I was resting in my security, catastrophe struck! A lumbering wave crept up from behind, its force wrenching me from my grip of the bunca, flushing me into the open sea where the enemy awaited. Stricken with panic, my impulse was to thrash through the water as quickly as I could, back to my precious refuge on top of the bunca. But I knew I had to be extremely cautious and not splash, signaling possible prey in the vicinity.

With nerve-shattering control I swam deliberately; stroke by stroke I glided through the water, causing barely a ripple on the ocean's surface. Not wanting to slow my progress, I didn't dare look behind me and check the proximity of the sharks to see if they were following me, but instead I made a beeline straight toward the bunca. Hauling myself up onto the hull, from my safe vantage point I scanned the ocean for the fins of the sharks and saw them nonchalantly swimming into the distance.

It took my heart a few minutes to resume its normal beating. But I couldn't wait any longer. I had to resume paddling, even with eyes open for other predators.

At approximately 2 P.M. I was startled by a subtle rumbling noise behind me. Turning around I saw that the monstrosity powering towards me was no apparition.

FOURTEEN

THE PRECIPICE OF DESPAIR

RACHELLE . . . 1:00 P.M., SATURDAY, MARCH 11, PLANE SEARCH. The drone of a twin-engine plane intervened, saving me from myself. I swung around, shielding my eyes from the glaring sunlight as I scanned the sky for the aircraft that for so many hours had been like an elusive beacon of hope. I saw it instantly; the sun glistened off the silver wing tips as it passed low over the sea coming in to land.

This is the moment I'd been waiting for with gripping trepidation. By embarking on this aerial search, I would soon face the truth on the destiny of my daughter. If this last-ditch effort were unsuccessful, then it would shatter my illusions and strip me of any vestige of hope that I might resolutely cling to. It was a traumatic process for me to set the wheels of destiny in motion. But ultimately it may save Michelle's life. I had to believe there was still a chance of finding her out in that ocean.

The roaring sounds of the plane as it came in to land drowned out my thoughts. I turned and headed back to the passenger shelter, willing my legs to continue walking. I was stricken with a crushing fear of facing the final outcome. If by some means it were within my power to delay the inevitable, I would have!

Dear God, let me hold onto my hope. It's the only thing that's keeping me functioning, I prayed. Without the belief that Michelle may be alive, I don't think I'd be able to go on. *Please God, let me find her out there.* I couldn't bear to find her dead or parts of the boat floating in the sea. How could I live with that, wondering forever what happened to her? *Only You alone know how much she means to me, God. Don't You think I've lost enough in my life already? Don't take her away from me as well,* I cried out as I walked back to the terminal.

"Ma'am, your plane is here. We are ready to go," one of the young boys said enthusiastically, eager to begin the adventure.

Yet again I found myself surrounded by a sea of animated Filipino faces, only too willing to assist me. The pilot and navigator introduced themselves and like a lost child I obediently followed them to the plane. I climbed aboard the aircraft with the distorted sense that somebody had crawled inside my skin and was automatically operating my body. Mercifully, I felt removed from the situation which was about to bless or destroy my life.

The Air Search Begins

I sat down in one of the seats at the front of the plane. People moved around me although I was not fully aware of them. The plane was relatively small, having only one seat on either side of the aisle. The tiny oval windows through which I'd soon be scanning the ocean were barely adequate for a clear view. The double glazing made me doubtful of the visibility once we were airborne. Within a few minutes everyone was seated and the plane was ready for takeoff.

The pilot turned and spoke to me. "Excuse me, ma'am. The Coast Guard has briefed us on the situation. I believe we are searching for a young lady who was carried out to sea in a bunca three days ago. The location where we have been advised to conduct the search is around the islands of Panay and Palawan. The currents would have carried her out in that direction, so we will start looking there. We have drawn up a flight plan which will crisscross over this entire area to make certain we achieve a thorough and comprehensive search."

"That sounds fine," I said in a flat, passionless voice that did not betray my fear. "How long can we stay in the air?"

"We have fuel for approximately two hours. By then we would have covered an extensive area."

"Have you ever done this before, I mean, search for people lost at sea?"

"From time to time, ma'am!"

"Did you ever find any of the missing people? . . . I think what I'm really trying to say is, what are the real chances of finding her alive?"

"Every case is different, so it's hard to say. Of course, several days have passed since she was missing. Obviously it would have been far better to conduct the search as soon as you were aware she was missing.

However, you must always cling to the belief that she is still alive and we will find her."

"Yes, I know. That's the only thing I have now to keep me going—faith!"

The motors roared to life, drowning out all conversation. My attention was diverted outside the plane. I peered through the window and watched the gathering of people who had congregated on the grass verge

---

"The awe I felt was all too soon replaced by an overwhelming sense of insignificance in an expanse such as this."

---

adjacent the runway. Many arms were waving energetically, wishing me luck. I felt a ray of warmth penetrate my heart, but I was unable to form a smile in return.

The plane taxied down the runway. I was instantly transported back to my enjoyable flight out of Sydney, when I was overflowing with the excitement and anticipation of seeing Michelle again and the expectations of this exotic holiday. The ironically cruel situation I now found myself in was inconceivable! How had it managed to go so wrong? Why was this dreadful thing happening to me? My very worst nightmares about my children and the dangers of the drowning seemed to have become a blatant reality.

We had liftoff. The tiny aircraft ascended into the air and shuddered as if in defiance. It wobbled, dropped several feet, but resolutely became airborne, gaining heightened momentum. Within minutes the craft had stabilized and we were cruising quite smoothly. I forcefully let out a lungful of air, unaware till then that I'd been holding my breath during takeoff. We rose fairly quickly into the uninterrupted blue sky.

In spite of myself, I was awed by the magnificence that unfolded before my eyes. Boracay Island lay below us, appearing so minute from my new perspective, a slither of land mass, a splinter of earth crowned in an infinite expanse of ocean, a precious jewel. The splashes of brilliant color converged on one another, defined like the colors of a rainbow. The emerald green of the lush tropical vegetation was in sharp contrast to the alabaster ring of white sand that encircled the island. It then merged into a glorious turquoise blue sea, melding into a deep indigo of the depths of the ocean. The immensity of the majestic skies crowned us like a heavenly blue dome.

The awe I felt was all too soon replaced by an overwhelming sense of insignificance in an expanse such as this. My mask of sheer bravado dropped; all of a sudden I felt so terribly ineffectual in the face of such abysmal odds. Exposed to the stark reality, I could see the futility of the monumental task ahead of us! The sea below stretched out like a never-ending global carpet of water, spreading out in every direction as far as the eye could see. The full realization hit me with the impact of a thunderbolt, severing any remnant of naive belief I'd held on to.

I knew in that instant that the only chance of finding Michelle out there would take a miraculous act of God to save her. How deluded I'd been to believe that once I had a plane to search for Michelle, I'd be able to locate her easily. I'd honestly thought from an aerial bird's-eye perspective, I wouldn't be restricted by limited vision as I was on land. I presumed from an elevated position I would be able to cover great distances and my sight would not be hindered.

Now this misguided notion was torn from where I had nursed it, feeding the belief with faith, torn from the heart of a mother. I felt a hopelessness beyond description. Silent tears trickled down my cheeks. I wiped them away hurriedly as they were clouding my vision, inhibiting my view of the ocean below. Although my heart felt as if it had turned to stone, I kept up the vigil of searching the water for Michelle.

My eyes burned from the concentrated effort of focusing on the water. The reflected sunlight glaring off the ocean pierced through my pupils like the white light from a soldering torch, making it necessary to rub my eyes every few minutes so I could refocus. The blustery winds had whipped up the surface of the ocean, creating a multitude of foaming white crests that overlaid the face of the ocean, resembling peaks of a meringue pie. Millions of whitecaps taunted me relentlessly, making my task almost impossible.

My eyes honed in on what I thought looked to be a boat. I strained to identify the object I was focusing in on, only to watch it break and merge with the sea. Not allowing disappointment to deter me, once again I sought out and scrutinized a segment of the ocean that somehow looked different from the rest. Could this be Michelle's boat? My eyes zoomed in, almost becoming telescopic as I tried to clarify what it was. The intrusive sound of someone's voice shattered the tense atmosphere.

"I can see something down there. It looks like a bunca off to the right hand side."

My heart skipped a beat. I felt my face flush as the blood rushed up to my head.

"Whereabouts?" I heard the pilot ask.

I jumped to my feet and within a fraction of a second I found myself peering out the portside window. Oh my God, I saw it too. It was a bunca!

"We'll turn around and take a closer look," the pilot said with a note of expectation. The plane tilted as it descended like an eagle circling in on its prey. *Dear God, please let it be her. Please let it be Michelle,* I pleaded. My eyes felt as if they were protruding out of their sockets as if they were on stilts, boring through the distance between us. I virtually stopped breathing, experiencing such an exquisite pinnacle of tension. As we descended, the boat became clearer.

"I can make out a person on board!" a jubilant voice cried out.

I strained to see more clearly, but I'd cried so much over the past few days my red and swollen eyes impaired my vision.

"Over there, waving out. Look! Can you see?" one of the boys said excitedly.

It was then I saw it! Sure enough, there was someone on board, alive and waving out to us. It was then I also noticed the sail which in my eagerness I'd ignored. "Michelle's bunca didn't have a sail!" I wailed.

A cry of anguish rose but froze in my throat, paralyzed by disappointment. I was unable to verbalize what I knew to be true. Seconds later, someone else in the plane obliged.

"No, it's not her. The man in the bunca is a Filipino." The heightened expectation we had all generated now plunged like a rock falling to the bottom of a pond. The rock lay immovable in the pit of my stomach.

A Needle in a Haystack

It took the crew several minutes to recover from the cruel blow and regain the discipline needed to forge on with our mission. Everybody took their places once again at the allocated windows and resumed the search. My vision was hampered by the body of the plane which prevented me from seeing directly beneath us. A devastating thought popped into my mind: What if we flew directly over Michelle and she was just a few feet out of my line of vision, hidden by the undercarriage of the plane? It was a grisly thought.

It seemed I'd been deluding myself that there was a chance we could find her; the stark truth was we were looking for a needle in a haystack. Feeling intensely frustrated, I left my position and went forward to talk to the pilot. Upon entering the cockpit I was instantly relieved to see the 180-degree vision they obtained from the dome-shaped windows in the nose of the plane.

"Can I sit in here with you? I can't see very well from the back," I asked the navigator.

"Of course, you can sit here between us," the navigator replied, clearing a space for me.

"What's that you're monitoring?" I asked, diverting my mind from the obvious fruitlessness of this search.

"I have worked out a flight plan so we crisscross over the entire area and not miss a patch of water. Can you see here?" he said, showing me a sheet of graph paper with zigzagged lines drawn across it.

"This is the area we have already covered," he said pointing to the diagram.

"Where are we now?"

"We are heading out towards the Cuyo Islands which are a group of four islands located due east. The biggest Island is the Cuyo Island. If you look over there, you can see the islands coming into view. The other three are named Dit, Agutaya, and Canipo Island."

"Do you really think it's possible she could have drifted out this far?" I questioned him in disbelief.

"I know it's a long way out; in fact, we're approximately one hundred and twenty nautical miles out from Boracay. However, the locals know these waters. Fishing is their livelihood and they know the tidal currents of this area intimately. This is where they recommended we search."

"Look, I trust your judgment. Besides I know nothing about this area."

The isolated cluster of islands were now looming up in front of us. My pulse began to beat faster. My imagination was fueled by the sight of these islands. Was it truly possible she could have made it this far and be waiting on land for us to rescue her? I waited in hopeful apprehension to see her little red bunca pulled up on one of these deserted beaches. Oh, the exquisite relief and indescribable joy I'd feel if this was the case.

Please God, let me see her bunca, some evidence that she is still alive. Don't take her from me, I implored Him. The plane swooped low over the desolated coastline. My eyes were riveted on the strips of ivory sand, half expecting to see Michelle's bunca there. My eyes transfixed

---

" 'Do you really think it's possible she could have drifted out this far?' I questioned him in disbelief."

---

to the beaches below, my hopes rose and fell with every life-like image I saw, then identified as something other than human. Strewn driftwood took on the possible form of a body or wreckage of a boat. Every object I clarified as not being either shattered my fragile expectancy.

Morbid thoughts crowded my mind. Were our endeavors in vain? Was our last ditch effort simply too little too late? With daunting clarity I realized this search was being carried out as much for me as for Michelle. With blatant honesty I asked myself, who could have survived that ferocious storm on the first night of her disappearance? With trepidation I acknowledged the truth: Nobody could have survived it! However, I knew I could have never lived with the knowledge that everything in my power hadn't been done to find her.

The terrible vision of my vivid dream flashed onto the screen inside my head. Michelle's body floating face down with her golden hair rhythmically swaying to the motion of the waves. I seemed to confirm some deep inner knowledge I fought hard to suppress. *No, no,* I screamed silently! *Don't torture me with this ghastly image. I can't bear to think of her life ending this way—in a horrendous struggle against the mighty power of the ocean, battling to save her own life, with the sea finally claiming her. . . .*

The pilot's voice announcing that we were approaching the last island in the group broke into my spiraling thoughts of doom, nudging me back from the precipice of despair. Another chance, another hope rose up feebly, and I grasped at it. Maybe right when we were about to give up, she would miraculously be found, in the eleventh hour, before the clock struck its last fatal hour? It happened that way in the movies. I wanted to believe that this was our one-in-a-million chance about to come true. The plane once again descended, sweeping over the speck of land which decorated an otherwise watery landscape. We went through the repetitive procedure of searching the island, but . . . there was nothing!

"I'm terribly sorry to have to be the bearer of bad news, ma'am, but we will have to return to base now. Our fuel is running extremely low. I wish we would not have to end this way but we've done all we can as far as an aerial search," he said, choked with emotion and sadness. Every word he said was like a knife that lacerated my heart. The plane lifted up and away from the island. Soaring into the sky, it headed back to Boracay.

Anguish numbed me, seeping through my veins like an injection of anesthetic, rendering me paralyzed. My brain refused to accept the finality of what this decision meant. I had mercifully entered a stupor, where the reality of this traumatic truth barred entry to my soul and remained on the periphery of my mind. However, I stubbornly held the sea in my sights as we made the sobering journey back to Boracay. I was determined to keep looking for Michelle until the last bitter minute, when I had no other choice but to accept defeat.

The majestic island of Panay rose up out of the ocean. The plane dipped and leveled up with the runway, a mere ribbon of cleared land among the dense vegetation. We wavered, shuddered, then did several kangaroo hops along the runway as the plane touched down. It managed to come to a relative halt before coasting back to the terminal.

I was no longer capable of acknowledging anything. Numbly, I uttered thanks to the crew who had accompanied me on this rescue mission. I felt like a walking corpse; my body was operating on automatic, far removed from the activity of life. I was only vaguely aware of the people who had gathered to greet me on my return. There was no need for any of them to ask the outcome. Our grim faces spoke the words our lips were unable to utter. . . .

FIFTEEN

DIVINE DELIVERANCE

MICHELLE . . . 2:00 P.M., SATURDAY, MARCH 11, CUYO EAST PASSAGE. I was so totally absorbed in my all-consuming struggle to reach the island before nightfall that I barely heard the subtle rumbling noise behind me. Turning around gingerly, I felt as if I had been suddenly gripped by an enormous imaginary hand which held me both frozen and incredulous for seven interminable seconds.

I couldn't believe my eyes! It wasn't an apparition. Coming towards me at full speed was a gigantic ship. My heart constricted in utter surprise as waves of shock washed over me. I knew I had to do something and quickly, but I was so dumbstruck I couldn't move. Only my eyes were free to view this stupendous moment. My heart was beating so hard and fast, I could feel gallons of blood race frantically around my body. If I didn't snap myself out of this hypnotic state, I would allow my surest chance of rescue in three days to pass me by.

Shaking my head wildly from side to side, I was brought out of my reverie. A series of rational thoughts now sped around my mind at lightning speed, then connected. *Oh, please let them see me! How on earth will I attract their attention?* I couldn't bear the thought of their not seeing me and my being left to watch the ship glide past me unnoticed as the other ship had. This was my last chance for rescue. If I made it to an island, the chance of attracting the attention of a passing ship was negligible. This was it! This monumentous event I had insufferably waited three days for was finally happening. I was going to be rescued!

Frantically I looked around for something I could use to capture their attention. If only I had a flare. I estimated the ship was approximately five hundred yards away and would probably reach me in about three minutes. I couldn't see any signs of life on board. What chance was there that a member of the crew just happened to be looking into the water? No, I couldn't trust my life on such a flimsy premise. I would have to think of another way to get their attention. But how? The problem was so colossal that it sent tingles of dread through me. I was at a loss to know what to do. I felt so powerless that tears of frustration stung my eyes. I would just have to pray that one of them would come onto the deck and look into the water. I was left with little other choice!

Instinctively I knew this vessel was bound for Manila! Don't ask me how I knew this extraordinary fact to be true, but somehow I just did. It wasn't a guess; it was information that had been given to me from the highest Authority, and I knew to believe it with absolute conviction. It was so incredibly strange nevertheless, because up until several seconds ago, I hadn't even the slightest clue as to my location.

This uncanny knowledge that the vessel was bound for Manila made it more than possible that I was still within Philippine waters. In my mind's eye I could see the map of the Philippines clearly, having studied it on numerous occasions when I was planning where Mum and I would holiday. I had been bewildered as to why, when there are seven thousand islands that make up the Philippines, I had managed to bypass them all.

Because of the powerful currents, I knew I'd been carried an extremely long way from Boracay. Until this morning I hadn't sighted any land whatsoever. To me that just didn't seem feasible. There was only one possibility, but it was rather farfetched. If I had traveled in a northeast direction from Boracay, then the reason I hadn't seen any land was that there wasn't any. There was just an endless stretch of water until a strip of islands formed the circumference of land and the boundary of the Philippines.

If this were the case, then these four islands were the Cuyo Islands and the last frontier before I hit the South China Sea and began heading towards the region of Southeast Asia. But this was pure conjecture, the only conceivable reason why I had not seen land. If my theories were correct, my life was in even more jeopardy than I could have guessed. If I missed this ship, and these were the last bastions of land for another thousand miles of ocean, I was as good as dead.

I couldn't let Mum go through any more days of grief and pain, thinking I was dead. I hoped she hadn't already called my sisters Angeline and Natalie and told them what had happened—that I was presumed dead after being lost in a boating accident. *My God,* I prayed, *surely she hadn't*. What would it do to them? My immediate family was extraordinarily close, and this news would devastate them. I couldn't let this happen. I knew I was alive, but I was powerless to let anyone else know. How ironic!

A terrible sense of guilt pervaded my every thought, eating away at me like an infestation of termites. How had I done this to Mum when I had promised her a relaxing, stress-free holiday? I was in a quandary as to what to do. I reasoned to myself it would probably be quicker for me to make it on my own to the island, which was now only about two miles away, and then I could pay a fisherman to take me back to Boracay. That seemed more logical to me than traveling all the way to

---

"If I missed this ship, and these were the last bastions of land for another thousand miles of ocean, I was as good as dead."

Manila, which would mean an extra day's delay. With each hour that passed without news, it would be confirmation to Mum that I couldn't possibly still be alive.

A flash of absolute logic struck me with clarity. What was I thinking about? Had I completely lost my mind? Here I was on the edge of death and I was debating whether I should let my only chance of rescue go by. I wasn't even sure if the island was inhabited and there would be a fisherman to take me back to Boracay! Well, a dead hero was not what she needed! She would have to wait the two days. I decided I was going to do everything possible to catch that ship to safety!

How stupid of me not to realize that they probably have a radio transmitter on board anyway. I could ask them to radio a message to Boracay Island that I had been rescued and was heading for Manila. I looked up at the ship with a mixture of relief, excitement, and a little apprehension. Was I finally going to be plucked from these treacherous waters and taken safely back to civilization?

Please See Me!

Abruptly, I turned to see a gigantic wave rolling toward me, breaking into a spray of white foam as it did so. I desperately tried to thrust myself and the bunca forward, hoping to ride the wave. Suddenly, realizing I wasn't going to make it, I tried to shield my head with my arm and brace myself as I was dumped in a torrent of foam.

Oh no, not again, I thought as another wave crashed on me, sending me sprawling over the hull of the bunca, into the sea. Thrashing wildly in a gasping attempt to resurface, my head finally broke through, coughing up the salty water I had just inhaled. While treading water I managed to stay afloat long enough to regain my breath.

I swiveled around to locate my bunca and the ship. Systematically I found them both and immediately made a swim towards the bunca. Finally reaching it, I hurled myself onto the arm of the outrigger and propelled my flippers in a turbulent motion going against the sea. I looked up to see that I was in direct line with the ship which was powering toward me, threatening to crush me under its bow if I didn't get out of its path.

Panic-stricken, I leapt into action, my legs and arms thrashing wildly, trying to tear through the curtain of water. My heart pounded with sheer terror as I wondered whether it was already too late. Would I be able to get out of the way in time? My would-be lifesavers had unknowingly become the instrument capable of causing my death. Instead of saving my life, they were about to end it as thirty tons of solid steel made mincemeat out of me.

God, save me! Please get me out of this. Don't let me die this way, I screamed. At the precise moment I uttered these cries for help, a ten-story wall of water lifted me and the bunca up like a matchstick, hurling us out of the path of the ship. Down I went once again under a barrage of water and resurfaced to see the ship gliding dangerously alongside me. I uttered a brief thank you to God for this spectacular miracle, one of the many that had been performed to sustain my life.

With outstretched arms, I grabbed the outrigger and hauled myself onto the slippery hull of the bunca. Straining my eyes, I urgently searched for any signs of life on board the ship. There appeared to be none. Where was the crew? I suddenly felt alarmed when it occurred to me that they might have put the ship on automatic pilot while they slept. But surely there must be someone awake at this time of day? Captains didn't leave their ships to steer themselves.

My eyes were riveted on the huge ship. All I could see was a massive bulk of steel, a sheer wall of metal reaching skyward as it passed alongside. I was unable to see the deck. As I looked down, my bunca suddenly appeared so feeble in the vastness of the sea and in contrast to the size of the ship. How I had managed to survive this long was a miracle mere words were inadequate to describe.

I came to a horrible realization but a very realistic one: Why would anyone be looking down into the water, especially for a castaway. But I couldn't face the shocking possibility of missing two ships in the space of a few hours. If they couldn't see me, then I would have to make them hear me. It was my last hope for rescue!

Inhaling deeply, I summoned up every scrap of strength in my body in an attempt to cry for help. As I started to scream, "Help!" I was shocked by the instant realization that I had no voice, only a hoarse whisper. I cursed my physical disability. How could my voice desert me now, at such a crucial moment? They couldn't see me, and now they wouldn't even hear me.

I was in dire straits! What could I do? I frantically ripped off my T-shirt and began waving it above my head like a lasso. *This just can't be happening to me,* I said to myself.

The monstrous rusty vessel sliced through the water alongside me; this in turn created a series of brutal waves which pounded my little bunca violently. *My God, was this to be my end? After fighting to stay alive for three days, I'll be slammed by the force of the waves into the side of the ship and knocked unconscious?* It was an all too real possibility.

Exercising the utmost caution, I swung myself over to the other side of the bunca, grabbing on to the rim of the hull for dear life—anticipating the necessity of abandoning the bunca should the ship crash into it.

Gazing up at the ship, I speculated who its occupants would be. Probably an all-male crew! My mind began conjuring up ghastly images of dirty, uncivilized people, maybe even pirates. Actually it wasn't a too farfetched thought. I remember being warned quite adamantly that pirates preyed in these waters. Not Captain Hook—1990s pirates! Anyone who was unfortunate enough to come into contact with these fiendish characters could likely end up tortured, raped, or even murdered for a little as a few pesos or just an afternoon's entertainment.

A disagreeable chill ran down my spine! The ramifications of my predicament struck me anew. The people I was trusting to save me, could in fact have far more dubious motives for wanting to rescue me. I had a lot of cash on me; maybe if I just gave them that and promised them more when we got to land, they would deliver me to safety, unharmed. When I really thought about it logically, what was the worst thing they could do to me? Kill me. Well, I rationalized, I'd be dead in a few days anyway, if I survived that long. It was hideous to think that they might rape me but it couldn't be worse than the torture I'd endured over the last three days. The fact was, I loved life more than anything on the face of this earth, and I was determined to continue being a part of it.

Hey, what was I worried about anyway? God had said He would save my life, not end it. What was the matter with me? Didn't I trust Him anymore? No that wasn't it. I think paranoia had distorted my thinking. *Of course I trust You, God,* I said in my head. *I just keep forgetting You are on my side. How stupid of me to think You would send someone to harm me! These people are here to help me.*

Relief flooded through me. I now felt confident regarding the people on the ship. I was in safe hands! Now that I had decided I wanted them to save me, would they?

It seemed to take an eternity for the ship to pass, but it finally did. I immediately resumed my position on the bunca, wedging myself in between the upturned hull and the remaining arm of the outrigger. With one hand gripped tightly underneath the hull, I used my free hand to wave my T-shirt top again, while simultaneously scanning the boat for any visible signs of life. I couldn't believe it: the ship was going past me. I could now see the stern as it moved away.

They were going to leave me here. It was cruel being so close to being saved, yet unseen. *Wait, wait for me,* I wanted to scream out. Nobody had come up on deck; nobody had seen me; I was doomed! I felt devastated, but I couldn't allow this catastrophe to break my spirit.

I wasn't going to allow myself to be swamped with disappointment. I'd pretend this little setback hadn't happened and I'd never seen the ship at all. It was simply a figment of my imagination, born out of my last hope to be rescued. This was the only way I could cope with this disastrous situation, since it looked like I wouldn't be rescued. The best thing to do was stick to my original plan of getting to the island and doing my best to survive.

I felt some of that old excitement fill my veins. I was still alive and life meant hope—what more could I ask? Besides, I truly felt exhilarated about making a life for myself on the island. This was going to be a challenge, as long as there weren't any cannibals. I was only a little less than two miles away; I'd be there in two hours. I wasn't worried about being alone; I liked my own company and generally preferred the company of animals immensely more than the company of people. Hopefully I could make many animal friends on the island.

"Riveted to their movements for any indication that they had seen me, I suddenly saw one of them point in my direction."

Answered Prayer

Although I decided to stick to my original plan and go to the island, I had still not given up hope of rescue by the ship. With one last-ditch effort I gathered up all my powers of concentration and willed somebody to come up on deck and see me.

Less then thirty seconds later, my prayer was answered. My mouth dropped open, my heart fell out of my chest, and my eyes lit up in astonishment as I saw the figures appear at the stern of the ship. It was just as if they had heard my prayer. I couldn't believe it was just a coincidence!

I furiously began waving my T-shirt in a desperate attempt to capture their attention. *They've got to see me!* I tried to scream again but it was hopeless; my voice was gone. Riveted to their movements for any indication that they had seen me, I suddenly saw one of them point in my direction.

Thank God, they had seen me! They'd seen me! His friend waved his hand in a signal of recognition. Right before my eyes my prayers were coming true. I could imagine God sitting up there on His throne witnessing this unforgettable scene, while all His angels in their flowing alabaster white gowns joined in the celebration, praising Him for the great miracle that He had just performed.

Thank You, God, I whispered in a voice choked with emotion.

A few more people appeared on the stern of the ship to join their mates in viewing what must have been an incredible sight! They probably didn't even believe their own eyes. What on earth would a white woman, holding onto a bunca, be doing out in the middle of the ocean alone? How extraordinary I must have appeared to them.

Come, come, they beckoned me with the motions of their arms, which I could see was definitely a welcoming gesture. These guys weren't pirates; I believed I was safe. They signaled for me to swim to the ship, which was continually moving away from me. No doubt having to stop a vessel of that size in midstream would take some doing. I watched with bated breath as it finally came to a relative halt about a half mile away. It seemed so far away and I wondered whether I would have the strength to swim there. Well, I would soon find out. My life depended on me doing so. My eyes were riveted on the people at the stern of the boat, as I prepared myself to leave the bunca.

I felt a sharp tug at my heart! I had developed a sentimental attachment to this hunk of wood that had carried me through the raging seas and delivered me basically unharmed. It seemed such a sacrilege to abandon it now. The bunca had become an extension of myself. During the day I'd learned to position myself in just the right way as to maneuver it in the direction I had been guided to go. At night I would securely wedge myself in between the red upturned hull and the lime green outriggers that held me safely in their arms.

Looking lovingly at my poor little boat, I felt I knew it intimately. It had taken on a personality of its own. How could I be so cruel as to desert it now, leaving it to the mercy of the sea. I wondered what would become of it? Would it just slowly disintegrate and be swallowed by the indifferent seas? My desire to save the bunca from its inevitable destiny had me considering how the crew could hoist it onto the ship and save my little bunca.

I felt myself suddenly break into a smile as I realized what a ludicrous idea I was entertaining. I had to concern myself with my main priority, me! It was with sorrow and a twinge of guilt that I said goodbye to my faithful friend. I prepared myself to leave and make the swim to the ship.

"God," I whispered as I looked towards the heavens, "You know I am about to make a very long and treacherous swim. I ask You to please put strength in my body to last the distance. I know I'm a strong swimmer, but without food or water for days I have no strength left. Without Your help I honestly don't think I'll make it. My mind is willing, but I fear my body is on its last legs, literally! And, God, please keep me safe from those sharks I saw a half hour ago. I'm terrified they are just waiting for me to leave the bunca before they make their move and also . . . "

Before I'd even had a chance to finish asking, an incredible surge of potent energy coursed right through me as if I were a battery being recharged sending tingling vibrations through all my nerve endings. And I knew it was God imbuing me with His supernatural powers to energize me.

Before this ordeal I'd always thought God was someone to chat with when I was in trouble. I couldn't have been more wrong. I felt so special—as if I were the only person in the world. That's the way God had treated me, as if I had my own personal relationship with Him.

Was that possible? In the last three days He had been by my side every mile of this journey; every minute of every day God had become my touchstone. I had heard Him speak audibly, not once but several times. He had guided and directed me in everything I had done and saved my life several times. He had picked up the bunca and turned it in the direction of the farthest island so I would then be in the ship's course. With seconds before contact He had thrown me and the bunca out of the path of the ship just before it plowed into us.

Too many acts and miracles to mention, but the predominant feeling was of protection and love. He surrounded me, making me feel reassured under such terrifying circumstances where there seemed no hope in sight. I always thought of God as I did Father Christmas. I couldn't fathom how on earth He could be everywhere at the same time and talk simultaneously to millions of people in different countries scattered throughout the world. Amazing!

It had confused me as a little girl and, to tell you the truth, it still made no sense. But I had come to the conclusion that there are not always answers to man's every question in life and all things are not supposed to be known, just accepted for what they are. Divine mysteries! This question of mine would go back into the too-hard basket.

Swim to Safety

Stunned and tingling all over by this sensation, I felt as if I'd been transformed into Superwoman. I felt invincible! I believed I could have swum the miles to the island had that been required of me. *Wow, it certainly pays to have friends in high places,* I thought to myself!

Without further hesitation, I slipped my T-shirt back on, tied a knot in the front of it, then looked at the stern of the ship, and waved to let them know I was going to swim to them. Then I slithered off the bunca into the glittering depths of the unpredictable ocean.

Adrenalin pumped through my veins. I was spurred on by a mixture of excitement and fear, realizing that sharks could be lurking just beneath the churning surface, waiting for any vibration in the water to signal a possible snack. I desperately hoped the two I had seen earlier had swum away by now, because I had no intentions of being lunch. My fear subsided as I became absorbed in my task of swimming to the ship.

As I propelled myself I was acutely aware I shouldn't splash in case one of those sharks would feel the vibration and come racing over to the source of the movement. I couldn't even begin to imagine what I would do if I saw the jaws of a shark coming toward me. I did not dare think of it. These thoughts as I swam along were not all-consuming but they lurked just below the surface just as the sharks did. I tried to keep my concentration centered entirely on synchronizing my arms in a breast stroke fashion, propelled mainly by the rhythmical motion of my flippers. I desperately endeavoured to keep all these motions flowing in momentum. I was aware not to make any sharp movements or splash too much, drawing attention from the predators.

After I had been swimming ten minutes, a burning sensation welled up in my arms and legs. I longed to stop! How much farther did I have to go? I looked up. The ship was still quite a distance away, maybe a third of a mile. I had started off energized, but now the stamina I had left was dwindling to a dangerously low level. What if, all of a sudden, my body just stopped, refused to go on? *I can't dwell on that now,* I thought. *I have to keep swimming.*

Ten minutes later fatigue had driven itself into every inch of my body, but I was almost there. I had to endure this torturous pain just a little longer. Suddenly I stopped; my body refused to obey. Overcome with total exhaustion, I was at breaking point! Right at this crucial moment, when rescue was in sight, my body betrayed me. After three days of battling to stay alive, how ironic it would be to be swallowed up by the sea and drown only a few feet away from safety. But I had no strength left to fight against it.

I would have liked nothing better than to submit, weep until there was nothing left, cry for all the mental and physical pain I had been through in these last three days, but I did not shed a tear. I was too afraid of becoming vulnerable; being emotionally weakened in my circumstances would have been my undoing, of that I was sure. I had held it all inside, but now I felt like a flooded dam about to burst.

I swallowed hard at the lump in my throat. I would have to wait. There was no time for tears now! I was so committed to my seemingly endless mission for survival but my body shrieked for relief. I had no choice but to stop and rest my aching limbs, if only for a minute until the burning stopped. Rolling over onto my back, floating in a spread-eagle position, I drifted along with the waves.

"After three days of battling to stay alive, how ironic it would be to be swallowed up by the sea and drown only a few feet away from safety. But I had no strength left to fight against it."

Half submerged, I wiped the excess water from my stinging eyes. Opening them, I gazed up at the bright orange blaze in the sky, its magnificence and ferocity blinding me. I adored the sun, but at this moment I wished it would slide behind a cloud and give me a break. Within seconds the sun had absorbed all the moisture from my skin, leaving my face taut and painful. With my face tilted toward the sun, I could feel the scorch of heat and realized how badly burnt I was. I had been roasted, almost as surely as in my dream of being cooked by the cannibals for their sacrificial feast.

Shielding my eyes with my hand, I turned back onto my stomach to locate the ship, making sure it hadn't left without me. I'd only rested for about two minutes, but it was adequate enough for me to have caught my breath and calmed my nerves.

With sheer tenacity I resumed swimming, this time lying on my back while simultaneously moving my legs up and down in a rhythmical motion, not unlike the way a dolphin would, I imagine.

This proved to be a very fast and effective way of moving, and it also gave my arms a chance to recover. Again I was reminded why the flippers were far more important than the bottle of water. I never could have made it without them. Thank God, I hadn't gone with my own instincts and grabbed the water bottle. I wouldn't have made it this far and be making this swim to rescue now.

I continually swiveled my head around to assure myself I was keeping on course. The constant wind whipped up the water, gushing it over my face. I repeatedly had to spit out gulps of salty water, at one stage almost choking from a mouthful. The salt from the water burned my raw throat and blistered lips.

What kept me going on this excruciating passage was the thought of a cool glass of fresh water at the end. It was like the piece of candy that was dangled in front of my face while I was swimming; it urged me on. I desperately tried to ignore the torturous pain that attacked every corpuscle and cell in me.

I played a little game, pretending I was doing a workout. I would set a goal of ten strokes for myself and then think, *Okay, Michelle, just ten more strokes. You can do it!* It was the only way I could reduce the mammoth task into manageable portions.

Totally spent of all energy, even that in my reserve tank, and in agony, I eventually found myself within a few feet of the ship. Feeling as if I were on the verge of death from exhaustion, I tried to pull myself back from the precipice. I couldn't afford to fall unconscious now. I had made it, reached survival and rescue; I wasn't about to give them up for anything. Turning back onto my stomach, I swam the last few strokes alongside the ship.

Treading water, I strained my neck to look up. Staring down at me in absolute amazement were a multitude of brown faces. Gasping for breath, I looked to them for directions as to what I should do next. My stomach churned as I quickly gauged the distance between myself and the deck of the ship. It must have been seven to eight feet. How on earth was I going to get up there?

Realizing my dilemma, they quickly threw a rope down the side of the ship saying, "You climb up!"

A dirty yellow rope, approximately an inch thick, unraveled as it fell down toward me. I was immediately reminded of Rapunzel's long, golden, braided hair being thrown down from the ivory tower. Leaning forward I attempted to grab hold of the rope.

Just as my fingers grasped the edge of it, I was abruptly smashed into the side of the ship by a savage wave. I felt my shoulder take the full force of the blow. Then as I moved away from the ship with the current of the wave I felt the shreds of skin attached to the metal fragments of the ship being torn away from my left shoulder as if a grizzly bear had gouged me with his ferocious claws. I opened my mouth to let out a cry of pure agony but it was strangled, silenced as I was engulfed in a torrent of raging froth. Struggling to reach the surface, I felt as if my lungs were exploding from the lack of air. I had to breathe!

At last the sea subsided and allowed me to resurface, and I convulsed in a fit of coughing. I was so close now to being saved, and yet still the struggle to stay alive and afloat was all-consuming. I didn't have the bunca to rest on now, there was nothing between me and the cascades of water that thundered over me. It would be so easy to just give in to the sea, to slip under, instead of carrying on this interminable struggle. God, it would be so very easy!

"With superhuman effort I lunged forward, arms outstretched, and managed to grab hold of the rope. So reassuring in my hands, I knew I held life."

Through salty liquid that filled my burning eyes, I tried to focus and find the rope. Like the pendulum on a grandfather clock, the rope swung back and forth in the wind. With superhuman effort I lunged forward, arms outstretched, and managed to grab hold of the rope. So reassuring in my hands, I knew I held life. With prune-like hands I grabbed onto my lifeline and attempted to haul myself up.

I stifled a sob at the futility of it all. It was useless! My arms ached and my shoulder throbbed. I didn't have the strength to put one hand in front of the other. The truth was, I couldn't have pulled myself up that rope if my life depended on it . . . and it did!

Looking distraught, one of the men called down, "Hold on tight. We'll pull you up." It was only then that I realized they spoke English. Peering up at them I noticed their eyes revealed the glint of excitement and discovery.

I held onto the rope with every scrap of strength I possessed for fear of dropping back into the sea that swarmed with deadly danger. I gritted my teeth in a snarl as the rusty fragments of steel from the ship ripped the flesh of my sunburned stomach and legs as they dragged me up the side. I was assaulted by pain so intense I almost let go of the rope but forcefully I yelled at myself, *No, Michelle, don't you dare let go!*

I knew if I did, death would be inevitable and I wasn't sure if I had the strength or energy to repeat this feat. This was a do-or-die situation! In a silent frenzy I willed myself to hang on. *Oh, God, help me, help me to hold on. You've brought me through these days of hell alive. Hold on to me for just another sixty seconds. Please . . . don't let me go.* My limbs felt like putty, completely saturated through to the bones. I was sure at any moment my arms would just fall out of their sockets as my rescuers hoisted me upwards. I tried to maneuver myself to put distance between my burnt, vulnerable flesh and scraping metal. My efforts, however, were in vain! As I tried to push myself away with my feet, the silicone flippers continually bent, preventing me from protecting myself. It was useless; I would just have to hang on and endure it. I'd suffered so much pain, both mentally and physically already but still I knew my threshold had not been reached; I could tolerate another thirty seconds longer.

Gritting my teeth, I tried to shut myself off from the torment that racked my body, as my skin was ripped to shreds. Craning my neck, I looked up to see how much further I had to go. I was close enough to look directly into the eyes of my rescuers. The rigid tension showed in their faces!

Suddenly I was touched by human hands grabbing frantically onto my outstretched arms in a desperate bid to haul me to safety. It was the most indescribably beautiful sensation to touch another human being, when I'd sometimes wondered whether I'd ever live to see one again. In that touch, all the purity and beauty in the world was revealed to me. I realized that no matter what creed or color, human beings are the same! I knew nothing about these people, but they had reached out and saved my life. There really was enough love in the world to go around.

In their enthusiasm to rescue me they were oblivious to the added pain they were inflicting on me as they hauled me up over the steel rim of the ship's deck, ripping the skin off my stomach. With two pairs of arms under my armpits, I was pulled on deck. For the first time in three days, my feet connected with solid ground!

Oh thank You, thank You, thank You, God! I've made it. The intense relief I experienced at that moment was indescribable, beyond comprehension. I was alive!

The hum of excited voices came to me as if through a haze, penetrating my ear drums. The only words my sodden brain grasped were "Americano Mermaid, it's a Mermaid." Repeatedly the words *Mermaid* and *Serena* resounded in my ears. What were they talking about? At this moment I really didn't care; at last my ordeal was over.

My quivering legs buckled beneath me. Ravaged by acute exhaustion, I succumbed to it. At long last I could give up the fight and sleep. Now that I knew I was safe I stopped struggling and welcomed the oblivion that washed over me. I was instantly engulfed in blackness; a kaleidoscope of flashing stars whirled around in my head as I slipped into unconsciousness.

SIXTEEN

A BATTLE OF WILLS

RACHELLE . . . 5:00 P.M., SATURDAY, MARCH 11, BORACAY ISLAND. I felt as if I had been pushed over an invisible barrier where I was immersed in heart-wrenching grief and feelings of inconsolable loss. I had withdrawn to somewhere beyond myself, where everything had taken on a nebulous quality. Images and reality were fused together in a distorted dimension. I could remember little of the boat trip back to Boracay. The excited chattering of the islanders had ceased. Carved into the silence was an atmosphere of doom.

As we approached the shores outside Willy's Beachfront Cottages, the splash of the anchor hitting the water shook me free from my stupor. I girded myself against the impact of being back on Boracay Island, returning without my child . . . defeated! Holding onto the edge of the boat I jumped barefooted into the three-foot water. Without warning a searing pain shot up my leg. Confused as to what had inflicted such pain, I wondered if I had trodden on a poisonous stone fish. Wading to shore I looked up into Rafel's face, who had obviously been waiting for our return.

"Oh no! What have you done to your foot?" she gasped.

Glancing down, I was shocked at the amount of blood streaming from the deep gouge in my foot. Within a matter of seconds it had colored the white sand to crimson. Two people were instantly at my side, supporting me as I limped back up the beach to Willy's Beachfront Cottages. The deep gash on my foot was seemingly a reflection, an outward manifestation of my bleeding heart. It seemed inevitable that the pain and wretched grief I felt inside would exhibit itself physically. I allowed myself to be escorted to a seat outside. Within seconds of sitting down, the open wound began oozing, forming a pool of blood on the patio floor. I watched with detachment as it gushed out with every palpitation of my heart. I was held mesmerized, observing the scarlet river flow from me.

Life is in the blood, the Bible says. It seemed therefore appropriate that the life force poured from me. *Where do we go when our time on this earth is terminated? Michelle, where are you?* I heard myself scream inside, watching as a bowl of water appeared at my feet. Someone took hold of my leg, a leg that had ceased to feel as if it belonged to me, and tenderly placed the foot into the antiseptically treated water.

Entranced, I allowed these kindly people to minister to my wound. Within seconds the clear water had turned into a blood bath. As someone lifted my foot out of the bowl, I noticed a deep inch-long wedge had been sliced into the side of my big toe. I was vaguely aware of a circle of people surrounding me, voicing words of sympathy and compassion. They were unable to penetrate my armor of self-preservation I had constructed to hold myself together.

A withered old woman appeared clutching a metal box. She placed it down on the table beside me, then with obvious difficulty managed to open the lid. I watched as the crinkled fingers rummaged through the contents, searching out the desired object. As it came into view, I gasped! I saw a large, ominous needle clasped between her fingers, while her other hand held a reel of cotton thread.

Immediately I acknowledged ownership of my foot and decided to reclaim it. There was no way I was going to allow her to stitch me up without anesthetic. *Let it bleed,* I thought! *With any luck I might die and be released from this unbearable torment.* Shaking my head violently from side to side, I snapped out of my apathetic state.

"No needle. I don't want you to stitch me up," I insisted.

The old woman looked offended at my lack of trust in her worthy skills.

"I sew up all the time. I do very good job for you," she said.

"No!" I shouted, louder than I had intended. Instantly regretting my lack of sensitivity, I quickly added, "Thank you very much. You're very kind and I'm sure you're very good, but please, no stitches for me. Just a tight bandage will do."

Robbed of her act of kindness, she regretfully accepted my decision and produced several clean bandages. Stopping the flow of blood was to prove no easy task. However, some twenty minutes later I had my foot bandaged and elevated, resting on a chair. The onlookers had now dispersed; for them the entertainment had passed and they could walk away from it. For me the suffering had only just begun.

Heart-Wrenching Grief

In the hours that ensued, I was totally consumed by my bereavement. I felt I no longer belonged in the realm of the living but in another level of consciousness, where my emotional and physical wounds disconnected from my essential self. As dusk fell, I found myself in Lotti's home, sitting at her dining table with her family. What had transpired during those several hours before dark were lost to me!

But for the moment that didn't matter. I was being nurtured by caring people whose hearts had been affected by my loss and who were mourning with me. They spoke to me of God's grace and His love for His earthly children. They believed with total conviction that Michelle had gone to be with the Lord, that she was safely back in her true home where He had called her to be with Him.

"We are all dying," Lotti theorized. "We are all living on borrowed time, and every day that passes brings us one step closer to home. It's all a matter of the appointed time God has planned for us to depart this world and join Him in heaven. Rachelle, it may help you and be a consolation to know that she's okay and beyond the cares of this world."

I sat and listened, acknowledging the good will in which these words were spoken. They comforted me, a stranger in their midst! The compassionate words and loving sentiments flowed over me like a soothing lullaby. I allowed them to penetrate and assuage my jagged senses, although I knew no words could heal the pain. Only time could do that work. I wasn't able to deal with the reality of losing my daughter just yet. I couldn't see my way towards any answers and frankly, the thought of having to make any decision about Michelle made me slightly hysterical. The only way I knew to temporarily escape this torment was through sleep; knowing that blessed relief awaited me, suddenly I was brutally tired.

❧ ❧ ❧

Sunday March 12 was a day like any other in the South Seas. The clear blue skies crowned the heavens, the heat of the sun hugging the body even at this early hour. It was a splendid morning where one should feel grateful to be alive. The lazy atmosphere of having nothing to do and all day to do it in prevailed in the air—for all except me.

Barefooted, I limped along the water's edge, sinking into the soggy, white sand as I did so. In vain, I attempted to keep the bandage on my injured foot from becoming wet. During the night, my toe had swelled up considerably, causing it to throb relentlessly. In a masochistic sense, I was pleased with the physical pain it was causing, as it drew my attention away from the more grievous emotional ache within my soul.

I had no idea where I was walking; all I knew was that physical movement seemed imperative in keeping my sanity. When I was motionless I experienced an overwhelming sensation of being pressed in on all sides. This feeling had the power to crush me if I allowed it. But I was in a foreign country among strangers, and I knew I had to hold myself together. I was in no state to formulate a plan or make any decisions. There was no tomorrow for me and my two younger daughters; our future had been shattered. The foundation of our lives in ruins. Would our wounds ever heal or would they just close over and form a scab, rupturing open again at every cut life inflicted on us?

I breathed in the fresh morning air, watching the Pacific Ocean gently lick the sands of the ivory shore. I was becoming increasingly concerned about the gash on my foot. I didn't want to take the bandage off for fear the gash had become seriously infected. Yet without antibiotics and fresh bandages it would undoubtedly fester. I knew how easy it was for a cut to become infected in these humid climates, and I could ill afford to let this happen.

Glancing up, I recognized I was opposite Lotti's bungalow. An overwhelming need for human contact washed over me and momentarily blotted out all else. A submerged, infantile longing and primal need for companionship unexpectedly surfaced. Instinctively I wanted to retreat back into the womb, curl up, protect my vulnerable self from experiencing the harshness of life. The desire to be cared for, nurtured, and loved, to have outer protective walls to cocoon and preserve me, was paramount.

I desperately sought an escape to avoid the sword of life which cuts away at the things we love and causes us loss. At this moment I felt incapable of facing this loss alone; it was just too great. The childlike part of my character wanted to be reassured it was okay, that everything would turn out fine. I desperately wanted to believe Lotti could fill this fearful need.

As I limped up her front steps, she appeared at the door welcoming me. I caught an expression of compassion flicker across her face. It was then I realized I must have looked tragic to her, the ravage showing on my face. Nevertheless, she managed to bestow a warm friendly smile upon me.

"Would you like a cool drink?"

"I would, thanks." I responded, grateful for her company.

As we drank Lotti rose to the task of consoling me with reassuring words. The ministering of empathy and compassion is what I had come to her to receive, and her presence had a calming influence on me. I acknowledged my need, realizing that if this accident had happened in Australia I would have been surrounded by a house full of family and

---

"When I was motionless I experienced an overwhelming sensation of being pressed in on all sides. This feeling had the power to crush me if I allowed it."

---

friends to comfort, reassure, and assist me in my search for Michelle. I would have had people to share this awful burden and not left to feel the terrible isolation I now experienced. Being alone in this foreign country, it was impossible to escape the feelings of utter desolation.

Then the enormity of what I was expecting her to fulfil occurred to me. No human being was capable of quenching such an intense need for solace. I was bereft; no one could mitigate my utter misery. God is the author of life and death, and it was to Him I needed to turn. Up until now I'd avoided seeking God's help. With the exception of several desperate pleas, I hadn't entered into genuine prayer.

I had never imagined it would come to this. I was still operating on my own natural strength. I'd been saving God as my trump card, a last-ditch effort if all else failed. Now I had exhausted all human endeavours, and it was blatantly obvious I had nowhere else to turn. My need to be comforted was all consuming. Lotti had done her best to balm my anguish, but to reach a state of mind where I was able to come to terms with the death of Michelle was beyond what any human could achieve.

A deep yearning came over me. I urgently needed to talk to God, to be in His presence and allow Him to minister to my aching soul. By this stage I truly believed Michelle had perished on the first night in the storm, but I still had resolutely held onto a trace of hope. I was compelled to go through the motions of looking for her, in case there may have been even a slight chance that she could have survived such an onslaught in as fragile a craft as she had set out in.

"Lotti, I really feel the need to pray. Is there a church on the island?"

"Yes, we do have one. It's behind Rafel's place. In fact there will be a service held at 9:30 this morning."

"Of course, it's Sunday, isn't it?" I'd completely lost track of what day it was. "Listen, Lotti, I really need a favor. Could you spread the word around and get as many people as possible to attend? I want to hold a prayer service for Michelle. I don't know if she's alive or dead, but wherever she is she needs our prayers."

"Okay, I think that's a good idea. I'll tell everybody and we can meet you there at 9:30."

"Thanks a lot, Lotti, I really appreciate everything you have done for me."

"It's the least I could do, Rachelle. Would you like to borrow my Bible?"

"Thanks so much. That's very thoughtful of you. I would. Hopefully I'll find solace in the Word."

She handed me a well-worn, obviously much-loved Bible. Holding it to my heart with both hands, I left Lotti's house and slowly made my way toward the church. Holding the reverent Word of God encased in this book touched me deeply and reunited me with the awareness of God. Tears of confusion and anguish poured down my cheeks.

Why, oh why, God, have You taken her from me? Please help me to understand why You didn't prevent this tragedy from happening. You've got millions of people in heaven. All I have in my life are my three daughters. Is it too much to ask for You to spare her? She's so precious to me. There must be thousands of old and sick people on earth who are just waiting to die. What purpose could possibly be served by her death, when she's so young and healthy and hasn't even had a chance to live her life yet? I feel so sad to think she will never know the joys of being a wife or mother. It seems so unnatural that a parent should outlive any of her children. How could You do this to Michelle? I feel so disillusioned by what has happened. I thought You were a loving and merciful God.

When I gave my life to You three months ago, I believed You would protect me and my children. You say in the Bible to trust and have faith in You, but how can I continue to believe in Your words after this has happened? You may as well take me too because I no longer have the desire to live in this world without Michelle.

I wrestled and argued my case with God as I continued along the trail on my way to the church. When people recognized me as the bereaved mother, they stood aside and allowed me to pass. Since this ordeal had begun, I discovered a peculiar phenomena: people became embarrassed by death or tragedy and they avoided my eyes and became

---

"How ironic it was to find myself in this place. What invisible network of circumstances had brought me to this moment in time and to what purpose? It was beyond my understanding."

---

tongue-tied. Mostly they completely steered clear of the bereaved person. At a time when a person most needed human contact and love, people were unable to face the dilemma of death and their own mortality. Perhaps it made them question where their destination would be if they too were taken suddenly. Up or down, heaven or hell? We have to stand back and acknowledge our own frailty and know that God is sovereign, Lord over all creation. Life and death is in His hands, not ours!

As I came into a clearing, there standing in a field of grass was a concrete building that resembled a church. It was not quite what I had imagined but a church nevertheless. I picked my way through the ankle-deep grass, looking up at this structure that was the house of God. I swung back one of the doors that leaned off one of its rusty hinges and gingerly stepped inside.

The building was not much more than a concrete shell with windows. In spite of its humble appearance, I held it in the same reverence with which I did the magnificent churches I'd seen in Europe. I believed it was not the outward appearance that mattered but the One who dwelled within. I walked halfway down the empty church and sat on one of the wooden bench pews that were facing a simple altar.

How ironic it was to find myself in this place. What invisible network of circumstances had brought me to this moment in time and to what purpose? It was beyond my understanding. My thoughts traveled down a road of memories and stopped at the first time I had entered a church—only three months earlier.

My Own Search for God

After many years of weaving through the occult, new age thinking, philosophy and psychology, reading literally hundreds of books on many varied subjects, in essence I was no better off. This knowledge fed my mind and my curiosity, but it never balmed the yearning of my soul or brought me any real joy. I was a more well-balanced person and was admired by many for my courage and achievements, but the stone lodged in my heart was no closer to being removed.

The understanding I had acquired through much study equipped me to intellectualize and rationalize my situation. In every circumstance I'd be able to analyze exactly what was happening and why, which in honesty did momentarily help, but there was no happiness or lasting effect, merely a superficial reprieve which had as much effect as a bandaid on a cancerous growth. The mental knowledge didn't have the dynamics to regenerate my soul. The puzzle of life remained with many pieces missing. I despaired of ever finding the crucial element to complete my understanding so that life would make sense to me and have a definite purpose and meaning.

In the midst of this quandary, I was on the brink of discovering the spiritual principle that would forever change my life and permanently transform me into a new person. The desire of my heart which I'd been searching for as long as I could remember—the thing that would absolutely satisfy my inner hunger, quench my burning desires, and give me the answers to unanswerable questions, the thing that would fill me with indescribable joy and peace—was now only a heartbeat away.

Throughout the past years I'd been looking for the food of life in all the wrong places. The golden truth had in simplicity been lying at my feet all along, but I'd been too blind and proud to see it. I was so intent in my own determination to find the truth that I had delved into complex human sciences and man-made opinions and theories. While I was reaching for the pie in the sky, I'd overlooked the orthodox way of finding God. It happened this way. . . .

Michelle had been in Japan for approximately six months. The girls went to school and I to work. On the surface life was acceptable, but inwardly I was crying out with loneliness. Under enormous stress, I carried a heavy workload as we neared the peak of Christmas advertising. With daily deadlines to meet, advertising was at its pinnacle; simultaneously I was compiling a twenty-four page business supplement entirely on my own. My brain had begun to short-circuit with the sheer pressure of it all. Leading up to Christmas, I had been beseiged by a series of catastrophes one after another. My health suffered both mentally and physically, driving me to near breaking point.

In the midst of this tense activity a fateful set of circumstances were propelled into motion.

On a sunny afternoon a friend invited me out to lunch. My spirits were high; I was singing along with the car stereo as I drove to the restaurant, very much looking forward to a pleasant outing with an interesting acquaintance. As I was driving around a winding bend in the road, without warning, my car struck a patch of oil on the road. I felt the grip of the tires lose their hold as I began to careen over the other side of the road into the path of an oncoming car.

As we sped toward each other on a collision course, in one frozen, heart-stopping moment our eyes met, seconds before impact. In that brief, timeless instant my life flashed before my eyes. I thought to myself, *This is it!* A split second later I felt myself thrown forward, my head smashing into the steering wheel with a powerful blow. After the car had come to a standstill, my first reaction was, *I'm still alive.*

I moved my legs and my arms tentatively. They seemed okay. Glancing down, I saw my blouse was covered in blood. Where was it coming from? Then I felt the warm liquid trickling into my eyes, thick oozing blood impairing my vision.

Oh no, not my face, I screamed inwardly in horror. Still strapped into the car by the seat belt, I leaned over and swiveled the rear view mirror toward me, then instantly regretted my decision. I had no forehead! It had been split open and was now crumpled back in a distorted bloody mess of folded skin on top of my head. I could feel myself slipping into unconsciousness when I heard shouts outside the car. "Open the door. Can you hear me? Unlock the door!" Obediently I leaned over and lifted up the lock.

The next thing I remember was opening my eyes and seeing paramedics around me, then hearing the wailing scream of the ambulance siren as I was sped to the hospital. They stitched me up, kept me for observation overnight, and then sent me home. My car had been reduced to an irreparably twisted wreck; they told me I was incredibly lucky to be alive. At that time I wasn't so sure; to die would have been an easy way out, a peaceful escape forever.

But it was not to be. I had to continue, to pick up the pieces once again. The despair of losing my uninsured car when I had only two more payments to make before owning it outright was a severe blow. I felt a bitter resentment when I had religiously made those payments over the past few years and was so near my goal of ownership. I had lost a car worth six thousand dollars—with no recompense. I took a week off work to recover, got a loan from the bank, bought another car, and carried on.

Then catastrophe number two fell upon me at a time when I was at the lowest and most hopeless point of my life. Picking up my mail after work several weeks later, I opened a letter that threw me into utter disbelief. I was delivered an eviction notice for the day after Christmas. This was inconceivable! According to the agreement with the landlord, the conditions of my rental only allowed for one child and not two. It constituted overcrowding, and I was being asked to vacate the premises in two weeks.

Outraged and in total confusion, I went to see the local magistrate to fight the eviction order but to no avail. A woman on her own was prey to further disaster and that would surely occur if I allowed myself to cave in. If I fell, who would pick me up and what would become of my children? I drove myself like a mechanical robot with nothing left inside of me but broken-down machinery that continued to operate, purely out of habit. I found new accommodations, and several girls from work volunteered to help me pack up, and we moved again.

I was brutally tired of our nomadic lives and longed for a sanctuary, a place to rest, a retreat from the harshness of life. I found none. The rent had to be paid! Many times during this period, without warning I would black out from stress. I found I couldn't remember what I meant to be doing. My clients' demands were still met, my company got a solid day's work out of me, my children were being cared for as best I could provide for them, and the landlord got his rent. But as for me, there was no one attending to me; circumstances dictated that my needs went unmet. I had no one to shoulder the burden.

Quite obviously there is only so long a person can carry on under this kind of pressure, and my days were numbered. My breaking point came one Friday morning!

My diary was filled with appointments with clients. We had a morning where Murphy's Law had been operating in full force, and by the time the children were ready to go off to school I was ready to go back to bed. Of course that wasn't possible. I had a briefcase full of artwork and layouts to put into production by ten o'clock that morning. These I had taken home to work on so I could keep my head above water. Feeling already frazzled, I opened the car door, threw my briefcase into the back seat, thrust the key into the ignition, and was ready to go. The car, however, was not!

I heard the ignition click over, but the engine remained dead. I sat riveted to the seat as an inward explosion of tension began to erupt. A million tightly-wound strings snapped, creating a trauma within, which I felt discharge through my entire being. Everything was caving in around me. Shaking violently I went back into the house, called a garage and requested assistance, phoned work explaining my dilemma, then sat down unable to do a thing to help myself.

I felt like a juggler who by his experience and skill attempts to keep the balls in the air and prevent them from falling around him. I also had tried to maintain the balance but I had no strength of will left to keep my life from collapsing. I gave up the struggle! My will to succeed had failed. All my striving had been in vain. In that moment of surrender I fell to my knees on the floor and let out a heart-wrenching cry for help directed at God, who I believed had ignored, deserted, and punished me relentlessly. My cry shattered the silence.

"My God, my God, why have You foresaken me?" I screamed out, feeling like a trapped and wounded animal. "I can't do this anymore by myself. Help me, please help me." I felt as if a hard outer shell inside of me had cracked, then completely broken open.

Through that opening poured a shaft of divine light. An amazing love flowed through my entire being, like a silent river of joy, filling every cell. The whole room appeared to be saturated with light; in that glorious moment I knew my cry had been heard in the heavens and had been answered. I felt the presence of my God, the God of Israel, the one I had sought for so long. The divine touch from heaven was real and tangible. I instinctively knew in that instant I had been miraculously transformed, and my life would never be the same again. In the darkest moment in my life a reprieve had come. I'd inadvertently turned the key to the door of life and allowed God into my heart.

Like the prodigal son, I had returned to my heavenly Father. After living my life my own way I approached Him, defeated, broken, weary in spirit and tired of carrying the load. Now I was only too willing to obey my Father and live the life He had planned for me from the beginning of time. He received me back with joy for I had been lost to Him, but now He had found me again. He then poured His spirit and blessings upon me.

All those painful years of searching were fruitless; I was looking for the truth in the writings and philosophies of man instead of relying on the provision God had made for His children.

How ironic! I had spent forty years in search of God. Through my own misunderstanding I had wandered in a spiritual wilderness similar to our forefathers in the desert before they found the promised land. I also had to wait forty years for God's promise to be fulfilled in me. I wanted to shout for joy and tell the world of my revelation. But that would have to wait. The knock on the door signified that the man from the service station had arrived to fix my car. The world would have to wait to hear of my discovery.

For the next few months I was carried along by the Holy Spirit of God. I felt a certain peace and assurance I had never known before. My life was still far from being what I would have wished, nevertheless I felt a serene acceptance of my situation. One of my colleagues from work was a Christian and gently persuaded me to come to visit her church. A resistance within me I couldn't explain prevented me, and I continued to decline her offer.

Driving around in my car one day feeling rather lost to the world, I headed my vehicle on a street which I had never been down before. I was struck by the peculiarity of what had influenced me to make that turn, as if an unseen force beckoned me there.

As I reached the end of the road, I was exasperated to discover it was a dead end and the road was almost too narrow to make a U-turn. Feeling discouraged, I sat there helplessly wondering what I should do.

Seeing a way through a narrow path, I thought I might drive through there when these words sounded in my head, "You have nowhere else to turn."

Looking up I saw the side of a large, modern, brick building. Right in front of me the words "Christian City Church" were clearly written.

The words reverberated through me. I spoke to myself, "It's true. I have nowhere else to turn." This time I received the message loud and clear.

"God, You're trying to tell me something, aren't You? You want me to go into that church," I said, dumbfounded by the simplicity of God's communication and His message to me. "Okay, if that is what You want me to do, I will obey."

With a new purpose I checked the local newspaper for the details of when the next service would be held. I committed myself to be present at that meeting. Not voicing a word to anyone, not even the Christian girl from work, I prepared myself for this willing act of entering a Christian church intentionally with a purpose in mind, although I knew not what it was and what to expect.

Sunday came! I dressed conservatively, and not without some trepidation did I enter this unfamiliar environment alone. Walking self-consciously through the double doors I was met by the overwhelming presence of God. As I moved toward a vacant seat I was bathed in all-encompassing love. I felt like a weary traveler who had wandered aimlessly along the highways of life, as if I had sojourned many years in a strange land without finding any rest and now had at last come home. I sat throughout the service attempting to contain the fire of love that had ignited within me and now burned with a hunger that only God could satisfy.

After the pastor had delivered his sermon, he asked, "If anyone here is hurting, if you feel lonely or empty and are tired of struggling in your life, then you need Jesus. He said He will restore the wounded spirit and be a balm for human suffering. If that is you, then come forward and receive new life and His bountiful blessings. There is no other name under heaven by which man can be saved. Only through Jesus can you receive salvation and eternal life. He said, 'I am the bread of life; he who comes to me shall never hunger and he who believes in me shall never thirst.'

"Please, come forward if you want to exchange your old life of heartache and suffering for a new life of joy. He will satisfy your deepest need."

It was as if the pastor were directing his words solely at me. I didn't need to be asked twice; nothing could have prevented my accepting his invitation.

Rising to my feet I walked toward the altar as if I were a bride about to meet my bridegroom awaiting there. Tears of unspeakable joy flowed unashamedly down my cheeks as I stood in the presence of two hundred people and received Jesus as Messiah of Israel, Lord and Savior. In that moment I gave my life to Him and asked Him to live in my heart. I became born again, not born of flesh but of the Spirit of God. From now on He was Lord over my life. I stood in the presence of the King of all men and accepted Jesus as God's Anointed.

No words I knew could ever express that blessed communion whereby through the grace of God I received His Son. I'd been forgiven of my sins and received eternal life. What greater joy could be had in the world than to know I was one with Him and through His death had been reconciled to the God of Abraham. I had received the treasure; Jesus was my prize. My forty-year dedication and pursuit of the truth had finally reaped the reward. I had been humbled and broken that I might turn to Him who created me.

"Behold, I stand at the door and knock. If anyone hears My voice and opens the door, I will come in to him and dine with him, and he with Me" (Revelation 3:20). This promise had truly been fulfilled. I was lifted from the dust of hopelessness into a new life of trust and faith and love and joy.

During the months that followed I allowed Jesus to nurture and teach me His ways. I experienced such exhilaration. My God was no longer far-off. He was not an idea or a dead, impotent God written up in the pages of the Old Testament. He was the God of the living. I had been united with Him and there was no separation. Through Jesus He had become a reality and now lived inside that empty space within me that was reserved specifically for His spirit. He shone a light of truth on my life and showed me how darkened my soul had become with man-made doctrines, traditions, and philosophies clogged with misconceptions and contradictions. I realized that only God's Word brought revelation and new life to the soul.

Now I understood what was meant by the "Kingdom of Heaven is within." I was experiencing this as reality. I realized all those years of believing in God, reading about Him, searching for Him was not enough to open the door to the truth. Knowledge of the things of God and knowing Him personally are two entirely separate things.

I discovered the mistake I had made by being a good person; it was not enough, for God expected me to act on that belief. I had to ask Him to come and take charge of my life and surrender my will to live my life, to make my own decisions which had continually led me into strife and heartache. I had to live my life God's way according to His plans and purpose for me. Surely He must have a better knowledge of what's right for me. I had tried it my way for forty years and failed miserably. Now I would do it God's way!

Jesus, God's Anointed from the beginning of time and spoken about by all the prophets, was the answer all along. He was the crucial missing part to my puzzle; only through Him could I be reconciled to God. Yes, Jesus was right when He said, "I am the way, and the truth, and the life; no one comes to the Father, but through me" (John 14:6, NAS). Human pride had corrupted my heart from seeing the truth, believing I had a better way than the one God had laid out for my life in the Bible.

From that point on my longing to know about Jesus was a burning, heartfelt desire. I had denied Him long enough. If He shed blood and died for me so I could stand without sin, clean before God, then I owed Him my total love and dedication. For the first time in my life I began to read the Bible. As I read the Word of God, it came alive. Certain verses would leap out at me, and the truth of the words would penetrate the darkness of my soul. Every word was precious, like treasure from heaven. I found comfort, love, and peace in those words, a far cry to what I had formerly believed was written there. It became my daily spiritual food. The answers to life's mysteries were strewn like jewels across its pages.

How could I have been so blind for so long? The emptiness I had carried within me all these past years had been miraculously filled to overflowing with the presence of God I had received through His Son, Jesus.

Have Faith

Only three months later, here I was in a humble church on a remote island in the Philippines pleading for my daughter's life. I placed the Bible on my lap and began rocking gently back and forth. The motion had a calming effect on me. For several minutes I was unable to do anything but nurse my shredded nerves. Gradually my mouth started to move and I began to pray, to beg for God's mercy on Michelle, myself, and my family. "Dear God, You know why I'm here—to plead for Michelle's life. Lord, if I've done anything to offend You, then please forgive me but don't punish me by taking Michelle from me. You know my heart and everything about me, so I don't need to tell You how much she means to me. Please let her live for her sisters and my sake."

Again, a flashing image of Michelle, floating face down in the water flooded my mind. "God, is it too late? Has she gone already? Are my pleas in vain? Only You know the truth; only You know her destiny. So if it's too late to ask You to save her, then please receive her into heaven and keep her safe until the day when we will see her again. Lord, I know she belongs to You. You created her, and she is ultimately Your child, not mine. I did nothing other than to raise this beautiful girl for You, but now it seems that You have staked Your claim, retrieved what was Yours and called her home.

"So if this be Your will, then I relinquish my earthly hold on her and offer her back to You and give You thanks, Lord, for the precious gift You lent to me. But if it is not Your will to take her at this time, then please bring her back to me. I know You are the Creator of the universe and every living thing. You have the power to save her. It's Your ultimate choice and decision. But please don't use her to teach me a lesson. I'll learn a better lesson if You let her live. I promise I will never ask for another thing in my life if You send her back to me."

My prayers swung wildly, alternating from one side to another; from being angry and challenging God for the enormous mistake He had made in selecting Michelle for death at her young age, then relenting and throwing myself on His mercy and grace, pleading for Him to save her.

I became humble and praised Him, offering Him my faith and loyalty no matter what the outcome. "Lord, I trust Your judgment and wisdom and realize it's Your will, not my will, that has precedence. Besides, who am I to say what is right or wrong? I want You to know, God, that no matter what, the love and faith I have for You are infallible. If this is Your will for my daughter, then take her back home. I commit her into Your care."

The vision of Abraham offering Isaac up to God in utter faith appeared in my mind. Without warning the most poignant words came tumbling into my head. "Have faith and trust in Me for all things, for you only have a piece of the puzzle, but I have the whole picture and know the plans I have for you."

"What do you mean by that?" I called out, realizing that I had spoken the question aloud. The voice did not respond, but I had the sudden distinct impulse to open the Bible. Without forethought I picked it up and flung it open at random. Where my eyes fell I began to read.

> *God is in the midst of her,*
> *she shall not be moved;*
> *God shall help her,*
> *just at the break of dawn.*
> (Psalm 46:5)

This passage triggered a flame of hope. Could I dare believe this was a message from God and truly conveyed something tangible that I could hold on to? In the frazzled state I was in, I wasn't sure. My faith was such, however, that I knew all things were possible with God. In

---

"In that moment, a sensation of extraordinary peace flowed through me and I knew my little girl was in God's hands, whether she was still of this world or had passed from it."

---

that moment, a sensation of extraordinary peace flowed through me and I knew my little girl was in God's hands, whether she was still of this world or had passed from it. All was well, and I had the feeling of being taken care of by my heavenly Father. I had submitted to His will. It was the only thing to do. The clay had no right to question the Potter!

SEVENTEEN

THE CAPTURE OF THE AUSSIE MERMAID

MICHELLE . . . 3:00 P.M., SATURDAY, MARCH 11, SOUTH CHINA SEA. Through the blurry veils of darkness and confusion I slowly returned to consciousness. Foreign voices shattered the earthly silence within my head. Groggily, I came to life! Where was I? Who were these people? I felt several hands slip under my back and legs; the dead weight of my body yielded to their strength as I was lifted off the cold steel floor of the ship's deck. Semiconscious with my eyes still closed, I knew I was being carried.

A cacophony of excited yet nervous voices shouted instructions to one another. Although they were speaking in a language I didn't understand, through the commotion I got the general gist of their conversation. It sounded as if they were saying, "Okay, turn left here"; "Be careful, don't drop her"; "Let's take her into the cabin." Then those words I'd first heard when I was dragged aboard rang distinctly in my ears, "Serena, Mermaid," a man said with a note of wonderment in his voice.

I could feel them struggling to carry my practically lifeless body. I was like a real-life rag doll, unable to keep any of my limbs from flopping around. In a matter of minutes I had deteriorated from total control of my body, strong and determined while I was still fighting the sea for my life, to total uselessness. As soon as I realized the battle was over and I was safe, I collapsed, knowing I could succumb to mental and physical exhaustion. I felt as if my brain had been sucked out of my head by a powerful vacuum cleaner; only my cranium was left intact, an empty shell with nothing inside, just a blank, dark space.

Crunch! A stabbing pain shot through my leg as the men carrying me accidently miscalculated the width of the doorway, crashing me into the side of the steel door. The pain quickly ceased, as if I had hit my funny bone; it hurt only momentarily then became numb like the rest of my body. After the multitude of blows my body had received and being constantly submerged in water for three days, I'd become almost immune to pain.

They delicately placed me on to a type of bunk on the bottom bed. At first the bed felt heavenly; it was such a relief to have support for my body, to let go and allow every muscle in my body to relax. While I was at sea I wondered if I would ever experience the feeling of lying down again. In the ensuing hours, however, the bed I had first thought was bliss became painfully uncomfortable. I realized with some dismay that I was lying on nothing more than a steel slab covered over with a piece of linoleum. Oh, I had dreamed of a mattress that would cushion my battered body, contouring into my shape, absorbing all the torn muscles and bruised tissue.

However painful, this was really irrelevant in the face of being alive and in safe hands. I knew now that these people would take good care of me; of that I had no doubt. I could sense it in their gentle touch, hear it in the tones of their compassionate voices. The intense relief I felt was overwhelming; I had fought the sea with everything I possessed, and I had preserved my life, with the obvious help from God, of course! I could now relax, give up the fight, and let other people take care of me. I was immensely grateful to hand over the reins to someone else at last. How blissful it was to rest in the cradle of security, knowing God had chosen these people to save me. Now I could sleep. Oh, how I had longed for this blessed moment.

Tender Care

Desperately, I called out for something my body needed even more than sleep. "Water" I heard myself speak, the words coming out of numbed lips. My voice sounded like a pathetic squeak. No sooner were the words uttered than I fell back exhausted on to the steel cot. I felt a soft, warm hand squeeze itself under the base of my neck, elevating my head up into a position that enabled me to drink. I felt a cool glass of water being placed against my bruised lips.

A spark of long forgotten joy was ignited within me. The touch and sound of human companionship and water were the two things I had most desired; I was now receiving them both simultaneously. The cool liquid rolled off my severely dehydrated tongue and slid down my throat, quenching my parched thirst. Greedily, almost in a frenzy, I gulped down huge mouthfuls of water. I just couldn't get enough—would I ever? It was not only my mouth that was dehydrated, but every living cell cried out for moisture. My eyes craved the liquid that allowed

---

"The touch and sound of human companionship and water were the two things I had most desired; I was now receiving them both simultaneously."

---

them motion; my cooked brain screamed for the life-replenishing elements; layers of torched and dehydrated skin begged to be quenched of their dying thirst. Even my hair felt as if it had the life burned out of it. How would I ever get it back to its usual silky condition? This kind and gentle stranger was reviving my almost dead body back to life. I wondered if he realized that.

Opening my eyes, I gazed around the room to get my bearings and familiarize myself with the surroundings. However, a wall of wide-eyed young Asian men stared anxiously down at me, blocking the view of the room. The burning curiosity about who or what I was was etched into their faces, evident in their sparkling brown eyes. I suppose I was a total mystery to them. They had found me in the middle of nowhere, hundreds of nautical miles out to sea, a half-naked, blonde-haired woman, wearing flippers, a bikini, and clinging on to what remained of a bunca. What on earth would they be thinking? Their faces revealed how stupefied they were. Chattering animatedly between themselves, they peered inquisitively down at me.

Again I heard them say, "Serena, Mermaid" repeatedly. The words registered in my mind but I was too completely exhausted to contemplate its meaning further. One of the young boys kneeling on the floor at the foot of my bunk attempted to pull off my flippers.

"Oooch," I screamed in agony. "Stop!" I said, adamantly gesturing with my hands the signal for stop. I couldn't believe how distorted my voice sounded; it was as if I couldn't speak English. The words that came out were thick and hoarse.

I saw by the expression on his face that I had offended him when he was only trying to help, so I relented. "Okay, but please be gentle!"

He nodded, plainly understanding me. Gritting my teeth in agony, I allowed him to remove the flippers from feet that were totally numb. Blue and purple bruises splotched the part where the rubber section of the flipper had securely gripped my foot, cutting off the circulation. It had left a deep indentation carved into my skin across the crown of my foot. As the flippers were removed, a rush of blood raced through my feet, electrifying them into a pulsating, tingling vibration of pins and needles so ferocious that they felt more like steel darts plunging into my flesh.

The ravaging pain was so acute that I could think of nothing else. At the same time I felt a measure of relief that I was able to feel anything at all. When the bunca capsized, my feet had throbbed incessantly after the first few hours of wearing the flippers. The next stage was a deep ache formed within the muscles and bones; after five hours they were numb. It was a terribly scary feeling, but my alternative was not much more appealing. The thought of my naked feet dangling in the ocean was a far more ghastly option. Hence, the extremely tight and uncomfortable flippers remained on my feet. The thought of getting gangrene or some other gruesome affliction had crossed my mind. I was afraid that the foot would be dead from the lack of circulation and may have to be cut off. I decided to risk the consequences. What other choice had I?

The sodden, deadened nerve endings encased in my foot were now activated by the rush of blood. They screamed in protest as they awoke from their deep sleep. I thought by now I had become accustomed to pain, but obviously I was wrong. Never had I anticipated pain like this; it was pure torture. And little did I know that this was just the beginning of the agony I would have to endure.

As the sea water began to evaporate from my skin the severity of my dehydration and burns became apparent. While I had been submerged in the ocean, the cool water had kept my body temperature down and my skin quenched. Now that I had been removed from the water my skin had become incredibly dry. Salt had ingrained itself into every pore, making my skin as taut and stiff as a piece of cardboard.

I suddenly felt suffocated by the claustrophobically small room jammed with people. The fiery heat radiating off my body made me feel as though I were sitting right on top of an open fire. The heat generating from my scorched skin seemed to eat up what little fresh air there was in the room. The extent of my burns made me worry. What if the damage was irreparable? Only time would tell. Anyway, this was not the time to worry about something as superficial as sunburn. I should be thankful I was alive with all my limbs intact and a mind that had remained completely sane! Considering the circumstances I'd lived through, it was nothing short of miraculous.

No Americano Mermaid

A young man who introduced himself as Marcial Batingas, the ship's oiler, said, "Excuse me, ma'am, I'll take this off so you'll sleep more comfortably," pointing to my money belt. I'd altogether forgotten that my money belt was still strapped around my waist; it had become an appendage, an extension of my body. I'd been wearing it for the past year while traveling extensively throughout Asia. It was so comfortable that I was barely aware of its existence.

He cautiously lifted me into an upright position while his mate leaned around my back and undid the catch on my money belt. I watched as he unzipped the pouch and pulled out the sodden items that were plastered together, obviously searching for some sort of identification.

Staring into their faces, I noticed their eyes held a thousand burning questions, as yet unanswered. Who was I? Where did I come from? How did I get to be in the middle of the ocean?

Recognizing my passport, he singled out this item for inspection. As he opened the cover, he read the details and looked at me dumbfounded then burst into spontaneous, gleeful laughter. Showing it to his shipmates, he spoke in Tagalog something I didn't understand, which caused them all to join in laughing. I couldn't fathom their strange sense of humor; it was all very much a mystery to me. The laughter that filled the small room was contagious, however, although owing to my cracked and bruised lips, I could only smile inwardly. I had no idea what was so funny.

As he lowered the passport to show his friends, I noticed that although the plastic covering that protected the photo and vital information had escaped damage, the inner pages had unfortunately not fared so well. Every stamped page was now a smudged inky mess. But at least now they knew who I was!

One young man who had evidently taken charge of this conversation looked first at the front cover, then at the photo, and lastly at me. "She no Americano mermaid. She is Australian," he said excitedly, pointing his finger at me.

Was it mermaid they were saying? Did they really think I was a mermaid? Surely they were joking! Or maybe not? I supposed it was feasible. Besides, what else were they to think? They had hauled me out of the sea, hundreds of miles away from civilization wearing no more than a bikini and flippers. My long blonde hair seemed to serve as verification that I must be a mermaid.

Their discovery that I was only a mere mortal shattered their fantasy. It must have been a terrible disappointment to them not to have caught the catch of a lifetime. They hadn't in fact captured a mythical half-fish, half-woman creature; they had simply rescued an Aussie castaway, a mere mortal. Now their chances of bringing a live mermaid back from the ocean for the eyes of the world would be dashed.

On the contrary, however, I detected an expression of relief on their faces as if they were pleased I was only human after all!

"Is that you?" he said in perfect English while pointing to the photo in my passport.

Suddenly it dawned on me that they spoke English fluently. I had imagined these cultured, mild-mannered young men to be brutal pirates—ridiculous! Although at that time my imagination was working overtime, the possibility of pirates preying in these waters and my being captured by them was not all that absurd.

"Yes," I said, only barely able to form the words. My jaws were tightly clamped together as if they had been wired shut. My own voice sounded foreign in my ears. I was scarcely able to form the word *yes*. It was almost as if I had forgotten how to pronounce it, as if I were the foreigner attempting to speak English while they fluently chatted away to each other in my mother tongue.

In three days I had reverted to infancy; I was like a baby, unable to feed myself, go to the toilet, walk, or even speak. It was infuriating to be so totally dependent on other people for my every need. This was a totally alien experience for me. Being such an active and independent person, I'd never been in a situation where I was completely reliant on another person for my well-being as I was now.

Even worse than this was being without my voice to ask for the things my body so desperately needed. The most ghastly aspect of my being mute was the frustration of not being able to tell them of my ordeal and relate the desperate urgency of getting a message to Mum on Boracay Island to tell her I was alive. Fortunately for me, my disability was merely a temporary impairment that I would recover from with water, food, and rest.

As I was lifted into a sitting position so I could have yet another drink of water, I noticed the terrible burns on my legs. Not only was I severely burnt and as red as a broiled lobster, but the top layers of my

---

"They had hauled me out of the sea, hundreds of miles away from civilization wearing no more than a bikini and flippers. My long blonde hair seemed to serve as verification that I must be a mermaid."

---

skin were badly wrinkled from three days of being totally immersed in water. My young skin resembled that of an eighty-year-old.

I knew the ship's crew had a thousand questions to ask me and I them, but at that moment sleep was the only thing I was capable of. Clasping my hands together in a praying gesture, I placed them against my cheek indicating I wanted to sleep. They seemed to understand my body language and many of them moved away from my bed and sat at a table on the other side of the room. A young man named Nelson Zurita placed a cool, clean sheet over me before leaving. He soon came back to place a bottle of fizzy orange drink beside my bed. I was so excruciatingly thirsty that I longed to pick up the bottle and gulp down its refreshing contents. As I made an effort to reach for it, however, I found I couldn't even extend my arm, let alone lift my head.

As my eyelids fluttered moments before the sleep my body so desperately craved engulfed me, I was filled with a horrible premonition. If I closed my eyes once, I may never open them again. I was terrified that I would slip into a very deep sleep or become comatose. I was more than likely being paranoid but I couldn't help but be scared of falling asleep, even though I was powerless to stop it.

The sensation of needing sleep overpowered everything else. Closing my eyes, I felt myself spiraling downwards; the force that was dragging me under was incredibly powerful as it drew me into its whirlpool. Down and down I kept traveling, unable to pull myself back up to the surface. Like being in a black, cavernous vortex, I felt myself whirl around and around until I was sucked forcibly into its core. I was terrified to succumb to its potent force, but I felt so utterly helpless to do anything else.

Please protect me from any bad dreams. Watch over and keep me safe while I sleep, I asked God silently before slipping into a black, dense slumber.

My ravaging thirst awoke me some time later; it was even more demanding than my need to sleep. Like an insatiable beast it took predominance over all else, requiring immediate attention. I don't know how long I slept but it felt as though I had returned from the dead. I made an exhausting effort to lean over and grab the bottle of fizzy drink next to my bed, when suddenly I felt a hand clasp mine.

"Here, let me help you" said Nelson the helpful young man. Lifting my head up, he put the bottle against my lips and poured the delicious orange drink in my mouth.

Now, fizzy drinks taken upside down, are most inadvisable; the effervescent bubbles exploded in my nose making me choke on the liquid. So he lifted me into a sitting position and patted my back until I had recovered from my coughing fit. The concern and sympathy generating from his warm brown eyes was touching. I didn't know whether to laugh or cry, and frankly I didn't have the energy to do either.

Something special passed between us, and in that instant I understood the folly of racism and prejudice. How can we segregate human beings into races, creeds, and colors? People are the same no matter where or what we are. This gracious man before me had more than likely experienced the same emotions as I had. He would have felt fear and love and probably had his heart broken; he would have experienced euphoria and happiness and most likely hate, the most destructive of all emotions. He went to work, he had a family, he brushed his teeth, ate, made love, lived, and would eventually die exactly as I would. If we are all God's children, then that would make this man my brother, my equal, my friend. Who knows? We might sit on the same cloud in heaven together one day and talk about the time he rescued me—that is, if there are clouds in heaven.

Looking him squarely in the eyes, I said, "Thank you for saving my life," with an unfathomable sense of gratitude.

His reply confirmed everything I would have expected from such a selfless character. "It is not I who saved your life, but God! Surely you must realize that." These blessed words reiterated everything that had happened during my ordeal. The supernatural miracles, the audible voice of God instructing me and breathing the promise of eternal life into my body, and His divine angels sent down from heaven to protect me. Although I knew beyond any doubt that I had not imagined any of this, Nelson's words were grounded in reality and I was the living witness!

"I can see how extremely painful it is for you to talk so I'll leave you to rest for awhile."

"No, it's okay. I know you must be dying of curiosity to know how I got to be stranded hundreds of miles out at sea."

All his shipmates now huddled around me for what would be a who, why, how, and when question-and-answer time. Although I was still exhausted, the pint of water which they had given me had loosened my tongue and enabled me to speak a little. Despite my exhaustion, after they had saved my life I felt obliged to explain my mysterious materialization to them.

Furthermore, there could be no rest for me until I got a message through to Mum to let her know I was alive. I was besieged by a nagging guilt to have caused her so much pain. She must be out of her mind with worry or more likely already grieving my death. How could I expect her to believe otherwise? I had been missing at sea for days now in horrendous conditions, with absolutely no protection or provisions. The possibility that I may have survived would be an inconceivable notion for her to uphold. For me it had been an almost impossible feat to accomplish, but with God's divine intervention I had survived.

The presence of something above me alerted my attention. Looking at the wire that ran around the top edge of the bunk I noticed some strangely familiar things. Unbelievably, there before me, hung separately with pegs on the wire, were all my sodden traveler's cheques, Filipino money, and our plane tickets. I was astounded at not only the obvious trouble they had gone to but also at their complete honesty. They had all the opportunity and certainly the need, but not a single peso was missing. I would reward them with material worth, and I imagined God would reward them too, but with heavenly treasures.

A group of about ten men sat on the floor around my bed listening avidly as I retold my horrific ordeal.

Nelson Zurita, the young man who had tended to me earlier, said, "I'm the assistant engineer. I understand English well, so I can interpret for the crew what you are saying."

I nodded my head in assent. "You are Michelle Hamilton from Sydney, Australia?"

"Aha," I murmured, pleased that all my vital information was written down in front of them and it wasn't necessary for me to relay the basics.

"So Miss Michelle, how did you get lost so far out at sea?"

Briefly I related my story. "You mean to say you have traveled all the way from Boracay Island to here, the Cuyo Islands, in that tiny bunca alone?" he said with an air of utter disbelief.

I heard him relaying my words for the benefit of the other men whose English wasn't as good. I heard the men gasp in astonishment as if they found it impossible to believe.

"So how long have you been floating out there?" Nelson said, obviously puzzled.

"If today is Sunday, then I've been at sea four days."

"No, today is Saturday."

"Oh, then maybe it's been three days. I honestly really can't remember," I said, aware that I had completely lost track of time out there. All I knew was that the minutes had seemed like hours and the days like months. I really couldn't be sure if it was three or four days; those few days had felt like an eternity.

"So where is your mother now?"

"I'm not sure, to tell you the truth. She is either on Boracay or maybe she has flown back to Manila. I truly believe she will still be on Boracay Island."

"Do you think she realizes what has happened to you?" Nelson asked with a concerned frown.

"To be quite honest, I think by now she couldn't help but believe that I'm dead. You know if God hadn't saved my life, then that is exactly what my destiny would have been. In fact I never would have made it through that terrible storm on the first night I was missing."

"You are lucky to be alive, Miss Michelle." The other men nodded in agreement, doubtlessly realizing they were witnessing evidence of a supernatural miracle performed by God.

"Nelson, I must get a message to my mother on Boracay Island immediately. Do you have a radio transmitter on board?"

"Yes, we do, but at the moment we are not getting a clear signal. There seems to be a lot of interference."

"Please try. I need to let her know I'm alive. I cannot rest until then. I know she will be in a state of panic, and I can't let her go through another minute of agony not knowing what has become of me. Do you understand?"

"Of course, Miss Michelle. You must be terribly worried about your mother and I assure you we will do our best to contact her. I'll go and get our Captain, Baudillo Pactao to come down and speak to you."

"Thank you, Nelson."

Aussie Ingenuity

After Nelson left, another young man quickly took his place sitting beside me; they all seemed so willing to be of assistance. After being alone and near death the warm compassion of these strangers deeply touched the core of my soul. After being so totally alienated from people, it was a moving experience to be part of the human race again. Life seemed so much sweeter for it. Right then I made a pledge to myself that when I recovered I would repay these people for saving my life in any way I could.

"Hello, ma'am, my name is Lusito Toniso. I'm the quartermaster on this ship," he said, greeting me warmly.

"Hello," I said, trying to smile without splitting open the bloody scabs that had formed on my lips.

"Are you hungry? Is there anything I can get you?"

"Well, I don't feel hungry but I'm very thirsty. However, maybe I should eat something if I want to recover."

The very thought of trying to chew and swallow lumps of food was painful. The state of my mouth was a bloody, horrific mess. A tray bearing two bottles of fizzy orange drink and a few mangoes was passed to Lusito who proceeded to skin and slice the mangoes into small edible portions. He fed me by hand as if I were a small child. I was overwhelmed by his extraordinary gentleness.

Lusito carefully placed a slice of mango inside my mouth. The cool sweetness of it on my tortured tongue was heavenly. Squeezing the ripe fruit against the roof of my mouth, I felt the mango dissolve into a juicy syrup and slide down my parched throat. The feeling was absolutely blissful. It instantly extinguished the raging fire inside my mouth. It tasted like nectar from the tree of life, and I was alive to enjoy it and would never take the simple things in life for granted again.

"Excuse me, Lusito. My skin is terribly burnt and is very painful. Would you by any chance have any moisturizer or something of that nature?"

He looked at me quizzically as if he was unsure what I meant.

"I need something to soothe my skin," I said pointing to my burnt face.

My skin felt not my own, but as if a taut mask had been placed on my face and stretched tightly over my cheekbones. I felt as though a mask covering my body had now shrunk several sizes under the heat of the torrid sun. The nerve endings directly under my skin's surface were pulsating with shock, screaming objections of pain for the punishment I had inflicted on them. Moisturizer was the only relief from this agony and was my dominating thought.

"I'm sorry," he said apologetically as he kneeled beside my bed. "We have nothing like that on board."

The thought of having to suffer this terrible pain for another twenty hours until we arrived in Manila was abhorrent. I cried out in a desperate plea, "Please help me. It hurts so much that anything will do. Even some butter would be okay!"

The distress so obvious in his face was answer enough to my question, but he spoke the words anyway.

"I'm very sorry, Miss Michelle, but we don't have any."

"Don't worry," I said patting his hand, not wishing to add to his humiliation. "I have another idea about what we could use as moisturizer and I know you have these in plentiful supply—mangoes! Could you please get some and cut the flesh up into long, thin strips? We will place them on my face to cool down the burning." I wasn't quite sure what healing properties mangoes possessed but if nothing else it would provide cool relief.

"Are you sure?" he said, looking surprised but at the same time happy that he could help me.

"Well at this stage I'm willing to try anything, even if it does seem a little odd."

A ripple of laughter filled the room; they were obviously amazed at my ingenuity. Necessity is the mother of invention, so they say, and this was the perfect situation to employ such a strategy. I felt a small smile creep on to my face. How ludicrous this was. I pictured the scenario through their eyes. They had rescued a would-be mermaid from out of the depths of the sea and dragged her on board. Sheltered away from the eyes of the world in the bowels of this ship, they had discovered their mermaid was in fact a mortal from Sydney, Australia, who had the passport to prove it. She presently looked more like the Loch Ness monster, and now to make matters more peculiar, she was requesting pieces of mango to be placed on her face.

"My skin felt not my own, but as if a taut mask had been placed on my face and stretched tightly over my cheekbones. I felt as though a mask covering my body had now shrunk several sizes under the heat of the torrid sun."

Looking through their eyes, I could see how strange I must appear to them. I doubted their families would ever believe them when they related the story; they would most likely think these men had been at sea too long and their imaginations had been working overtime. I could hardly believe what was happening myself; in a matter of hours my circumstances had altered so dramatically. Only hours ago I was stranded in a watery deathtrap, totally isolated from civilization, completely alone, clinging to life with my every breath. And without warning a ship had come into my path and dragged me on board, and suddenly I was surrounded by people, bathed in the warmth of human compassion and love, quenched with water, and filled with food.

It was unbelievable! In the blink of an eye, in the beat of a heart, I had gone from death to life, cold to comfortable, thirsty to satisfied, lonely to comforted. All I could do was marvel at life and the unexplainable hand God dealt me. What an awesome chain of events to comprehend. I had imagined that in a few hours I would have been on the island trying to make a life for myself like a modern-day Robinson Crusoe, not on a Filipino fishing vessel bound for Manila.

Lusito proceeded to delicately remove the mangoes from my face, then sponged me with cool water to remove the sticky residue. My skin felt so incredibly tender I was almost too scared to touch it. If extreme care wasn't taken, the skin on my face might well slip off my bones, like the meat off a well-cooked chicken.

I began to further investigate with the tips of my fingers the other painful parts of my body. I let out a whimper as I massaged the glands on my throat which had swollen enormously, jutting out as if I had swallowed a couple of golf balls. My fingers moved up gently to examine my cracked and swollen lips; they had enlarged to such an extent that they felt as if they had been blown up by a bicycle pump. I was suddenly overwhelmed with curiosity to see what I looked like. Although I was a little apprehensive at what I might discover, I nevertheless wanted to survey how much damage had been done.

With considerable effort I rolled over on to my side and beckoned one of the boys to assist me. A man who had previously introduced himself as Maximo Hilario jumped to his feet and came rushing over to see if I was all right.

In a rasping voice that felt as if it had been ripped raw, I asked him, a little embarrassed by my own vanity, "Would you by any chance have a mirror on board?"

"Yes, we do. You wait here and I'll get it for you."

In an instant he was back, kneeling beside me holding an antique oval hand mirror. He gingerly slipped his free hand around my lower back, cautiously aware of my sunburnt skin, and helped into an upright position. A groan of pure agony involuntarily escaped me. I knew I was not going to look like an oil painting, but I was unprepared for the shocking sight that was reflected in the mirror.

All I could see was red! There wasn't a part of my face that had escaped the sun's torturous rays, from eyelids to earlobes to the crown of my head. I had been sizzled like a sausage on an Aussie barbeque. The only part of my body that had avoided being burnt was the limited coverage my bikini had afforded me. Peering into the mirror I wondered if the damage done to my skin was irrevocable. Would I be scarred for life as a permanent reminder of my brush with death? It seemed pointless to worry about it now; besides I was lucky to be alive at all.

I lay there contemplating whether my need for a drink was greater than the pain it would cause me to change my position. Every movement was agony but my thirst took precedence over all else. Placing the mirror down I leaned over to scoop a cup of water from the steel cauldron that had been placed beside my bed. I had felt I was being a hindrance asking them to bring me a glass of water every five minutes, so I had suggested that they fill a large vessel of water. They had certainly carried out this request to the letter and brought me a huge kitchen cauldron. It served my purpose perfectly as it seemed no amount of water could ever quench my raging thirst.

Captain Baudillo Pactao returned from the radio room with disheartening news. "Excuse me, ma'am. We have been trying for the last hour to contact both Boracay and Manila, but we are unable to make contact

---

"Peering into the mirror I wondered if the damage done to my skin was irrevocable. Would I be scarred for life as a permanent reminder of my brush with death?"

---

with either of them because there is so much static in the frequency. I am very sorry that we have been unable to get through, but rest assured that we will keep on trying."

"Oh, okay then," I said with frustrating acceptance, resigning myself to the fact that there was nothing else I could do.

I awoke suddenly as a searing pain attacked my abdomen. A groan escaped my lips. Pressing my hands on my stomach I tried to ease the pain, but it didn't help at all. Nelson came rushing over.

"Miss Michelle, what's the matter?" he said, his face crumpled in concern.

"I don't know. Could you please lift me up?"

I resented feeling so utterly helpless, being so totally reliant on others to help me to do the simplest of things. Placing one hand behind my back and one on my neck, Nelson gently lifted me into a sitting position. The physical pain was unbearable, I felt I was going to die. Quickly drawing my knees up to my chin I wrapped my arms around them and sat rocking to and fro in an attempt to make the pain subside. As my eyes met Nelson's, I noticed how worried he looked.

"Don't worry. I will be okay soon" I said to dispel his fears for me. "Would you mind leaving me alone for a minute?"

"Sure," he mumbled in dismay as he walked away. Relieved to have been left alone, I sat whimpering to myself, while rocking back and forward in a cradle-like motion. I knew I must have sounded like a wounded animal but I didn't care. There was some merit in groaning aloud when you felt sick; somehow it made you feel better.

Normally, I was not the kind of person to panic easily, therefore I logically tried to reason why I would have such severe cramps. After being on an enforced fast for several days, then being crammed full of mangoes and fizzy drink, this was probably the cause. The effort of trying to stand up myself proved to be beyond my capacity.

Yet again I had to ask for assistance. Nelson appeared before me as obviously he had been assigned to look after me.

"Could you please show me to the bathroom?" I asked, mildly exasperated. He cast his eyes downward and appeared embarrassed.

Several seconds passed before Nelson got up enough courage to announce that they didn't have one.

A little perplexed I repeated his answer, "You don't have a toilet!"

"Well unfortunately it got blown off the ship in the last storm."

"So what do you use instead" I asked despairingly, hoping that he wouldn't say the side of the ship.

"Don't worry, you come with me," he motioned.

I swung my legs around so I faced him as he called his mate over to assist him, then together they placed their arms around my back and under my armpits hauling me to a standing position. When people said their legs turned to jelly, I had always wondered exactly what that had meant, and now I knew! This was the first time I had stood on solid ground in four days. My bruised feet tried desperately to hold up my quivering legs. My knees buckled under me, and I practically strangled Nelson as I collapsed, leaving his neck to support my entire weight.

Apologizing profusely, the men regained their supportive hold of me as we hobbled outside. Nelson pointed to a pair of very worn blue and white thongs, indicating I was to put them on. Together we staggered along the side of the boat. The deck was extremely slippery, looking as if it had just been hosed down. I was momentarily blinded by the dazzling whiteness. The foggy world outside appeared to be very ominous. Peering up into the sky, I was captivated by a canopy of stark white, which appeared to blanket my surroundings. It was as if the heavens had been covered in snow; not a patch of blue peeped through the clouds.

We stopped outside a steel door. Nelson leaned over, sliding the door open. Inside I noticed three other Filipino men. Nelson turned to me and announced, "This is the kitchen!"

What are we doing here? I thought. Feeling dazed I couldn't muster the energy to ask questions. I was afraid if he released his hold I would have collapsed.

They began speaking amongst themselves; I couldn't understand what they were saying but by the expression on their faces I presumed it was about me. While Nelson was talking, the other men kept turning to stare at me with wide eyes full of confusion.

Scanning the room I saw boxes of vegetables in one corner and several sacks in another, probably containing rice or flour. There in the main cooking area, to my disbelief, was a young man with a hose in his hand, washing his hair. It was an incredible spectacle. I blinked again to see if I was imagining it, but, no, there it was, a circus before my eyes. Two chicks were scurrying around the kitchen, as three big cauldrons bubbled away on the stove, probably lunch—most likely the other chicken! If I had the strength, I would have laughed but could only manage a grin.

The grin quickly disappeared when Nelson motioned with his finger in the direction of the kitchen and said, "The toilet is in that corner."

Hey, was this some kind of a joke? Surely they didn't expect me to go to the toilet in the kitchen. Maybe they do usually go over the side, but being considerate of me thought it might be a little inappropriate, not to mention embarrassing.

Wincing in pain as another series of cramps attacked my abdomen, all embarrassment fled. I tried to concentrate on alleviating the pain; anything would do at this stage. This was so humiliating!

I finished up, hosed down the floor, and staggered to the door, thanking them for their consideration. Nelson led me back to the hard little bed. I felt degraded, disgusting, and in dire need of a shower. I wondered what the shower would be like? Oh well, right now I didn't have the energy for any more surprises.

EIGHTEEN

A LONELY VIGIL

RACHELLE . . . 9:00 A.M., SUNDAY, MARCH 12, BORACAY ISLAND. For the first time in days I experienced a measure of tranquility and acceptance. I didn't know if the words I'd read were a promise of deliverance for Michelle or not, but during that time spent with God I'd submitted myself to His will, accepted His final judgment, and still maintained my belief that He was a righteous and loving God. If the death of a sparrow didn't go unnoticed by Him, then how much more would He care for Michelle?

I became aware of the seats being filled as people streamed into the church, though I was blind to them; they were on the periphery of my world. I heard prayers being offered up for Michelle's life by the tiny community. I felt inquisitive eyes bore into me, and it made me feel uncomfortable being the focus of so many strangers' attention. I wanted to be out of the spotlight.

Before the service was over, in an impulsive action, I stood up and walked self-consciously out of the church. I considered returning to my bungalow, then instantly decided against it. What could I do with myself now? David was my answer—that's who I wanted to talk to. I wanted his advice. I couldn't think rationally.

I found him sitting on the patio of his beachfront bungalow, talking to several German travellers. He stood up and came forward to greet me.

"Hi, Rachelle, how're things going? Have you had any news yet?"

"No, there's been nothing," I said dejectedly. "To tell you the truth David, I don't know what to do now."

"Here, sit down. Don't worry. Together we'll think of something. What's your embassy doing about this?"

"They say there's nothing they can do, as they don't have the resources to conduct an aerial search."

"Maybe they don't, but America has a huge military base in Manila. They are bound to have planes and helicopters available."

"I'm sure they have, but I'm not an American citizen. People are dying here every day, so what's the life of one foreigner?" I said bitterly.

"That's not true, Rachelle. I think that while you're only a distant voice on the end of a phone your plight seems remote and unsubstantiated. If you were there in person and demanded they took some positive action, they would be compelled to do something about it. They wouldn't easily be able to fob you off when you are standing right in front of them. You know there's really little else you can do for Michelle on Boracay. After four days the search teams begin to get discouraged and lose incentive."

"I'm sure you're right, David, but I don't have the strength to go to Manila alone. What would happen if someone found her and I wasn't here?"

You Must Go!

A powerful anxiety rose up, rendering me paralyzed. The shocking thought of leaving this place where I felt the essence of Michelle was like turning my back on her, deserting her in the eleventh hour. How could a mother abandon her daughter? A betrayal of such magnitude at this time was unthinkable! I felt as if I'd be selling her out, and the mere mention of it made me sick to the pit of my stomach.

"David, I can't do it. I can't go. I won't desert Michelle, not now."

"Yes, you can go, and you have to, for Michelle's sake. Look, Rachelle, I'm going to be honest with you. I can't tell you why but I believe it. Some deep inner knowledge tells me that Michelle is still alive. It may sound completely unrealistic, but it's a gut feeling that I've got. If there's even the slightest chance that this is true, then we must keep on searching for her and not give up. You've got to go to Manila and stir them up, get someone to take action. Until you have exhausted every avenue you musn't give up hope," he challenged. "Michelle's counting on you, so let's make some plans, shall we?"

David had broken his toe the previous day and was in agony. To top it off, my toe was pulsating like a lighthouse beacon, so together we limped up the steep incline to The Hump Resort, which was situated on the hillside overlooking the expanse of Boracay. Supporting each other, we hobbled up the bush track, making an odd looking couple.

While David made arrangements with Ray, the proprietor, I sat in the quaint hilltop restaurant, gazing over the treetops out to sea. Despite my distress, I couldn't help marvel at the spectacular view from this vantage point. Directly below us, the land was densely covered with

" 'You've got to go to Manila and stir them up, get someone to take action.' "

lush vegetation. The palm fronds which overlapped each other created a canopy of emerald green foliage. Beyond the trees lay a horizontal strip of brilliant white sand, fused with the inviting turquoise water which stretched out seemingly forever. To my left I saw the island of Panay jutting out into the open sea.

The expanse of the ocean was never ending! A sickening weight of defeat descended over me. How would we ever find her? Was I exerting my will against unrealistic odds? When I was confronted by the ocean, I was reminded of its enormity and had to face how truly impotent I was. The fight suddenly went out of me, like the air being expelled from a balloon. I was left empty and dispirited.

Even if I were successful in persuading the Australian Embassy to organize an aerial search, by the time they would be able to get it underway at least five days would have lapsed since Michelle was missing. I'd heard of people lasting for weeks out at sea, so I didn't think I was being pessimistic and giving up early; it was just that I couldn't deny the facts. The people who had managed to survive long periods of time lost at sea, usually had the advantage of an inflatable life raft, which was almost unsinkable. They were also generally equipped with food, water, and provisions.

Michelle's flimsy seven-foot canoe was in no way seaworthy to combat the open ocean. I found it almost impossible to conceive how the bunca could have stayed afloat. I imagined the first big wave created by the onset of the storm would have swamped the makeshift bunca, either sinking or capsizing it. I knew it would be nothing short of a miracle for her to have survived that first night at sea.

Was I on a fool's mission going to Manila? What real chance was there of her surviving this long? Was I defiantly unwilling to accept the blatant truth?

I felt I was pitting myself against the hopeless odds. Each step I took was leading me to the inevitable. Once again I experienced the feeling that she was lost to me forever. Any feeble attempt to deny this was sheer human bravado. But I didn't feel ready to give her up just yet.

Please, let me go on pretending there's hope for a little while longer, I pleaded. I wasn't yet strong enough to face her death, so for the moment I'd allow myself to be caught up in David's plans and continue with the futile act of human striving. The fight was at least keeping me from collapsing altogether.

Ray took up the challenge and moved into action. He contacted several airlines and finally arranged a flight for 2 P.M. that afternoon; meanwhile he busied himself writing letters of introduction to valuable contacts for me in Manila, so I would have the support of people who could assist me. A grim seriousness clouded the atmosphere. Sitting at the table I watched David and Ray making plans for my future. I felt detached and disconnected from them and the thriving evidence of life that surrounded me.

The very act of leaving Boracay symbolized that I had accepted defeat. It was an admission that all was lost, an indication that I had given up the fight, leaving Michelle to her destiny. How could I desert my child, turn my back on her, and walk away? That's exactly what David and Ray were planning for me.

Don't make me leave here, I groaned from within, *I can't bear the thought of relinquishing my vigil.* To leave meant letting go of Michelle and leaving her for dead. The crying ache inside was tearing me apart. I wasn't sure I was capable of standing upright on my own two legs, let alone of journeying to an unfamiliar city. What they were asking me to do was beyond my capacity to carry out. I wouldn't go. They could bury me in the Philippines with her; I'd refuse to leave her.

"Rachelle, good news! We've managed to get you on that flight that leaves at 2 P.M.. We also have contacted Mr. Frazer from your embassy who will meet the plane so you won't have to be left on your own. Rachelle, are you okay? Did you hear what I said?" David asked.

"I heard but I am so afraid. I don't know how I'm going to get through this. I just want to run away from it all and hide somewhere."

"Rachelle, you won't break down. Pull yourself together. If you want to help Michelle, you must go to Manila and get assistance for a full-scale search."

"But by the time it would take them to organize a search, at least five days will have gone by. Tell me, David, the honest truth: What real hope do you think she has? You're not stupid; you know the odds as well as I do. You saw the size of the boat she went out in. She would have had no protection whatsoever. How in the world could it have stayed afloat? David, can't you understand it would kill me to hold out false hope only to be let down. Please tell me the truth; do you really believe there is even the slightest chance that Michelle could still be alive?"

"Rachelle, why do you think I'm going to the trouble of getting you to Manila to get a search started if I didn't think there was any hope? Michelle's a very unique lady. From the short time I spent with her I was so impressed with her. She's a fighter and wouldn't give up easily and neither should you. You owe her every chance of survival, don't you think?" he said, his words cutting me to the very core.

"Of course I do, and that's why I've agreed to go. But the overwhelming odds she's up against seem so daunting. Every time I think of her I see her challenging the sea barehanded for her every breath. It's a living torture for me. I feel so totally useless. I keep hearing her voice calling out my name, screaming for me to help. It taunts me every second."

"I can't pretend to understand how you must be feeling because I don't, but we musn't let these feelings render us powerless to help her. We must go on. You would never forgive yourself if you didn't do everything humanly possible to find Michelle. That's one thing I do know. I'll walk you back to your bungalow so you can pack up your things while I finalize your tickets and the documents you will need," he said with a note of finality which conveyed he wouldn't take no for an answer.

"How's your foot holding out? Do you think you can make it back down the hill okay?" he asked.

"Do I have a choice?"

"Do any of us really choose the things that happen to us? I think not. Come on, let's go now. There's not a lot of time left before your flight."

We thanked Ray, then supporting each other like a couple of invalids we trudged down the steep slope and made our way back to the bungalow. A silence laden with heaviness fell between us. As we approached the bungalow we saw Rafel coming towards us.

"Have you any news of Michelle yet?" she asked with expectancy.

"No, there's not, but David's convinced me to go to Manila and seek the help of the Australian Embassy and anyone else who is willing. I'll be leaving here about 2 P.M. I'm not able to pay our bill," I said apologetically. "Michelle has all the money on her in the money belt, but I promise as soon as I get back to Australia I'll send what I owe you."

"Don't worry about that now. You can pay me whenever you are able to. What I'm more concerned about is that you haven't eaten for days. If you're traveling to Manila you must keep your strength up. I'll order you something, shall I?" Rafel said sounding concerned.

"Honestly, I don't think I could keep anything down, besides I really don't feel hungry, but thanks for being so thoughtful."

"I'll tell you what, I'll bring you something and you can just pick at it if you want, okay?"

"That would be fine, Rafel." And she headed back to the restaurant.

"Well, Rachelle, I'll leave you here in good hands. I'll be back in about half an hour. Do you think you can be ready by then?" David asked gently.

"There's not really that much to pack. I'll be ready. Thanks, David, for all your help. I don't know how I would've coped without you."

"It's nothing. I'm only pleased I'm here to be able to help you. Take care. I'll be back soon."

Mourning

I watched him walk away from me. My immediate instinct was to run after him. I'd learned in the past few days to lean on his strength as my own resources had long been depleted. I felt the familiar fear rising in me, but I knew I had to face this ordeal on my own from now on. I willed myself to produce the courage to endure this nightmare.

I walked up the wooden steps of our bungalow and gingerly unlocked the door. Stepping inside, the intense emotions I experienced were explosive. There seemed no more room inside me to contain the anguish, and that any moment I might burst. Like a boiling cauldron they spilled out over and over, erupting through every pore in my body. This was the dreaded moment. I was giving up defeated, succumbing to the truth. My daughter was dead! The darkened bungalow became a tomb in the bowels of the earth. The walls seemed to close in on me so that I could barely breathe.

God help me. Help me to do this thing. I managed by some superhuman effort to control the desire to fall down into a heap and never get up again. Consciously, I took a mental inventory of the task ahead. With sheer determination I succeeded in taking control and set my mind to work.

I had two backpacks with assorted toiletries and clothing to pack. Raising the mosquito net to one side, I tied it back then lifted both packs onto the bed. I couldn't as yet bear to touch Michelle's belongings, so I proceeded to place my own clothing and goods into the bag. I was deliberately taking my time, delaying the moment as long as possible before I had to handle Michelle's things. It reminded me of when Granddad died. Grandma left her beloved husband's things untouched in his wardrobe for two years before she had the heart to touch them. This, I realized, was going to be one of the most difficult tasks I had ever undertaken in my forty years of living.

Well, I couldn't avoid the ghastly task any longer. I zipped up my turquoise backpack, swinging it down off the bed and placing it by the door. The unthinkable had happened; I'd have to go home and leave Michelle in the Philippines.

Her black backpack lay open on the bed and resembled her coffin, where I placed what remained of her to rest. Her trifle belongings became symbolic of Michelle's body which was now lost to the world. The room had been transformed into a cemetery, and in it I was burying my beloved daughter. Fondling each article which still retained her special smell, I lovingly folded each one up as neatly as I could and placed it in her pack.

I picked up Michelle's hairbrush! Her long, golden blonde hairs were entrapped in the bristle teeth. With my fingertips I gently pulled out one strand. As it yielded to my tugging, the hair slithered from its confines, and I held it up in the air with the pressure of my thumb and forefinger. I wanted to caress her head so much, but all I had left was a few loose strands of hair. That would have to suffice for the rest of my days.

A knock on the door stopped me from collapsing into total despair.

"Rachelle, sorry to intrude but I've bought your lunch. Where would you like me to put it?" Rafel asked, entering the room with a tray laden with delicious smelling foods.

"Just leave it on the table. Thanks Rafel." Glancing over at the sumptuous food I said, "That looks more like a feast for two. I'll never be able to do it justice."

"Don't worry, eat what you can. Everybody on the island is praying for Michelle. I know it's not much of a consolation for you, but it may help you to know it's our belief that wherever she is, God is watching over her and will keep her safe with Him. Whether in life or death, He'll be caring for her."

"Thanks for your kind words and I do believe you, but right now I'm hurting too much to be philosophical. You know I also believe in God, but this has been a severe test of my faith. My love for Him has not altered; this has only shown how delicately we are connected to life. I find it so difficult to comprehend that my daughter, a healthy young woman in the prime of her life and so full of vitality, with everything to live for, could be snatched from this world at God's calling without a moment's notice. It's made me realize that our days are numbered and we never know when our time's up.

"It still doesn't seem fair to me though. Rafel, I haven't told anyone this but when I sat in the church this morning, I relinquished my ownership of her as her earthly mother and gave her into the hands of God if that was His will. I can't fight His authority. All I ask is that He takes care of Michelle wherever she is and that He gives me and my other children the courage and desire to go on."

"Rachelle, you are a very brave woman and God will greatly reward such faith in Him. Although this awful tragedy has happened to your family, your faith hasn't wavered and your trust in God is an example to all of us."

"Rafel, you're wrong. I'm not being brave. I could never express to you in words how much Michelle means to me. Not only is she my daughter but she's also my very best friend. I just realize to fight against God's will is foolishness. My perception of God is that He's a loving Father; if He wasn't, He wouldn't have sacrificed His own Son for the salvation of mankind. I feel I can trust Michelle into His care. All I ask is that He heals the pain and gives me another purpose to go on living."

"You do have other children, don't you?"

"Yes, I have two wonderful daughters and know I have them to go home to, but I can't bear to think about them at the moment, knowing that I'll soon have to face them, and tell them the truth. I can only deal with one thing at a time! I'll have to cross that bridge when I come to it."

"I'm sorry, I didn't mean to upset you."

"That's okay. It's bad enough that I have to go through this, but when I think of what it will do to my daughters—losing their big sister—it tears me apart!"

"Rachelle, I wish there was something I could do to comfort you but I know there's not. Time's the best healer. Just know that we all do care and we'll help you in any way we can. I don't want to distress you further, but unfortunately I have some disappointing news I have to tell you. I feel you have the right to be told the truth. As you know, on the first day when Michelle was missing my father took out one of our fishing boats with some friends to look for her. He returned only an hour ago after three days of searching. He did a thorough exploration of the outer islands and I'm sorry to be the one to have to tell you, but he found no trace of her."

Another piece of damning evidence drove yet another nail in her coffin, desecrating any remnant of hope I may have defiantly clung to.

"Thanks for being honest with me. I know I can't run away from the facts any longer. Rafel, would you mind leaving me alone for a moment. I want to say goodbye to my daughter."

"Of course, I understand. Please try to eat something though, won't you? If you need anything I'll be at the restaurant," Rafel murmured as she respectfully ushered herself out of the bungalow. With a devastation too terrible to describe I resumed burying my daughter's remains inside her backpack. I was holding myself together only by a supreme act of will. There were only a few toiletries yet to be packed away when I heard footsteps outside the door.

"May I come in?" I heard a deeply accented male voice call out deferentially.

"Yes, the door's open." A robust, handsome Filipino man stepped into the room. "Ma'am, I'm Rafel Gelito's father, Willy. I hope I'm not intruding but I felt I had to speak with you before you left. Please accept my heartfelt sorrow at the loss of your lovely daughter. We ventured out as far as we felt the currents could have carried her, but after three days and nights of finding absolutely nothing we were forced to return home as our fuel was getting low. Everyone on board was extremely upset that we didn't find her. We've had to come home empty-handed and bring you the bad news. I promised the crew I would personally come to see you and express everyone's sentiments, so you can be assured we have done everything in our power to find her."

"Thank you, I appreciate everyone's effort. You've all been very kind. I'll never forget you all. By the way, did you ever get to meet my daughter?"

"No, I never had the pleasure," he answered, looking apologetic.

"Here, I have a photo of her. Would you like to see it?"

Not waiting for his reply I unzipped the side pocket on my pack, pulling out a sheath of recent shots of Michelle taken in Singapore. I barely glanced at them as I passed them over to him. He gingerly took them from me and stood staring into the photograph. I watched silently as the expression on his face crumbled, tears spilling down his soft brown cheeks.

"She's very beautiful. You must be very proud of her. I'm so sorry we couldn't have done more," he said pressing the photos back into my hand. Touching my shoulder gently, he moved to leave.

"Farewell, ma'am. May our Father in heaven grant you the understanding and peace to accept your great loss." He turned away soberly and disappeared out the bungalow door.

The photograph in my hand was wet with his tears. Now I dared to look into the smiling face of my darling girl. Oh, she looked so happy and alive. How could we have ever known only one week ago that we had only a few precious days left to us? I was so grateful that our last days together had been filled with such joy. We had spent every moment in each other's company, and I had told her on many occasions how much I loved her. It was a small consolation that our last moments were spent in this way and there were no regrets that I never had the chance to say I love you. Bringing the photo up to my lips, I kissed the face of my cherished daughter, then turned back to my onerous task of packing.

I placed the photo on top of her clothing and began to zip up her backpack. The words tumbled out of my mouth, "Lord, I commit the spirit of my daughter to You. Please keep her safe in Your loving care until the day when we can meet again. Please give me the strength and faith to accept Your ways. Lord, the worst thing is that I'll never know what happened to her. It's the unfinished ending and the agony of not knowing that will burn in my soul as an unanswered question. If it's in Your will, please let me know what became of her because until then I'll just be living in a limbo and will never be able to heal." Taking hold of the silver zipper, I began to pull it around, sealing the coffin closed.

"Goodbye, my darling. I love you. There will not be a day that shall pass that you will not be remembered." My legs buckled under me and I fell to the floor. The shocking thought that I was leaving her, alone in a foreign land while I journeyed home to Australia, was unthinkable.

Grief took over, and I sobbed hysterically. *I can't go and leave you all by yourself in the cold, lonely ocean. I want to take you home with me. Oh Michelle, where are you? I want to keep you safe and warm.*

David found me in a heap on the floor. What I was terrified of happening just had. My resolve had crumbled; my courage deserted me. The thought of leaving Michelle in the Philippines by herself forever without her family was horrendous.

Through the blurry veils of grief, I heard David's voice say "Rachelle, snap out of it. Pull yourself together. You've got the rest of your life to mourn for Michelle if she's not found, but right now you can't let yourself go to pieces when there's still hope. Don't you think Michelle deserves that chance?"

I heard him call out, "Would somebody please get a glass of water."

I felt a cold glass being pressed against my lips as he urged me to drink the cold water which marginally restored me.

"The boat's waiting," he said urgently. "It's time to leave. Just sit there and compose yourself. That's better," he said soothingly.

When I had gained a measure of self-control, I stood up on shaky legs. Refocusing on the horrendous ordeal ahead of me I knew I had to be strong. I noticed someone had removed the backpacks and taken them out to the waiting boat. Hobbling to the door, I turned around to say one last goodbye, then walked out of the tomb and into the bright tropical sunlight.

Several people had gathered on the beach to bid me farewell and wish me good luck in Manila, although I only saw them as an indistinguishable mass of blurred faces. Only David and Rafel's faces were clear to me. I spoke to them as I limped down to the waiting boat. "Rafel, I feel I won't be returning to Boracay. I'll be leaving Michelle in spirit here with you. Please say prayers for her and remember her always. She belongs to the Philippines now; she has become a part of your country. I have come to love your people. Please thank them for the love and concern they have shown Michelle and me. When I get back to Australia I will have a plaque made, and I would like you to place it on the front of our bungalow in Michelle's memory. Would you do that for me please?"

"Of course, it will be an honor. We will never forget the both of you. Take care of yourself. Go home and find solace in your two other children. They will help you overcome your grief. Goodbye and God bless you," she said, her words filled with compassion.

As I looked to David for strength, he averted his eyes. Being so typically male he avoided the emotion of the moment and instead gave me practical, last-minute instructions. "Don't worry, you'll be okay when you get to Manila. The consulate officials will be there to meet you. Don't forget you have all those letters of introduction should you need any other assistance. If anything happens here, we will be sure to call the embassy immediately. Don't forget what I told you: be strong. Michelle needs you!"

Once again I journeyed to the airfield at Caticlan; only this time there was no purpose or anticipation, only deathly defeat and an emptiness that seemed to wind on forever like a dark, lifeless tunnel. I was on my way! My dream holiday had lasted a total of nine days, four of them a hellish trial that I would never have contemplated when I leafed through those magnificent glossy brochures on the flight to the Philippines.

NINETEEN

SAVED

MICHELLE . . . 9:00 A.M., SUNDAY, MARCH 12, ABOARD THE *ALYSS STAR*. As I bent my head to avoid hitting it on the top bunk, my eyes instantly filled with flashing stars. Oh no, I could feel myself going down for the count once again. I blinked, trying to regain focus as my knees collapsed beneath me. I slumped to the floor. I felt myself being lifted into the bed. Then I muttered thanks and fell asleep.

I awoke some hours later but hovered reluctantly on the edge of waking. Pretending to still be asleep, I watched my rescuers through half-closed eyes. The room was almost completely dark except for the flicker of a candle burning. Huddled around a table in one corner of the room, the men were playing a game of cards. I felt as if I were peeping into the intimacy of their circle. Unbeknown to them I watched on, listening to the resonance of their boisterous voices which filled the room.

I couldn't believe my good fortune at having being rescued by such kindly people. I was extremely grateful for the hospitality and care they had shown me; they had treated me as well as they would have one of their own. These people had so little themselves in the way of material wealth and possessions, but they were rich in their love of God, family, friends, and country. I admired their devotion and drew strength from their continually smiling faces.

I couldn't help thinking about everything I had been through the past few days. It seemed bizarre in retrospect, how that one snap decision of mine—not to call it a day and bring the bunca in when I dropped Mum off to shore—had monumentally changed my life. I was compelled to believe that this was no accident, but a destiny preordained by God. I remember while in Singapore Mum had excitedly told me of the new discovery in her life, Jesus! She reckoned it had completely transformed and renewed her whole life, and I had to admit she did emanate an inner peace I had never seen before.

At the time I found what she was suggesting all rather preposterous. How could one man, born two thousand years ago, have the ability to dramatically change one's life in the twentieth century? Unless of course He was who He proclaimed to be, the Son of God! I believed everybody had the right to their own opinions and religious beliefs; however, I did not have to accept them myself.

Now after the supernatural happenings I had experienced, and witnessing firsthand the dynamic power of God at work during my ordeal, the evidence of His existence was impossible to ignore. When Mum had suggested the true divinity of Jesus and His purpose in coming to earth—for the salvation of mankind for whoever believed in Him—I remembered politely rejecting the likelihood of this being true. At the time I had declined her invitation to seek more understanding on the subject.

Lying here now, I realized if she was willing to share with me now what she had learned and understood of the Scriptures I would be readily open to listen to what she had to say. Ironically as I recall in my moment of imminent peril, unconsciously I had struggled to remember Jesus' words as I was taught in Sunday school. I now recognized the truth that God wasn't an entity sitting on a throne up in the sky, surveying His creations. No, He was very real and had proved that to me beyond a doubt. He had audibly spoken to me, giving me directions and instructions, fortifying me both mentally and physically. I had a sense of security in the most diabolical circumstances, but most of all I had a promise that He would save me, and He kept His promise. I had grown to love, trust and have 100 percent faith in Him.

What greater demonstration of loving care is there than to send down four of his angels to protect me throughout the night and keep me safe from the man-eating sharks. As further evidence, He had physically and supernaturally lifted my bunca into the air, spun it around 180 degrees and propelled it in the direction He wanted me to go, directly against the force of the oncoming waves—an impossible feat to perform by man but easily possible with God. No, I could not deny this overwhelming amount of evidence confirming He had supernaturally intervened to save my life. Why, I was yet to find out!

Physical Needs

A pain jabbed me out of my contemplations. For the first time in four days I felt hungry! Now that my mind had been freed from the preoccupation of survival, this bodily need made its presence felt. Grumbling and groaning like an old man, my gnawing hunger demanded attention.

In a harsh whisper I called out, "Excuse me."

This gained the attention of the chief mate, and Pedro Casilag swiftly rushed to my bedside. "Yes, ma'am."

"It seemed bizarre in retrospect, how that one snap decision of mine—not to call it a day and bring the bunca in when I dropped Mum off to shore —had monumentally changed my life."

"I am very hungry. Do you have anything to eat?"

"Yes, sure, what would you like?" he said, welcoming the opportunity to help.

"How about a Burger King Whopper with extra pickles and ketchup," I said jokingly, amazed my sense of humor was still intact.

"You really want a hamburger?" Pedro asked, knowing it was beyond anything he could produce.

"Yes, more than anything. I'm ravenous but I'll settle for some sticky rice if you have some."

"Sure, we also have some curried chicken if you would like a little."

I wondered if this was the chicken I had previously seen scurrying around the kitchen floor. Oh well, who cared? I needed a little protein to restore my energy levels.

"Okay, that sounds good as long as it's not too spicy. My throat couldn't handle it," I replied as I beamed him a grateful smile which instantly cracked open the cuts in the corners of my mouth. It was worth it. It was true that a smile was contagious because his worried frown broke into a spontaneous smile, revealing a set of gleaming white teeth.

"Don't make me laugh. It hurts," I said pointing to my cut and blistered lips. Once again he made me smile as he departed from the cabin.

I was still utterly exhausted; the acute stinging of my burnt skin pained me with a vengance. I dreamed of the moment when I could lavish thick, creamy moisturizer all over my body to balm the scorched layers of flesh. I envisioned myself standing under cool jets of water, rinsing away the dried grains of salt which had embedded themselves into my every pore. The heavenly relief of being clean was something I urgently craved. It overpowered everything, even my desperate need for sleep.

Pedro returned bearing a plate of food. Placing it on the floor carefully, Nelson and Pedro gently raised me into a sitting position, each movement causing me inexpressible agony. Every muscle and tendon had been ripped apart, from the nape of my neck to the base of my spine. Even the simplest task of holding my head up was excruciating. The plate of food set before me consisted of two chicken drumsticks and rice covered in a curried sauce. The meal could hardly be described as gourmet, but considering that a matter of only hours ago I doubted that I would ever have a meal again, this looked pretty good to me. It tasted wonderful.

"How long before we reach Manila?" I asked.

"Our scheduled arrival time is around 2 P.M. this afternoon!"

"Could you do me a favor, Nelson? I know I have already asked you so many times, but could you please try the radio again to see if the frequency is clear. You know how urgent it is for me to get my mother this message. I know I am being a nuisance asking you every hour, but as you can imagine it is terribly important."

"Of course I understand. It is no trouble! We are getting closer to the mainland so we should be able to make contact fairly soon. Don't worry, Miss Michelle, we'll get your message through as soon as it's possible."

"Thank you, Nelson," I said, relieved that the burden of getting the message through had been taken from me. "I think I will try and get some rest now" I said looking forward to a few precious minutes of sleep.

Sleep seemed elusive, out of my reach. After a short space of time I would awaken startled, still thinking I was in the bunca with the seas crashing around me and I had allowed the powerful, magnetic force of sleep to drag me into its custody. It was impossible to convince my weary brain that it was now safe to sleep. I was wound too tensely to relax enough for sleep. My every thought now was consumed by anxiety and worry for Mum and how she would be coping with my death. I was desperate to let her know how very much alive I was.

Time! It was only a matter of time. I could not wait to tell her of all the amazing experiences that had happened to me while I was at sea, although it would take a lifetime. I knew how very fortunate I was now to have a lifetime. Awaking some hours later, the longest sleep I had had so far, I found myself feeling better. I knew it was only an artificial feeling of well-being and within minutes of waking, any energy my body had gained would be drained all too rapidly. I realized I would need a few days of complete rest to recover and allow my wounds to heal.

At this moment what I severely needed was a shower. I felt so incredibly dirty. My mouth was a sand-pit and my teeth felt as if a fungal moss had grown over them. I was completely repelled by myself and wished I could crawl out of my own skin. Being a naturally clean person, I found going without daily hygiene for as long as four days was abhorrent.

An affinity had grown between Nelson and me. Although he couldn't have been a day over eighteen, already he had the maturity of a much older person. Compassion and a natural love for his fellow man flowed from him. For these reasons I asked Nelson to help me to the shower.

With the utmost care I was helped to my feet. I never imagined it would feel so weird to have solid ground beneath my feet, but it did. Placing my feet in the thongs that Operito Abique, the other quartermaster, had lent me, I prepared to walk to the shower. My legs were so wobbly that I leaned against Nelson for support. As he slid open a steel door off the sleeping quarters a gust of hot, acrid air blasted against my face. Moving into an enormous chamber he closed the door behind us.

I was utterly stupefied by the sight that met my eyes! Literally thousands of small dead fish were strung along the hundreds of wires that ran the length of the room. The putrid fishy smell and scorching hot air bombarded my skin, infiltrating every orifice. Breathing was impossible, but I was determined to be clean, however painful the process may be.

Gripping tightly to the steel bannister I dizzily made my way down the winding staircase. My legs shuddered dangerously under me, threatening to give way at any second. Despite Nelson supporting the greater part of my body weight, still I could barely sustain the dead weight. The acrid heat and thundering noise coming from the ship's engines reverberated off the steel walls of the room, suffocating and deafening me with mighty blows. I had an overwhelming desire to run back up those stairs and out of that room which stank from the smell of dead fish. I wished I could transport myself out of this claustrophobic room and onto the ship's deck where all my senses could drink in the pure sea air. Would I ever be released from this continual pain that tormented me?

Suddenly I heard the voice of my conscience saying, *Stop feeling so sorry for yourself. Be grateful you are alive!* I realized how very true this was; I had survived my ordeal basically unscathed, with all my limbs still intact. Who could ask for more than that?

A Changed Life

After I showered we staggered back up the stairs. I stopped suddenly and turned to him. "I want you to know that I think you are one of the kindest and most compassionate men I have ever met. I hope life treats you kindly," I said sincerely.

"It does and saving your life is one of the highlights of my life. I feel honored to have been able to help you, Miss Michelle."

We both looked into each other's eyes and smiled, an honest warm smile that filled us both with love and happiness.

"You know, Nelson, it was only yesterday, while I was out at sea that I kept saying 'Why is this happening to me, God?' Now twenty-four hours later after you've saved me, I'm thinking the very same thing. There must be a reason I'm yet to find, why I had to experience that horrendous ordeal. Now it seems as if the coin has flipped over to the other side and I'm being lavished with human compassion, friendship, and goodwill. There must be some logical reason why this has happened to me, too, don't you think?" I questioned.

"Of course I do and God will tell you the reason soon enough. In the Bible Jesus' words are 'Follow Me, and I will make you fishers of men' (Matthew 4:19). Go home to your friends and tell them what great things the Lord has done for you and how He has had compassion on you."

"Do you really believe that is what God has in store for me?"

"Yes, I do, and I'll tell you what else. I think God has something great planned for your life."

"To be honest with you, I don't know what the future holds any more. I feel like an infant without any preconceived ideas, a child ready to learn all over again. I've changed so much already Nelson; I can feel it. In three days I feel as if I've been to heaven and hell and back, faced death constantly and experienced more emotions than most people do in a lifetime. I can never go back, never be the same! Can you understand what I'm saying?"

"Yes, I can and I think you're right, you have changed. Nobody could hope to go through such a horrifying experience as yours and come out of it unaltered. But the essence of your character, the real Michelle, will always be there."

"I hope so. I used to like her." We both laughed at my egotistical joke.

Totally sapped of all energy, I lay back down on the bed and slipped into a fitful sleep almost immediately, but not before reminding them to try the transmitter once more.

"If only they could get a message through to her that I was alive, this process of anxiety and bereavement could be halted. I didn't wish for her to feel one more minute of anguish. My ordeal was over; I wanted hers to be too."

I could see Mum's face clearly behind my closed eyes, as if she'd been projected onto the back of my eyelids. Her face was filled with fear; her eyes revealed their torment; she looked so incredibly tired. I needn't have speculated on how she would be feeling right now because I knew her too well. The pain I felt at having hurt her so much was like a physical ache in my heart that wouldn't go away. If only they could get a message through to her that I was alive, this process of anxiety and bereavement could be halted. I didn't wish for her to feel one more minute of anguish. My ordeal was over; I wanted hers to be too. Mum had already been through so much; for me to have put her through this nightmare was a deep source of guilt for me, a terrible burden I had to bear on my already weakened shoulders.

A muted voice reached my ears, pulling me from my deep thoughts.

"Miss Michelle, wake up, wake up!"

"What is it, Nelson? Is there something wrong?" I said, springing instantly to life.

"We managed to get a connection on the transmitter. You can send a message through to Manila now."

In the radio room Captain Baudillo Pactao said to me, "Please write down on this piece of paper your full name and where your mother is staying on Boracay Island and we will pass this information on to Manila. We have told our boss, Mr. Bobby del Rosario of the Irma Fishing

Company, what has happened and he wants to speak to you right away. He's on the phone now. Are you up to speaking to him?"

"Okay, sure."

Through a crackly line, in a shaky voice I spoke to Mr. del Rosario. He was very sympathetic and explained that his sister would meet me at Navatos Fishing Port and escort me to the Coast Guard station where I could report the incident and call the embassy. He told me the story had already leaked out over all Manila and would I mind if the press interviewed me when I arrived. I told him nonchalantly that I didn't mind, only that they respect my urgency in getting a message through to my mother first. He said he understood completely. I thanked him and hung up.

All the young crew members were chatting animatedly, excited that I had spoken to their boss and how proud he was of them that they had saved my life. I imagined this would be extremely good publicity for them.

"Michelle, would you like to go up on deck? You can see mainland and Manila clearly now. We are almost there."

"Okay," I said, happy to be almost back in civilization, where I could get things accomplished more quickly. The Australian Embassy would be a lifesaver; surely they could help me locate Mum if she had left Boracay.

Dropping myself into a swivel chair in the bridge room, I gazed through the glass windows out at the sea that stretched before me to the shores of Manila. The sight of the midnight blue water and the huge waves smashing against the bow of the ship sent my stomach a-flutter. The ocean now terrified me, and I felt nauseous with a sick fear. Would I ever be able to admire its beauty again, ever bathe in its tropical waters, ever sail across its turbulent seas? At this moment it seemed unthinkable. The sea had been my enemy, a deathly predator for three long terrifying days. How could I ever be friends with it again?

TWENTY

LIFE OR DEATH: THE BLATANT TRUTH

RACHELLE . . . 1:00 P.M., SUNDAY, MARCH 12, MANILA. The boat pulled away swiftly into deeper water. Was it possible that only seven days ago Michelle and I had sat side by side in a bunca similar to the one I was in now as we made the last leg of our journey to beautiful Boracay by sea?

Our plane had arrived in Iloilo, the capital of Panay. We were greeted by throngs of excited Filipinos, all cajoling each other for our patronage to ride in their jeepneys to the other side of the island where we could catch a motorized bunca to Boracay. As we stepped out of the air-conditioned plane, the tropical heat hit us in a series of waves.

My first impression was vibrant splashes of color. Growing out of the sunburnt earth, the lush green palms stretched skyward. In the distance the segregated paddy fields looked painted onto the landscape. The natives wore huge cooli hats to protect themselves from the fierce sun as they trudged behind their lumbering bullocks plowing the fields. We were herded into one of the waiting jeepneys, the form of motor transport. The manner in which they were adorned and brightly painted was a reflection of the gaiety and expressiveness of the Filipino character.

A crowd piled in, swinging backpacks onto the roof. Several travelers boisterously scrambled onto the roof for a better view. As we traveled along the bumpy road the dust rose up, laying an orange covering over everything. It was dusk by the time we eventually arrived at Caticlan and had to make the short journey by sea to Boracay at twilight.

Excitement was running high as half a dozen travelers loaded their packs into the waiting buncas and set off to the island retreat. We could only just see the outline of Boracay silhouetted against the night sky. Our temporary shipmates hailed from an assortment of countries: Germany, Sweden, USA. We attempted to converse in broken English, each sharing his personal tales of good fortunes, narrow escapes, and intrepid adventures. Lights from the various beachfront settlements decorated the night. Distant music floated through the velvety air, piercing the silence that reigned over the ocean. Michelle and I were tense with anticipation as we envisioned ourselves on this exotic island and the delights we were about to experience.

Nine days later, here I was taking the same journey back to Caticlan in vastly different circumstances. The laughter and happiness of that moment was all but a distorted memory. I was leaving Boracay alone, but my daughter would remain here forever.

Goodbye, Michelle

Before I knew it we had arrived at the airport. I had been lost within my thoughts, far removed from the external happenings. I fluctuated between having the courage to face what I must and wondering how I could possibly manage to carry it out. At the crucial moment when I had to board the plane I was seized by feeling the latter. Being physically removed from the place where Michelle lived her last hours was like turning my back and walking away from a graveside.

I was incapable of boarding the aircraft. Petrified, I stood frozen to the spot, feeling as if every single cell inside my skin was a moving vibration, erupting its lethal venom of fear through my body. Caught up in a vortex of indecision, I felt powerless to take the first step forward which would ultimately propel me towards what seemed an abysmal future. I was deserting her, leaving her amongst strangers. To be on Boracay was to be near to her, but circumstances dictated I leave this place. How could a mother make that choice?

It required more than I had within me. David's words floated back to my consciousness, hovering around the edges of my awareness: *Defeat is in the mind. You have to keep fighting for Michelle's sake.* I felt someone take hold of my arm, guiding me towards the plane. Inside I was silently screaming, *No, don't make me do this! I can't go through with this!* But nevertheless I found myself being led onto the plane and resisting like a rebellious child.

The fuselage rumbled as the aircraft revved to its maximum.Although we bounced along the makeshift runway, the vibrations finally ceased as we became airborne. Within seconds I could see the tops of the palm trees, then the bleached expanses of beach converging with the ocean, hundreds of miles of it. The island looked nothing more than a minuscule droplet of fertile earth against the immensity of oceanic blue liquid.

I was instantly struck by the possibility of seeing Michelle's bunca as we flew over the sea from Boracay to Manila. A flood of hope shot through my veins! Like a drug it was transforming me, elevating me to a level of renewed anticipation. I became alive with the alluring suggestion. Unbuckling my seatbelt I walked up the aisle and spoke individually to all the passengers, pleading for them to look out for a small boat which could very possibly belong to my daughter who had been lost at sea five days earlier.

I felt inquisitive eyes search out mine, delving into my wretched thoughts, trying to fathom what it would feel like to be the parent who had just lost her child. Sympathetic glances and words of consolation were uttered, though I wasn't listening. I didn't need their pity; I needed their help. All that I required of them was to enlist their eyes to scan the ocean surface where mine could not. To my relief they were more than agreeable. I observed their faces pressed to the windows, eager to be of service to a grief-stricken mother.

By the time I had returned to my seat and looked out the window, to my dismay the plane had gained considerable altitude. We were now flying so high above the ocean it resembled a gigantic blue carpet, where nothing distinguishable could be seen. I was distraught that we could fly right over Michelle and she would see us but we wouldn't be able to see her. I wrestled with the terrible irony of this happening for some minutes, then gave up the mental anguish.

I realized it was futile to pit myself against something I had no control over. Of course I was far from accepting what had happened, but I had to believe God had His reasons and at this time in my life I hadn't either the wisdom or ability to see into eternity and judge what was right or wrong. I questioned if I really believed He knew us intimately and could intercede on our behalf. Or was I just paying lip service to a deity I didn't believe really could intervene or physically act in human affairs. It was a tough one!

I sat with that question burning into me with the intensity of a blowtorch. People proclaim they believe in God; when confronted with death or disaster, they turned to God, pleaded for His help to rectify the situation or produce a miracle. But did they really believe He had the power to do what they asked or the faith to know He could? In this very confusing situation I found myself faced with the same conflicting questions, forced to confront what I truly believed. The faith I believed I had was put to the ultimate test. These crucial questions flamed within me, demanding answers!

Deliberating this question, I finally broke through from indecision into clarity. "Yes, Lord, I do believe You have the power, and I will not withdraw my trust in You. I don't know why this has happened to my darling girl. I know she's Your child as well, but because my understanding is so limited, please give me the heart to know You better and the strength to accept Your will, and please heal the pain."

Tears of humility flowed gently down my cheeks, the conflicting emotions and oppressing disillusionment had lifted from me and in their place I felt a reassurance and serenity. An unfathomable tranquility seeped through my entire being; like cool water it extinguished the inferno that had raged over the past five days. At last I felt a measure of peace.

I gazed out the window and was astonished to see the most magnificent rainbow. For a moment I just stared at it, then instantly it struck me as being strangely significant. I had never seen anything like it before! It was only a miniature rainbow shaped like a boomerang; the seven colors were so vivid and well-defined. It was as if God had placed it in the sky for my benefit alone.

I clung to this sign from heaven. God was acknowledging His promise; He had heard my prayers and all was well. I was reminded of what the rainbow represented. God had created the rainbow for Noah to see after the earth's destruction by the Great Flood. It symbolized His eternal promise that He upholds those who have faith and love Him. It seemed uncanny the way this extraordinary-shaped rainbow appeared in the sky as if for my eyes only.

For the first time in days I felt fortified sufficiently enough to turn my thoughts to my two younger children who were still innocently unaware of the tragedy that had taken place. My arms suddenly felt empty and I longed to hold them. The fierceness of a mother lion to protect her cubs gripped hold of me. I urgently yearned to take solace in their sweet innocence, to touch them, hug them, and sincerely appreciate the precious gift given me through my children.

What wonderful thing had I ever done to deserve these treasures to fill my life with love and joy? One moment in the act of love these children were conceived and grew to perfection. They are truly the mark of God's great work. He had fashioned them in His likeness, then offered them into my care. What a priceless gift!

I experienced a twinge of guilt! How blasé I had been taking everything in life for granted. Never again would I take life for granted or forget to tell the people I love how much I appreciate and cherish them. One never knows the day or hour when our loved ones will be called home. I took comfort in the fact that Michelle and I had spent those wonderful last days together; they would be memories I'd treasure forever.

The question remained, however: How would I tell my children what had happened to their big sister? It would surely break their hearts. Hypothetical conversations raced around in my head. *Now, girls, please sit down. I have something to tell you. You're obviously wondering why Michelle hasn't come back with me. Well, she loved the Philippines and the people so much she decided never to leave there. She is very happy where she is, and God is looking after her now.*

The focus of my own grief suddenly diminished as I was struck by the anguish that would be inflicted on my girls. My concern for them was a blessed relief as it took the emphasis off myself and made me consider what effects this shocking news would have on them. They were still trying to deal with the loss of their father due to our recent divorce. Sometimes life seemed so incredibly cruel, but I knew they would be relying on me to hold us all together especially during the initial shock.

Being responsible for the welfare of children always had a way of carrying me through the impossible. Thank goodness I had them to go home to, or I could never have left Boracay.

Manila . . . and Civilization

I had the sensation that we were descending. Glancing out of the window to confirm my notion I saw the city of Manila ahead of us, the tall buildings of Makati standing out against the skyline. It felt as if a motor inside my chest had kick-started my heart. From the relative calm I had maintained during the flight I was abruptly thrust into a frantic panic. The thought of being in Manila on my own under such deplorable circumstances was more than I could cope with. I suddenly found it difficult to breathe; I felt I was being smothered by the claustrophobic confines of the tiny aircraft. Thank goodness we were coming in to land as I desperately needed to be freed from this steel entrapment.

As we rolled slowly into the plane's berth, I found myself standing at the door, immediately impatient to be the first off. In the space of only minutes I was off the plane and walking across the tarmac towards the terminal. There were no customs to go through as it was a local flight so I was free to pass straight by.

Slinging one backpack over my shoulder, I managed to half carry, half drag the other one toward the barrier. My eyes instantly met a gentleman who was obviously seeking me out. It could be none other than George Frazer from the Australian Embassy. The expression on his friendly face indicated he recognized me. As her stepped forward he alleviated me from the burden I was dragging behind me.

"You must be Ms. Hamilton? I'm George Frazer and a representative from the New Zealand Consulate has also come to meet you."

"Hello, thank you for meeting me. I appreciate that."

"That's okay, is this your only luggage?"

"Yes."

"We have a car waiting out the front. Here, let me carry that pack for you."

"Oh thanks." I willingly allowed these two men to take control of the situation and bear some of the weight of responsibility from my shoulders.

Mr. Frazer had a pleasant, true-blue Australian face, if there was such a thing. His expression was warm, and the eyes behind the glasses were full of compassion; I imagined him to be totally without a bone of malice in his body. No doubt this was one of the more unpleasant duties he had to perform in the official role of Consulate. I was so relieved to be in the company of my own countrymen and found it reassuring to be back at last on the mainland in the protection of officials who had the power to help me.

I was bewildered as to why the New Zealand Consulate representative was present. I knew I had only contacted the Australian Embassy, so how did they know of my Kiwi background? The question went unanswered; I was only grateful to have their presence I decided, as I followed them out to the waiting vehicle.

It was a shock to my system being immersed back in civilization. During the past nine days I had had the sensation of being stranded on a distant planet. It had been difficult to believe the world still existed outside Boracay. Unsuspectingly I was now thrown amid the crazy Filipino rush-hour traffic, where thousands of people converged like ants, scurrying in every direction accompanied by a deafening cacophony of sounds.

The manner in which Filipinos drove their cars was unparalleled by any other culture I had witnessed. As if they had only just received their car horns for Christmas, they weaved in and out of the traffic, beeping them continually as they went. The vehicles seemed to be conducting excited dialogue between themselves, a kind of automotive morse code conversation. This traffic fever flavored the tapestry of bustling Manila. Commuters hung out of every imaginable type of vehicle; the city rush hour was certainly something to experience.

I found the diversity from the tranquility of the island dramatic. It was as if I'd been transported from the moon and deposited in the middle of a three-ringed circus. Spellbound, I observed the affray from my position of obscurity behind a car window. Agile pedestrians had developed ingenious techniques of dodging between cars as they sped through red lights with their horns sounding to warn everyone of their intent. Multi-colored jeepneys decorated the streets which were jammed with city workers returning home. We drove through the winding traffic, and both men, sensing my distraction, allowed me to adjust to this energetic environment before they asked me the barrage of painful questions which we all knew must eventually be asked.

I had become engrossed by this exuberant race of people, who lived out their lives close to reality. There were very few embellishments in the lives of these people, but my admiration of their quick, fertile minds, their sense of humor, and positive acceptance of their place in the scheme of things was sincere. Even in extreme poverty laughter was heard above the clatter of daily life. They extracted great pleasure from the simple things. A flicker of transparent clarity flashed into my mind: the Western World could learn a great deal from the Filipinos, with their spiritual values and sense of community caring!

The raw, pulsating tension had waned for the time being. The company of people from my own country had a pacifying effect on me; at last I felt a measure of safety even though it was false security, a temporary haven.

Eventually we arrived at a huge compound where an armed guard stood erect in his duty of protecting the entrance. As we approached, the uniformed security patrol recognized the car, opening the formidable gates immediately. I was shocked to see the heavy weaponry he carried, especially since I presumed this was a suburban area. Evidently the diplomatic families and other important persons who lived within the walls needed security and protection.

Enclosed inside the compound were homes, streets, in fact a complete suburb where international delegates and businessmen could reside in seclusion. As we cruised past magnificent Hollywood-styled homes, it came as an abrupt awakening to see such a sharp disparity of living standards in such close proximity. I made no comment of my perception; this was common in modern cities all over the world. The rich and the poor living on top of each other in sprawling overcrowded areas was a fact of twentieth-century living. As the diplomatic car purred up the driveway, a valet appeared from nowhere to attend to his duties.

Stepping into the sanctuary beyond the reinforced doors, we found an atmosphere of cool, tasteful luxury. The gleaming marble floor resounded as our footfalls shattered the silence which was heavily laden with a prevailing sense of sorrow. The fresh flow of air conditioning enveloped me, and it was welcoming to be in such a meticulous environment after enduring a hectic, sweltering day.

I experienced an acute sensation of unreality. After spending seven harrowing days on a remote island, the present surroundings I now found myself in appeared somehow superficial to my unaccustomed eyes, as if they belonged in a doll's house. I was bombarded with the revelation of how very little material possessions mattered when it came down to the value of human life.

I was ushered into a spacious lounge room tastefully furnished in subtle natural tones. The elegantly decorated room was in stark contrast to the casual jeans and track shoes I was wearing; they seemed to emphasize the unforeseen circumstances that brought me here. I felt distinctly out of place in the unfamiliar setting although my hosts were doing everything possible to help me feel comfortable.

Delicious hors d'oeuvres and refreshments were offered by George's wife, a petite beauty from Laos. I absently picked at the food but had no appetite; it was merely a diversion to fill the apprehension. I was simply delaying the moment when I would be expected to relate the traumatic events of the past few days.

Acknowledging the Truth

For a brief time I had been absorbed by the sights and sounds of downtown Manila, but now that distraction had passed. My real purpose for being here thrust itself back into the forefront of my mind, dominating every other thought. We all were putting off broaching the grim subject of Michelle's disappearance, delaying the inevitable with pleasantries that were merely superfluous. Nevertheless, the distressing topic had to be discussed. I was again on center stage and was expected to retell the story all over again, detail by agonizing detail. In a few moments I would be submerged back into the well of crushing emotions.

"I imagine this is going to be very upsetting for you to have to talk about, but unfortunately we need to know the exact details of the accident. Do you feel up to telling us exactly what happened?" Mr. Frazer asked, concerned, realizing what he was asking me to do.

"Yes, I think so. There will never be a good time to do it, so I may as well get it over with. Then we can get a search underway as soon as possible. Where do I begin?" I said, absently searching through my mind for a starting point.

When did this tragedy begin? Did the process start with the decision to go to Boracay, or was it when we chose to hire the boat on that fateful day? It was more likely the wheels for disaster were set in motion when Michelle elected not to come in early but rather to continue to sail around the island. At what precise point had an innocent day's outing turned to catastrophe? These questions most probably would always remain a mystery. In a fleeting thought, it suddenly occurred to me, if these incidences were preordained before birth, then this was a *collison with destiny,* and it would have brought us to this place regardless of any futile attempts we may have taken to avoid this divine appointment.

I decided a starting place for the story to be told was with our decision to go the Philippines.

Stammering out the first few words, I tentatively began, "On Tuesday when we had been horseback riding, we had discovered the remote beauty of the other side of the island and decided to hire a boat the next day and sail around to it. However the next day the wind was so blustery, we decided to postpone it until the next day. On Thursday morning the weather conditions looked perfect, and we hired a bunca from the owners of the bungalows where we were staying. We had planned to picnic around the other side and do some snorkeling there. We were so enthusiastic about the wonderful day ahead of us," I explained in a voice quivering with raw emotion as I recalled the events of that morning that would forever change my life.

Every single detail of that fateful day was etched into my mind and no doubt I would churn over again and again in the years to come the terrible circumstances that had taken my daughter's life. I would forever relive the moment when Michelle had dropped me back to shore and I had asked her to come back in with me. If only I had been adamant about it, this may never have happened and I wouldn't be sitting here now. The thought of Michelle lying on the bottom of the ocean conjured up grisly images that triggered a chilling sensation, congealing the warm flow of blood in my veins.

"You musn't torment yourself with guilt. There was no way you could have known the outcome. It was not your fault! Don't blame yourself!" Mr. Frazer comforted me.

"I don't really, but to know I could have prevented it and didn't kills me."

"Don't dwell on that now. You'll only upset yourself more. By the way, can you remember what time Michelle set out in the boat alone?"

"About ten thirty was the last time I saw her alive!" Sobs of inconsolable grief that I'd held in check burst forth like a fountain. Powerless to comfort me, my hosts compassionately waited for my tears to subside before I could continue the story.

"We are very distressed by what has happened," he soothed. "My job frequently involves having to deal with matters similar to this, and it never gets any easier. When an Australian loses his life over here, we all feel saddened. If there is anything we can do to help you through this rough time, please don't hesitate to ask. We will do all we can to help." I sat up.

"Actually there is something you can help me with. That's specifically what I've come here for. I want an official, full-scale search mounted for Michelle immediately. The search up until now has been sketchy and insufficient. Several fishing boats went out looking for her but found nothing. As you already know, I hired a light plane to search for her, but after two hours they found no trace of her. Apart from these two limited attempts to find her nothing else significant has been done. How long would it take for you to authorize a search and get it underway?"

"Rachelle, if I may call you that, it's distressing for me to have to tell you this, but as I explained to you on the phone before you left Boracay, unfortunately we have neither the resources or equipment to carry out a search of this nature."

"There must be something you can do! I was told there are American military units based right here in Manila. They must have aircrafts and helicopters available. Considering the urgency of the situation, couldn't you ask them if they could make a plane available? After all, they are our allies. Please do whatever you can," I pleaded, the desperation rising in my voice.

"Those aircraft you're speaking of are military planes, not civil, and we have no such policy to request assistance for private searches. I'm truly sorry, but I don't know what else to suggest to you. You have already conducted an aerial search around the supposed area where she went missing and found nothing." Shifting uncomfortably in his chair and looking at me sympathetically, he said, "She's been gone five days now, hasn't she? The chances of finding her are . . ." He wasn't able to finish what he was going to say, and his words hung in the air like a death sentence.

Devastated, I slumped in the chair trying to comprehend the impact of his condemning words. It was perfectly clear to me he thought the situation was hopeless; his verdict seemed final. He believed Michelle would not be coming back.

Too choked with emotion to speak, I remained silent. I realized, *This was it. I have come to the end of the road and there is nowhere else to turn.* A feeble objection rose up in me, then collapsed; I had no impetus left in me to fight back. I had to acknowledge the finality of Michelle's destiny: My beloved daughter who was lost at sea had obviously drowned in the storm on that first night. The reality that I had attempted to deny for days now surfaced, and I had to accept it.

Inwardly I'd feared this all along because my thoughts had kept returning magnetically to the crucial scene in my dream where Michelle had become the embodiment of that lifeless doll floating in the ocean with its eyes missing, where the soul of its occupant had so obviously departed. I felt so infuriatingly ineffectual; if only there were something more I could do! Now I had to face up to the fact that Michelle was dead, but at least I could salve my conscience by knowing that I had done everything possible to save her.

Although I had suspected the truth all along, making this admission outwardly caused an eruption inside me.

"She was such a beautiful girl, so special . . ." I mumbled, speaking to no one particular.

"I'm sure she was," someone commiserated.

"You know, I'd come on this holiday to rest and spend time with Michelle. If only I could have foreseen what would happen. I can't believe she's dead; it's still impossible to accept. You know, she was only twenty-two and had so much life in her."

I continued with a limp smile as I remembered what was already a memory. "She was always such a daredevil, trying to extract as much out of life as she could. She wasn't afraid to take a risk or speak her mind even though it did sometimes get her into trouble. Her blatant truthfulness often shocked people, but that never stopped her. She radiated such an air of confidence she was able to get away with it. Strangely enough this actually endeared people to her. Michelle had always loved to travel, and one of her dreams was to backpack through America. It was a country she had a strong affinity for, but now I guess she never will."

I rambled on absent-mindedly, neither desiring or requiring a reply. They considerately allowed me to pour out my heart to them. "It seems such a terrible waste, such a loss, not only to me but to the world."

"It does seem so senseless, especially someone so young with so much to live for. I wish there were something I could do or say that would make you feel better, but at times like this, words seem so inadequate. Do you have any other children?" he asked.

"Yes, I have two younger daughters back in Sydney, and I absolutely adore them, but they will never replace Michelle. One child can't replace another. We were more like sisters. The age difference between us wasn't that great. Michelle was like a star that shone brighter than the rest. She was like a magnet that drew people to her unconsciously and held them spellbound in her company. I know this sounds like a mother talking, and you're probably thinking I'm biased, but I would often glance over at her at a party and she would have unwittingly attracted a group of people who were drawn to her. Tell me, how could all of that vibrant energy and charisma just disappear off the face of the earth? Where has she gone?" I said, knowing they were unable to supply the answers.

"She sounds like a wonderful girl. I wish I'd had the opportunity of meeting her. It must be so painful for you. There are no simple answers when something like this happens. You just have to believe she's safe and in good hands."

"It's that very belief that has carried me through this tragedy. I do have faith and believe she is in heaven with Jesus," I affirmed.

"If you have faith, you have everything! Keep hold of that. It will see you through. What are your plans now? Have you made any?"

"No, I had all my hopes pinned on your being able to organize another search, but you've just told me that's out of the question. So there's little else that I can do here. Only I can't face going home just

---

"Now I had to face up to the fact that Michelle was dead, but at least I could salve my conscience by knowing that I had done everything possible to save her."

---

yet. I think I'll stay here for a while to put my thoughts in order and try to come to terms with this before I have to go home and break this devastating news to my children. They only have me to rely on. I'll have to be the strong one, to comfort them though the loss of their big sister and help ease their pain. It destroys me to think of how this will affect their lives. This will seem so unjust to them. How will they ever trust in anything again? It's too awful to even think about."

"You'll still have each other, and in time you will all heal and learn to trust again. The best thing for you to do now is take it easy and rest. We will assist you in any way we can. No doubt you will need replacement passports, tickets, and travelers cheques, and we'll see to it that these are organized for you."

"Thanks very much. I feel too upset at the moment to even think about anything else. Right now all I want to do is go to bed and sleep and not have to face any of this."

"Under the circumstances, that's completely understandable. Do you have any sedatives to calm you?"

"No, I think I would have swallowed the whole bottle by now if I had."

"Don't do a silly thing like that, will you? We'll get a doctor to call on you in the morning if you like. He will be able to prescribe something to help calm your nerves."

"Thanks, I think that would help."

"I'm sorry to have to bring up the subject at a time like this but it has to be tackled. No doubt you will be traveling back to Australia soon so I have to ask you. I'm sure you realize the chances of Michelle's body being found are fairly remote. It's an enormous ocean out there and it's highly unlikely, but if she is found, what procedures would you like us to take? Would you prefer her body to be sent back to Australia so she can be buried at home?"

His words plunged into my heart like a dagger. My darling girl was now being referred to as a corpse. A tormented scream rose in my throat, and I was unable to answer him. How could he expect me to answer such a gruesome question? At that moment I wished the ground would open and swallow me up.

The sound of ringing bells reached my ears as if they were coming through a hazy fog. Mr. Frazer's words barely penetrated the sanctuary where I had retreated inside myself, unable to deal with this cruel reality.

"Excuse me for a moment. I have to answer the telephone."

Left alone with the questions reverberating around me, I felt as if I had been thrust into a spiraling black tunnel that had no end. Thank God, the phone had rung and prevented me from answering him, because to do that would be to accept her as dead and lost to us forever.

I couldn't believe this had happened to Michelle, the baby that had grown inside me, the tiny creature I had nurtured at my breast, the one I had watched tenderly grow step by step into womanhood, the human being I knew more intimately than any other on earth. I could always read her feelings by the expression on her face; every gesture she made was familiar to me. I loved the way Michelle threw her head back when she laughed or the way she blushed deeply when caught off guard. The intensity and laughter in her expressive green eyes would never look into mine again. I wondered if these unique characteristics that were so much a part of her personality were still a part of her where she was now.

Michelle, where are you? If only you could come back and tell me that you are all right, I could spend the rest of my days in peace. If by chance you can see me or hear me now, please know that I love you dearly and will always miss you terribly. Goodbye, my darling. My thoughts and love are with you always. I wept.

The sound of heavy footsteps snapped me out of my thoughts. George's ecstatic voice shattered the gloomy silence.

"Michelle's alive! They found her floating out in the middle of the ocean. It's an absolute miracle, but she's been rescued by Filipino fishermen and apparently is alive and escaped without serious injury."

Rising to my feet in triumph, I threw my hands into the air as a fountain of profound joy burst forth from within me. Tears of intense relief and thankfulness flowed from me. An absolute miracle had been performed by the living God! With arms outstretched toward heaven I cried out loud, "Praise God! Oh thank you, Jesus, thank you for saving Michelle!"

TWENTY-ONE

OUT OF THE DARKNESS

MICHELLE . . . 2:00 P.M., SUNDAY, MARCH 12, MANILA. On wobbly legs that barely supported me I finally stepped onto truly dry land . . . Manila! A multitude of outstretched hands reached for mine, assisting me off the gangplank and onto the deck.

Instantly I began to feel dizzy and disoriented, fearing that I would collapse if I didn't sit down. A mass of people swarmed around me, directing questions to me at machine-gun pace. Remembering my rescuers, I turned back to wave a last goodbye to the men who had saved my life and delivered me to this destination. A woman in the crowd strode purposefully towards me; she was obviously Mr. Bobby del Rosario's sister. Thank God, someone was here to help me! She recognized me immediately, probably because I was the only fair-headed, sunburnt person among them.

"Are you Miss Michelle?"

"Yes, I am."

"I'm so pleased to meet you. I'm Susan. My brother Bobby del Rosario, who is the owner of your rescue ship the *Alyss Star,* told me what happened to you. I just can't believe it! It's so amazing that you survived all that time without food or water."

"Yes," I nodded agreeing with her, too exhausted to make conversation.

"Anyway, there is plenty of time to tell your story later. My brother told me you urgently need to get a message to your mother on Boracay Island."

"Yes, that's right. She doesn't yet know I'm alive," I conveyed anxiously.

"Well, I'm at your service. I have my car over there," she said pointing to a shiny black jeep. "I'll take you anywhere you want to go."

"Thank you, that is very kind of you. First, I think it is best if you take me to the police so I can find out if my mother has reported me as a missing person and let them know that I was lost but now I'm found."

She looked at me and smiled, knowing I meant this in more than just the physical sense. "If I may suggest, I think it would be best for you to go to the Coast Guard station first, because if your mother has filed a missing person's report, it would be lodged there. Also they have very modernized equipment and would be able to telex your message straight through to Boracay."

"Okay, that sounds logical. Is it far away?" I said, knowing that every second was precious and there was not a moment to waste.

There could be no rest for me until Mum knew I was alive and well in Manila. I was frantic to tell her about my miraculous rescue and my even more miraculous ordeal. Right at this moment she was probably preparing for my funeral. For Mum to discover I was alive would seem as if I were returning from the dead. Every passing minute must seem like an eternity when one is waiting for news to find out if your loved ones are safe.

The worst possible discovery for Mum would be to learn that I was dead but at least what had become of me would be certain and she could begin to heal. However, I knew the waiting game and uncertainty of not knowing what happened to me would be an unbearable torture. She must have thrashed out a million different scenarios when I didn't come back, forever left to wonder what had become of me. Was mine a quick painless death, or did I suffer horribly before death finally engulfed me? Did I drown or was I eaten by sharks? The ghastly thoughts which must have possessed her mind instantly filled me with palatable guilt, especially since her holiday was for the sole purpose of rest and recuperation.

Notify Mum!

It had now been four days since I had been missing. How could she possibly still hold on to the hope of my being alive? Every passing hour to Mum would most surely confirm my death. The joy and relief I knew she would feel at finding I had been restored to her was unimaginable; I was anxious for her to know the truth.

As I climbed into the back seat of the jeep, Susan introduced me to her friend whose name I didn't register. Switching on the ignition she drove off, leaving a cloud of dust behind us. I answered as best I could the stream of questions Susan hurled at me, although most of my an-

---

"Right at this moment she was probably preparing for my funeral. For Mum to discover I was alive would seem as if I were returning from the dead."

---

swers were monosyllabic. Sensing my exhausted voice trailing off in a sigh, she tactfully left me to rest while she drove speedily to the Coast Guard station. Wearily, I leaned back against the seat and closed my mind to everything except the faint mumbling of their conversation in Tagalog.

After fifteen minutes of extremely bumpy travel along the unsealed back roads of Manila, we finally arrived at the Coast Guard station. Susan helped me from the jeep, and I braced myself for another round of tedious questions. Where are you from? How did this happen? Where is your mother? I felt so incredibly weary of answering this continuous stream of questions, questions, questions! I would have to endure another couple of hours for the sake of my mother. Then it would be all over and I could sink into a nice soft bed, wrap the cool linen sheets around my body, and drift off into an oblivious sleep.

With sluggish movements, as if I had been drugged, I hauled myself out of the jeep and staggered into the station. Susan motioned for me to sit down while she explained the situation to the officer on duty. I watched his face contort in bewilderment and he turned to stare at me as if he had difficulty in believing her account of my story. Obviously unsure of what action to take, he left the room.

Susan explained to me that he didn't speak very good English and would get the lieutenant in charge to assist me. I heard a sudden yapping noise behind me and turned around to see what it was. My face lit up at once as an adorable little German shepherd puppy came scurrying around the corner, sliding on the shiny floor. This fluffy bundle of joy stood before me wagging his tail incessantly, begging for attention.

Clicking my fingers together I called out "Come on boy" and he came over to me, licking my toes and hands excitedly. I felt the strain of torn muscles in my back as I leaned down to swoop him up in my arms. I felt my spirits lifting and momentarily forgot not only my mother but my aches and pains as well as I embraced this warm, furry bundle of life. This tender act of affection touched my heart in such a way it made me realize the significant importance of the simple pleasures in life. It struck me instantly that from this moment on I would see everything in a new light and appreciate God's bounty of which I had previously taken for granted.

"Miss Michelle." The sound of my name being called out brought me back to the core of my problem. "The lieutenant is out of the office for about half an hour on business. Do you wish to wait for him?"

"It seems I have little choice," I said, trying to conceal my frustration that someone wasn't available to help. "Well, Susan, if I am going to have to wait for half an hour, do you think I could possibly use their telephone directory? I want to alert the Australian Embassy and call the airport. This way I'll be able to find out if my Mum has left Boracay Island."

Before she had time to answer, the officer in charge came to my aid, having overheard me. He escorted me over to the table where I sat down while he brought me the telephone directories.

Without thinking I opened the cover and started with the A's for Australian Embassy. It suddenly dawned on me that the directory was printed in English not Tagalog as I had expected. Thank God for that! I located the number quite easily and dialed it immediately.

I felt a flutter of raw nerves buzz inside my stomach. I was about to speak to someone from home, who understood me perfectly and had the power to help me. What a glorious sense of relief this would be! After the first couple of rings a recorded message came on the line saying "I'm sorry but the Australian Embassy is closed at the moment and the phone is unattended. If you call back on Monday to Friday between the hours of 8:30 A.M. and 4:30 P.M. our office will be open then."

No! It suddenly occurred to me that it was Sunday and nobody would be there. Now what was I going to do? I racked my brain for an answer while the message droned on. I was at a total loss as to what to do next and was about to hang up the phone when the taped voice stated if there was a real emergency—and they emphasized this—then I should leave my name, number and the reason for my call and they would get back to me as soon as possible.

I questioned myself—did I fit into the category of emergency? It automatically struck me as what a stupid question this was. How much more desperate did a situation have to get before it was classified as an emergency? Yes, of course, this applied to me. The phone beeped, signaling me that it was ready for me to leave my message.

Suddenly I was at a loss for words. I didn't know where to begin. Embarrassed, I hung up the phone and thought about what I was going to say and where I could be contacted. I had no idea which hotel or, for that matter, where I would be at all. The most reliable and convenient place where I could be contacted was right here at the Coast Guard station. I asked the officer to write down the phone number and address and proceeded to call again. This time armed with the correct information, I related my ordeal and my urgent need to contact my mother, who I believed was still on Boracay Island.

Now that I had dealt with that important task I felt some measure of relief; however there was still one more job to do before I could relax and that was to call the airlines.

I carefully extracted our damp and partially disintegrated airline tickets from my money belt. With difficulty I studied Mum's British Airways ticket, barely able to read the smudged type. As I held it between my shaking fingers, I guessed that she wouldn't have flown home to Australia yet, which meant she was still on Boracay Island or had flown to Manila. I decided to call Philippine Airlines to check whether my mother had flown from Boracay to Manila in the past few days. I read out Mum's passport number but didn't have much luck with her ticket as several of the numbers were illegible. The receptionist reassured me that I had given her sufficient information but that it would take awhile to verify if the ticket had been used.

An eternity seemed to have passed as I waited for her to come back to the phone. Now that I was compelled to sit still, I began to feel awfully nauseous. I realized I needed food to strengthen me as I hadn't eaten more than two mangoes and a few spoonfuls of rice in more than four days. I felt extremely weak and knew it would take a lot more than one meal and a good night's sleep to repair my depleted body and return me to my former good health. However, something to eat would sustain me for the next undoubtedly grueling hours.

Without warning a dizziness surged through me, and a loud throbbing noise began to ring in my ears. I closed my eyes; momentarily, it was dark like a black screen which abruptly became covered in a mass of twinkling stars which flashed on and off as they whizzed around inside my head. I tried repeatedly to erase these stars and refocus my eyes but it was hopeless. I experienced the sensation of spiraling downward and knew I was about to blackout.

Crunch! The phone fell from my hand onto the table, shattering the silence with a loud clang and the elbow which had been supporting me slipped from under my chin; my head slumped forward. I immediately sensed people beside me and a hand was placed on my forehead.

"Are you okay? Is everything all right?" they asked me with concern as they lifted me upright.

Disconecting myself from the fuzzy haze that had overpowered me, I forced myself to answer "Yes, I'm all right," dispelling their fears for me.

"Would you like to lie down?" one of the officers kindly asked me, seeing the evidence of my weakened state. I felt myself yielding to his suggestion and almost said yes. There was nothing in the world I longed for more than to lie down and sleep without the fear of dying, yet still I had to endure until these tasks had been taken care of.

"No, I won't, thank you, but I would like a glass of water please," I asked, hoping it would revive me long enough till I would be able to get something substantial to eat. He scurried off and returned with a large, cool glass of water.

"Hello, hello. Is anybody there?" I heard a faint voice calling through the telephone receiver.

Jarred back to the purpose of my call I picked up the handpiece and apologized, explaining that I had accidentally dropped the phone. "What did you find out?" I asked eagerly, waiting to hear some news that would confirm or deny my assumptions.

"Well, the data on the computer says that the ticket is still unused, although it is possible she may have purchased another ticket from a different airline."

I wondered if that were likely; to my knowledge she had no money as I had all our cash and travelers' checks in my money belt. Perhaps someone on the island had lent her the fare to Manila? My mind assimilated this information and calculated the likelihood of this being the case. I couldn't think; it was all speculation, and I doubted I would get any further information from the airline inquiries clerk.

"Oh well, thank you for your help," I said, disappointed that neither of my phone calls had resulted in bringing me closer in my search for Mum.

I heard a motor vehicle pull up, and a car door slammed. A Filipino man with short, sleek black hair entered the station. Although he was not overly tall, his presence commanded attention; he was obviously the

---

"My phenomenal journey to the brink of death brought me to the outstanding discovery that God was real."

---

lieutenant. Striding over to the officer on duty, he conferred with him for several minutes then threw a surprised glance in my direction and strode into his office.

Susan explained to me rather apologetically that she would have to now leave me in the care of the lieutenant because she had to pick up her little girl. Obligingly, she offered to return later and help me find a suitable hotel for me to spend the night. I thanked her and told her not to worry, that I would catch a taxi to the nearest hotel possible. Susan told me that her brother would be in contact with me as soon as I was rested and felt well enough. He wished to meet the mermaid his employees had gallantly rescued!

"Well, Michelle, we have completed the formalities here. Would you like to get something to eat? You must be very hungry," the aide asked.

"Now that you mention it I'm absolutely famished. I haven't been able to relax enough to think about food until I had relieved my mind of the nagging duty to inform my mother I was alive."

Taking hold of my arm he helped me from my chair and we walked into the foyer. I asked Lt. Fernando del Rosario to leave a message with his officers that if the Australian Embassy called to tell them I was out getting something to eat and as soon as I knew the hotel where I would be staying, I would call here at the Coast Guard station and leave the necessary details with them. The Lieutenant translated all this to his officer, who nodded his head in acknowledgment. He held the door of the taxi open for me as I stumbled into it ungracefully.

Walking out through the throngs of people, without warning I was struck with an extraordinary sensation: Here I was a part of the human traffic again. Yet I felt apart and separate from these people, as if I didn't belong to the human race anymore.

Aside from the severe burns on my face and the staggering gait, I wondered if anyone guessed the catastrophic ordeal I had managed to escape from. I felt different; surely I must look different!

My phenomenal journey to the brink of death brought me to the outstanding discovery that God was real. I had talked personally to the Creator of the universe and saw the undeniable supernatural miracles He had performed for my eyes only; then in an instant I had been deposited back to the land of the living. How could I not be transformed forever by what I had lived through? It was indelibly carved on my mind for all time.

Live Life to the Fullest

I could never turn back the clock. I could never erase the past four days. Would I ever feel I belonged to this earth again? Would I ever be an average, normal person? At this moment I doubted it. In an instant I had been plugged back into the mundane world of daily living. From my observation people appeared to be walking around in a state of deathly sleepwalk.

I felt as if I were the only person who appreciated being alive. I wanted to shake them, wake them up, and tell them to be glad to be alive; to take hold of their lives and live in joy in the fullness of this wonderful gift. But, no, they wouldn't understand. Would anybody?

My past life seemed a blur. Until that moment, I realized I hadn't been living each day to its capacity. I would never again take for granted each morning sunrise when I'd been given a full twenty-four hours to live, to experience the euphoria of just being alive. Its very gift to us by our Divine Creator is a miracle in itself. I would never forget that every breath I took was a gift from God and a continuing example of His grace.

When the waters threatened to cut off my air supply, I realized then how very precious each and every breath was to us. For a reason only God alone knows, He had chosen to sustain my life and save me. I intuitively felt that God had a plan for my life and He would expect me to be faithful to that promise I made Him—that I would devote the rest of my life to serving Him in repayment for restoring my life to me.

The tasty meal left me feeling satisfied and marginally better. We left the restaurant in search of the second most urgent need on my agenda—a hotel, which meant a refreshing shower and blessed sleep in a proper bed. I couldn't wait!

Darkness had now fallen over the city and the streets of Manila were lit up like a Christmas tree. The city pulsed with vitality and the sidewalks were crammed to capacity with thousands of smiling, exuberant faces. Clubs, pubs, and restaurants were on every corner, beckoning business their way. The teeming crowds of people were a swarm of action like the drones in a hive. I instinctively sensed an undercurrent of danger and was pleased I was not walking the unfamiliar streets of Manila alone, but that Lt. del Rosario was still wearing his official-looking uniform, escorting me. We climbed into a cab and instructed the driver to take me to the nearest hotel.

Bone-weary, the very real threat of collapsing was ever present. As we walked to the entrance, I felt a pang of regret as tears of absolute exhaustion welled up in me, but I wouldn't allow myself to break, not now, not so close to finding a place to rest. I was thoroughly glad to have the lieutenant at my side, supporting me and being in the front line. The capacity even to keep my eyes open was fading fast.

As we began to walk, I suddenly became aware that every fibre of my being was saturated with exhaustion. Reality became a distorted daze. Even my vision was clouded by a hazy veil. Beneath me my trembling legs refused to carry the weight of my lifeless body any further, threatening to give way at any moment. Buckling at every step I had to fight to command them to keep moving. "Just a bit longer," I cajoled my aching limbs. My weary lids fluttered closed as I walked along the streets of Manila, opening again only when the lieutenant directed a question at me. I responded with monosyllabic answers, then returned to my thoughts of what a relief it would be to finally be alone.

My need to be cared for was paramount. Instantly a yearning for Mum came over me. I felt as if I had reverted to a sick and helpless child, totally reliant on the care and attention I knew only my mother could give me. I imagined her washing my hair, soothing away the pain in my body with the touch of loving hands. No request would be too great. She would lather my skin with moisterizer and then she would make me a cup of chicken soup and tuck me into bed. I blissfully imagined myself crawling into the haven of sleep and hibernating for six months.

How dearly I wished her to be here with me. *Soon,* I thought, *soon we will be together!* She would give me all that special attention and love that only a mother can. Thank God, I would now have the opportunity to say all the things I should have and tell her how very privileged I was to have her as my mother—appreciation we children don't express enough. Only when we are threatened with losing something we love can we fully appreciate its value as we should have in the first place. I was extremely fortunate to have been given a second chance. I never again would go without telling those around me how much I loved and appreciated them.

The lieutenant's voice broke into my chain of thought as he said, "Here we are." A hotel loomed up in front of me. At this stage I didn't care if it was a cowshed as long as I was able to lie down and sleep. Lt. Fernando booked me into the hotel under his name.

My heart took a dive as I read the sign on the elevator, "Sorry, Out of Order." This was the last straw! It was all too much for me. I began to shake with an inner rage at the obstacles and complications which seemed to be deliberately hindering me from getting any rest. I felt like doing something childish like throwing a tantrum and smashing a plate, which would do absolutely no good but would have the desired effect of making me feel better. I wanted to scream out my distress and have someone carry me up those flights of stairs that I believed I wasn't capable of climbing myself.

No, I'd have to endure this one last trial. Just a few more minutes and it would be over and then I could stay in bed for two whole weeks if I wished to. Little did I know that the immediate future held a crazy series of events which would not allow me one minute's peace, let alone two weeks of recuperation!

I asked Lt. del Rosario what level we were on so far. "Three," he said with a slight grimace, empathizing with me at the test ahead. I could barely place one foot in front of the other. It was going to take a supreme effort to make it to the sixth level. A voice in my head responded to my question: *The same way you left the bunca and swam unaided a mile into the arms of your rescuers on the* Alyss Star *when you were suffering from severe exhaustion.*

"You're right," I answered myself. "I did it then and I can do it now." With that resolve, one by agonizing one, I climbed the stairs—each step a minor victory over my body's determination to give up.

The fourth level was difficult, the fifth downright painful and the sixth pure agony. The muscles in my legs were afflicted with an acute burning sensation which I had come to know so well. With my jaws clenched tightly together I gradually ascended the last of the stairs. I felt like one of the walking dead; what spurred me on was the lure of the soft bed that awaited me on the sixth level. The pinnacle of achievement was reached when I placed both feet on the landing of my level. The lieutenant firmed his grip around my waist, supporting my full weight as he half dragged, half carried me into the room.

He opened the door wide and there before me was a sight for sore eyes . . . a bed! I staggered over and flopped down onto it like a limp rag doll. I lay there gasping for breath, unable to do anything else but wait patiently until the burning sensation boring into my limbs had subsided.

While I rested the lieutenant adjusted the aerial and attempted to get a clear picture on the archaic black and white television set. It was a tremendous relief having him to help me; however, now that I was safe, I had the overwhelming desire to be alone, for even to speak was an effort.

I think his perceptive nature sensed this, because immediately after he had handed me a bag of his own personal clothing for me to change into, he made a move to leave. I was about to shake his hand when I realized it was absolutely too formal for the occasion. Leaning over I gave him a hug. Quite surprised at my display of affection and gratitude, he said looking rather embarrassed, "If it's okay with you, Michelle, I'll call you tomorrow morning to see how you are."

"That's fine, I'd like that. You can be my early morning wake-up call, but please don't call too early as I plan to sleep in!" I said attempting to make a joke. "The way I feel now I will probably go into a comatose state and sleep forever."

"I hope not. You get a good night's rest and I'll see you tomorrow. Good night, I'll see myself out."

"Thanks, thanks for everything. Bye." He disappeared, the door closing softly behind him.

Finally I was alone! This state had proved to be as elusive as water in a parched desert over the past two days. It seemed rather ironic that only three days ago at sea I had hungered for human contact, craved for the comfort of conversation, and now all I wanted was to be left alone with my thoughts, the complexity of which made me shudder.

I looked longingly at the bed. My immediate needs were in conflict with one another. My body cried out for sleep but I also had the overwhelming desire to be cleaned first. I toyed with which one would be the most beneficial. Being clean took predominance; I knew I would not be able to sleep properly otherwise. However I decided to take a short rest before attempting the daunting task. I staggered back toward the bed, flinging garments of clothing off as I went. I gingerly lowered myself onto the bed, my body still a mass of bruises, torn muscles, and burnt skin. It wasn't quite the luxuriously soft bed with the white linen sheets and featherdown pillows I had been dreaming of all those long nights at sea, but it was certainly an improvement on the linoleum covered steel floor where I'd slept on the ship. I lay there feeling every ache and pain but nevertheless soaking up the measure of comfort it offered.

The images on the television screen flashed before me. The background hum was reassuring although I wasn't actually listening. Staring up at the ceiling, I realized that my body was still rocking to the cradle-like motion of the sea. I willed myself to stop! Even now rest eluded me!

Churning over and over in my mind was the call to the Coast Guard station which as yet I hadn't made. I had to find out if there was any updated news from Boracay. Had Mum received my message yet? Was the Australian Embassy aware that I had been rescued? Had they received my message? Were all businesses and departmental offices closed on Sunday?

Fernando and I had been gone from the Coast Guard station for about two hours; in that time a message could have come through. I knew I should call straight away but I just didn't think I could go through the rigmarole of explaining yet again my story to whoever answered the phone, especially if they didn't speak English. My best bet was to wait until Fernando returned, then simply ask him. Yes, that's what I would do!

My eye caught sight of a painting on the wall depicting a tropical scene. The moon shone its illuminating light down on the turquoise water making the foaming surf glisten like a glassy green wall. The palm trees were leaning to one side, their fronds in wild disarray. The scene was that of a stormy night on a tropical island. Gazing at it intently, I felt the bile suddenly rising in my throat. Nausea swept over me; I was going to be sick! Swinging my legs out of bed I hurriedly shuffled my way to the bathroom where I vomited violently several times. After returning to the bedroom I turned the offending painting face to the wall. I just couldn't bear to look at it; the memory of my ordeal was too fresh, like an opened wound which hadn't yet healed.

My entire body felt so dehydrated; the sun had literally sucked every vital juice out of me. I had consumed gallons of water and yet I still felt an unquenchable thirst. My skin had been torched; it craved moisture. A quizzical thought crossed my mind; during the days at sea I didn't fully realize how severely burnt I was. Even my dire thirst had become secondary as the struggle to stay alive dominated every other bodily need. Now, however, every cell in my body demanded immediate attention.

Walking back to the bathroom I delved into the bag of toiletries I had purchased on my way to the hotel. I withdrew bottles of shampoo, hair conditioner, toothpaste, soap, and a comb. I had been dreaming about feeling clean for days; it was now within my grasp, only minutes away. I set the temperature at lukewarm and stepped under the deliciously invigorating spray. Oh, what sweet relief! The blessed liquid soothed my body, soothed away the aches and pains. How I welcomed this water sprayed over me, contrary to my feelings in the ocean. I stood slowly rotating myself under the jets; at that moment I didn't think anything could eclipse this revitalizing feeling. After this, I would certainly sleep soundly.

Lessons Learned

The sound of the phone ringing interrupted my twilight sleep. *Who could this be?* I wondered. I picked up the jangling instrument.

"Hello? Hello? Is this Michelle Hamilton?"

"Yes, speaking," I answered. It was strange to be using the telephone again.

"Michelle, I have someone here who wants to speak to you."

My intuition immediately told me it was Mum. A tightness gripped my throat as I waited for her to come on the line. Would she be overwhelmed with happiness and relief or hysterical and angry with me for going out on the boat alone when she had expressly told me not to go out too far?

"Michelle, is that you?" she said in a voice that betrayed her emotional state.

"Yes, Mum, it's me."

"Thank God, you're alive! I couldn't be absolutely convinced until I had heard your voice for myself. It's unbelievable! You're not hurt, are you?"

"Well, I still have all my limbs and I'm alive, so, yes, I guess I'm okay!"

"I just can't believe you are alive and in Manila. It's truly amazing—I never thought I would see you again. Praise the Lord for this miracle. This is surely an act of God."

Mum's voice was quivering with emotion as I gave her the name and room number of my hotel. Coincidentally, in the huge expanse of Manila, Mum's hotel was only just around the corner. Providence had brought us one street away from each other!

Having completely accomplished my cleansing ritual I stepped onto the bathroom scales. Tentatively, I watched on as the numbers swayed, finally settling on 110 pounds. This was nothing short of staggering, for in three days I had lost twelve pounds. I laughed inwardly to myself, *Trust me to do it the hard way!*

Propping myself up on the pillows I waited anxiously for Mum to arrive. How desperately I had longed to see Mum when I was at sea; now that the moment was almost here I felt peculiarly apprehensive. Would she be really angry at me, or would the relief that I was alive and well overshadow all the other emotions? I hoped it would be the latter.

The physical and mental exhaustion over the past few days had left my mind blank; it was as if a wall has come down and blocked out what was too terrifying to remember. I was too scared to think about what had happened because to do that would cause me to re-experience all the terror I had finally escaped from. At this stage I did not dare retrace my steps down the petrifying path which I had traveled. It was a weird feeling just to lie here in idleness without having to fight for my survival. I found the inactivity threatening; as soon as I shut my eyes I thought of myself back at sea, especially as my body continued to sway to the rhythm of the ocean's waves.

I had miraculously been restored to an ordinary, everyday life, although I would never view it in the same way again. The miracles God bestows upon us everyday would not be taken for granted ever again. No, I was not the same person who was put out to sea a few days ago. I had returned, transformed by my experience. Now I marvelled at the wonders of my body, its precise mechanisms, its incredible endurance, and its ability to adapt to circumstances in order to survive. My eyes had adjusted to the salty water and my body's stores had sustained me, although not a morsel of food or a drop of fresh water had passed my lips. In the fight for survival my entire being had supported my struggle and maintained life.

What a precious possession we are given when God bestows us with a body and a mind, molded after His own image. Truly our bodies are the temple of God with the Spirit of God dwelling within. From now on I would treat it with the utmost respect. By His love for me He proved that I was never alone, never out of His sight. This confirms the scripture for me that I have since come to know: "Are not two sparrows sold for a copper coin? And not one of them falls to the ground apart from your Father's will. But the very hairs of your head are all numbered. Do not fear therefore; you are of more value than many sparrows" (Matthew 10:29–31).

Through what I had experienced I know that God cares for each and every one of us with tender love, compassion, and mercy. I now realize I had been previously living my life solely for myself, never giving a thought to the God who had given me my life. Only when I had totally given up my human effort to save myself, when I had become completely depleted of all energy and totally powerless to overcome or change my circumstances, only then did I turn and cry out to God for help, asking with a humble heart for His help. The Bible says: "My grace is sufficient for you, for my strength is made perfect in weakness" (2 Corinthians 12:9).

God couldn't work while I still had supreme confidence in my own ability. He needed me to come to Him as meek and helpless as a little child; I understood that now. In His lovingkindness toward me, He heard my desperate pleas. Only when I had surrendered up my life to Him, promising to do His will and not my own, did He answer me.

Yes, I could see it clearly now. I had to be made aware of my human weakness and realize only by the power of God, through Jesus Christ, could I be saved both physically and spiritually. I marvelled at the lovingkindness He must have for me: He commanded His angels to stay with me and protect and comfort me during that horrifyingly lonely night. Yes, God is real and true to His word to those who believe in Him. Why He chose to save me can only be understood in the light of the scriptures which I have now studied since returning home to Australia.

> For this purpose I have raised you up, that I might show my power in you and that my name might be declared in all the earth for My own name sake. (Exodus 9:16)

> For all things are for your sakes, that grace, having spread through the many, may cause thanksgiving to abound to the glory of God. (2 Corinthians 4:15)

I had promised God that for saving my life, I would live every day for Him and make my existence a living sacrifice. I would be worthy of Him as a willing instrument in the divine plan He had for my life. I vowed my best to live up to that pledge.

The sound of male voices outside my room aroused me out of my meditative thoughts. I snapped myself back to the present. Summoning up every last ounce of strength, I willed myself to get up and answer the door.

This is it, I thought.

Gingerly I turned the knob and pulled the door open. Flanked between two dark-haired gentlemen, who I guessed to be embassy officials, stood my mother. All prior anxiety about what she might say instantly vanished at the sight her. I had never been more pleased to see anyone in my life. A stab of guilt robbed me of my joy as I noticed the dark circles under her eyes and acknowledged the grief I had unintentionally caused her. We looked deeply into each other eyes and we understood beyond words what we were saying in our hearts. Jubilant tears of relief flooded Mum's eyes as she moved toward me, eager to hold the one whom she had thought she would never hold again. My heart was pounding hard as we held each other, a surge of unadulterated joy engulfing us.

"Let me have a look at you. Do you know, Michelle, I thought I might never see you again. Praise Jesus! He has returned you to me," she cried.

"I know, Mum. It's true. I owe my life to Him. My being alive is a living testimony to His might, His compassion, His grace, and His unconditional love. I can't wait to tell you all the miraculous things that happened to me at sea. You are going to be speechless. I am still utterly spellbound myself!"

It had been only five days since Mum and I had seen each other, but in that short space of time both of us had looked right into the face of death and survived.

You will be adrift in a sea of loneliness, discontent, fear, and guilt until in humility and desperation, you realize your total dependence on God. Even from within a mighty tempest, you can experience the infinite love of your Creator and cry out, "I need you Jesus to be Lord of my life!" He will hear. He will save.

For You cast me into the deep,
Into the heart of the seas,
And the floods surrounded me;

. . .

Yet You have brought up my life from the pit,
O LORD, my God.

EPILOGUE

SINCE MICHELLE'S TRAUMATIC EXPERIENCE and miraculous rescue, she and her mother have not returned to Boracay Island. Upon arriving in Manila, they were inundated with interview requests from newspapers, magazines, and television networks. Within a short time the media had dubbed her "The Aussie Mermaid."

Following a special ceremony honoring the crew of the F/V *Alyss Star,* Michelle and Rachelle returned to Australia where they were reunited with Rachelle's two younger daughters, Angeline and Natalie. During the following eighteen months, Michelle and Rachelle wrote this account of their ordeal giving testimony to God's grace and power. They currently reside in Perth, Western Australia.

ABOUT THE AUTHORS

MICHELLE AND RACHELLE HAMILTON spend much of their time in public speaking and are currently writing their second book. Michelle and her mother, Rachelle, enjoy traveling, sightseeing, and reading.

Three other ladies complete the Hamilton family—Michelle's two sisters, Angeline and Natalie, and Michelle's cat, Nikita. The Hamiltons live in Perth, Australia.

The typeface for the text of this book is *Times Roman*. In 1930, typographer Stanley Morison joined the staff of *The Times* (London) to supervise design of a typeface for the reformatting of this renowned English daily. Morison had overseen type-library reforms at Cambridge University Press in 1925, but this new task would prove a formidable challenge despite a decade of experience in paleography, calligraphy, and typography. *Times New Roman* was credited as coming from Morison's original pencil renderings in the first years of the 1930s, but the typeface went through numerous changes under the scrutiny of a critical committee of dissatisfied *Times* staffers and editors. The resulting typeface, *Times Roman*, has been called the most used, most successful typeface of this century. The design is of enduring value to English and American printers and publishers, who choose the typeface for its readability and economy when run on today's high-speed presses.

Substantive Editing:
Michael S. Hyatt

Copy Editing:
Cynthia Tripp

Cover Design:
Steve Diggs & Friends
Nashville, Tennessee

Page Composition:
Xerox Ventura Publisher
Hewlett Packard LaserJet™ III

Printing and Binding:
Maple-Vail Book Manufacturing Group
York, Pennsylvania

Cover Printing:
Strine Printing Company
York, Pennsylvania

Practical Help for Family Issues

The Focus on the Family ™ Guide to Growing a Healthy Home
Mike Yorkey, General Editor
ISBN:1-56121-020-X
Hard Cover, 350 pages
Family

FOCUS ON THE FAMILY is North America's most prominent Christian ministry in providing practical help and insight for the problems facing families.

Now, Mike Yorkey, editor of *Focus on the Family* magazine, has assembled some of America's leading Christian family advocates to produce this important book.

In this single volume, you'll find chapters by: Dr. James Dobson, Larry Burkett, Gary Smalley, Jean Lush, Dennis Rainey, David Hocking, Connie Marshner, Ruth Senter, Ron Blue, Dale Hanson Bourke, Josh McDowell, Jay Kesler, Ted Baehr, Grace Ketterman.

Growing a Healthy Home is a home encyclopedia that addresses the issues every family faces: marriage, husbands and fathers, children, teenagers, mothers and wives, family activities, education, family problems, and current issues.

This volume is one of the most comprehensive and practical books on the family ever published.

For Further Reading

From His Wife's Point of View, What Was Job Really Like?

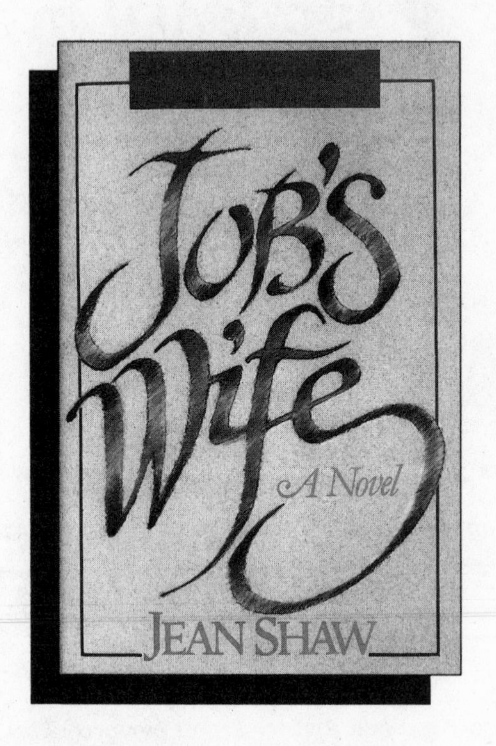

Job's Wife: A Novel

Jean Shaw

ISBN: 0-943497-96-5

Trade Paper, 146 pages

Biblical Fiction

JEAN SHAW, AUTHOR OF *A Second Cup of Coffee*, retells the familiar story of Job from the perspective of the one person closest to Job—his wife.

This is a novel filled with emotion, excitement, and encouragement—a perfect gift for women.

Imagine What Noah's Story Would Be Like, If It Were Set in the Future?

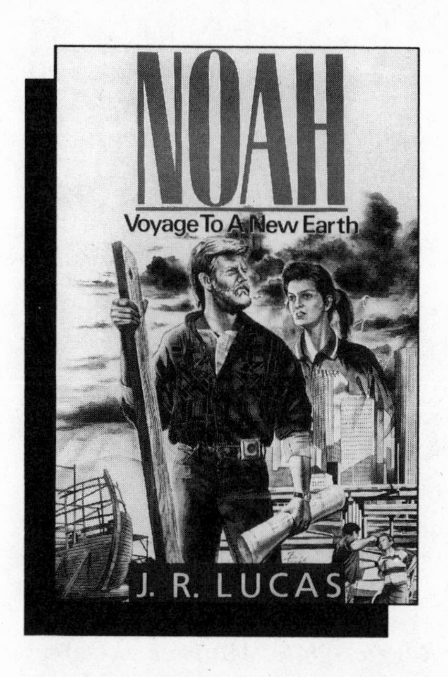

Noah: Voyage to a New Earth
J.R. Lucas
ISBN 1-56121-053-6
Trade Paper, 272 pages
Novel

SURROUNDED BY A SOCIETY OF CORRUPTION and depravity, besieged by a culture infested with homosexuality, venereal disease, immorality, and spiraling into gross depravity: One man stands faithful to God—Noah.

J.R. Lucas chronicles the powerful saga of God's judgment and Noah's stalwart obedience. Fashioned in a setting of the future, Lucas guides you through the doubt and frustration of a seemingly impossible task—the bitter anger and murderous violence of an opposing culture. He tells of one man's overwhelming fatigue and subsequent dependence upon a sovereign God.

Step into the world of Noah. Experience the struggle. Share the vision and task of preparing for the voyage to a new earth.

J.R. Lucas is the author of *The Parenting of Champions*. He lives in Missouri with his wife Pam and their four children.

For Further Reading

A Great Defensive Lineman Devoted to Jesus Christ

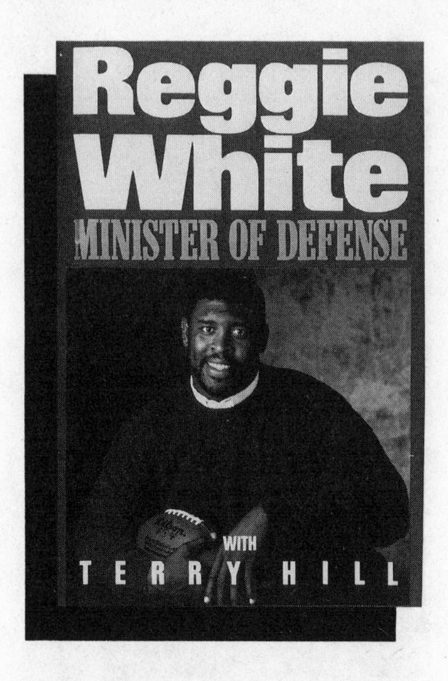

Reggie White: Minister of Defense
Reggie White with Terry Hill
ISBN 1-56121-087-0
Hard Cover, 224 pages
Sports autobiography

HE'S BEEN CALLED THE PERFECT DEFENSIVE LINEMAN, the best player in the NFL, even the best to ever play the game of football. As Defensive Player of the Year, and Pro Bowl MVP, He is one of the most celebrated athletes in sports today. And he's a man with a determined commitment to excellence—to doing his best in everything win or lose. *Minister of Defense* is the story of Reggie White—the story of a man devoted to his wife and family, a man devoted to Jesus Christ, and unlike so many athletes today, a man who truly deserves to be a model for youngsters and a benchmark of character and principled living for us all.

The book includes sixteen pages of full-color photos and is a perfect gift for sports enthusiasts of all ages.

A graduate of the University of Tennessee, Reggie White is a defensive lineman for the Philadelphia Eagles. In the off-season, he and his family live in Maryville, Tennessee.